# On Reporting the News

# On Reporting the News

**WILLIAM E. BURROWS**

Department of Journalism
New York University

New York • New York University Press • 1977

**Library of Congress Cataloging in Publication Data**

Burrows, William E.    1937-
   On reporting the news.

   Bibliography:  p.
   Includes index.
   1.  Reporters and reporting.  I. Title.

PN4781.B78     070.4'3     76-16472
ISBN 0-8147-1009-3

Project Editor:  Nat LaMar

Manufactured in the United States of America

For Jo

# CONTENTS

vii

# Contents

# PREFACE

This book grew out of lecture material prepared for a course on basic news reporting I began teaching at New York University in the autumn of 1974. I had no idea at that time that any of it would be published.

In preparing the lecture material, and then expanding and refining it for publication, I had at least one enormous advantage: I had never read a reporting textbook. I was therefore unaware that dullness and humorlessness were tantamount to prerequisites.

I later scanned three or four of our leading books, and although all of them treated the technical material decently, they all had what was for me a serious shortcoming. None had character. I marveled at the fact that those who were in the business of teaching aspiring reporters how to write interestingly seemed to be such plodders where their own writing was concerned. It was as though the authors had written their books on the other side of an opaque curtain, first explaining in wearying detail what a new lead is, and then clipping and pasting something from the Associated Press to illustrate the point. In at least one such book, the "examples" are set in narrow margin to simulate the way they look in a newspaper—column after column of stories which the students I've talked with can't get through. I can't get through them, either.

News reporting is a serious affair, but this doesn't mean that it has to be pondered like original sin or taught like geometry.

Every page written on the subject doesn't have to drip with persistent self-righteousness and a stiffness that potentially good writers can only find intimidating. Nor should reporting be reduced to a pseudo-science and structured like organic chemistry—an unhealthy trend that has grown since Vietnam and Watergate. There are now whole chapters in basic reporting books devoted to polling, the use of such hardware as Video Display Terminals, and other technical stuff, all put in at the expense of what, for lack of a better word, can be called "soul."

Reporting the news is an art and a craft, and it always will be, irrespective of polls, computers, data-retrieval systems, video displays, scientific sampling procedures, and the rest. This is not to say that such things don't have their place, but a basic reporting book that gives students information on how to use hardware at the expense of setting the moral basis of the profession—of translating news coverage into a human dimension—misses the mark. I have seen entire chapters titled "What Is News?" or something like that. Not here. If you don't know what news is after reading the following chapters, I will have failed miserably. But that definition ought to seep in slowly through interesting example rather than be pounded in through pronouncement.

You will therefore not see diagrams of newsrooms and copy flow charts (go to your local newspaper, where they'll be delighted to show you the works, live and in color), any reference to Video Display Terminals (which you can learn to operate in a day or two), or specific instructions on reporting for the wire services, radio, or television (since all news reporting involves the same basic elements, and this is a basic reporting book). Similarly, you will not see reference to reporting women's liberation, men's liberation, black liberation, gay liberation, environmental "liberation," or any other kind, since (gasp!) there's no special trick to handling these areas once the basics have been learned. A reporter who has mastered the basics can cover anything; one who doesn't have a solid grounding in the essentials can be taught how to cover women's liberation until doomsday and he or she will still foul up.

Every story in this book was made up by me, as were the names of the characters, so any resemblance to actual persons, living or dead, is purely coincidental (usually). There are at least four good reasons for inventing examples of news stories rather than pirating them. First, I think it allows a much better "match" with the textual instructions because they were custom-made to go with them. Second, it allows absolute simplicity, which ought to make the stories as clear as possible. Third, it permits characters to move from one chapter to another which makes them more lifelike and therefore more interesting. Finally, it encourages (I hope) the stimulation of humor and imagination through example. I should also say, in all honesty, that writing them was more fun than clipping stories from the newspaper. I would feel differently, I suppose, if this was a book on how to clip stories from the newspaper.

*On Reporting the News* is not "complete," but then again, neither am I. I haven't read it all, I haven't done it all, and I'd be able to run much faster if I had four legs. This is simply a compilation of what I believe to be the most basic and important material on reporting. It is based on a decade of reporting and writing, on the help and insight of an awful lot of excellent professionals, and on plenty of observation and introspection. It is also based on teaching experience. You learn a great deal about yourself and your craft when you have to explain both to others in such a way that they not only understand it but enjoy it. I see in my students' problems my problems, so I have to ask myself how I would have wanted to be taught.

This book is divided into four parts: Theory, Practice, Specialty, and Survival. The first attempts to set the philosophical and perceptual basis for the technique that comes later. I believe that reporting students ought to think a little about their and others' perception, about the moral basis of libel, and about the true nature of the craft before they write a word. They ought to do a little pondering about what it is they're getting into. The second deals with general technique as it applies to every kind of news reporting. The third concentrates on specialties—beats—starting with the underappreciated and deceptively easy obituary, and ending with politics and government, which is comprehensible to very few (the participants included). Some points are repeated, under differing circumstances, for emphasis. Some toes, including those of lawyers, politicians, movie stars, public relations persons, scientists, soldiers, bureaucrats, athletes, and journalists themselves, get lightly but firmly stepped on. The last part, Survival, offers some practical advice on the care and feeding of colleagues, including editors, and on making it through that difficult first year.

There are places in here where the tone is direct: You should do this . . . you should not do that. I in no sense mean to "talk down" to the reader. Yet a book which sets as one of its goals the development of reporters who will not mince words can hardly expect to achieve that goal by mincing words. It is impossible to teach forthrightness through equivocation.

In the same vein, I would have no reason to expect my students to become effective political reporters if what I gave them on politics consisted of a sterilized civics lesson and omitted the often devious role of political packagers, the manipulation of polls, and the fact that an awesome number of politicians are liars. Similarly, I don't think a conscientious teacher can talk about the virtues of journalism without also discussing *its* vices. It is inherently impossible to teach balanced reporting by chest-pounding—by holding up the best in the profession for emulation while pretending that the clunkers don't exist. Telling a child over and over again that he looks like a demigod and thinks like a genius is no way to produce a well-adjusted adult. The holier-than-thou mentality so prevalent in journalism today is dangerous because it results in the same kind of gross distortion, fatuous in-breeding, and self-righteousness that we, as journalists, are the first to pounce upon when we notice it elsewhere. The message is that improvement can come only by recognizing our shortcomings and then working to correct them, not by pretending that the shortcomings don't exist. It seems to me that taking such an approach, far from talking down to students, amounts to talking *up* to them—that is, treating them like serious adults who can cope with the complexity of reality.

Although *On Reporting the News* has a lot of "me" in it, I am, in turn, the product of many others. Some of them were unaware that this was being written. Some are no longer here. Still others have changed jobs, or careers, or have retired since we last met. Obviously, neither they nor those who consciously helped make this book possible bear responsibility for its deficiencies. But its strengths are their strengths. This, then, is my opportunity to settle what is in many cases a very old debt.

At *The New York Times:* Raymond Anderson, William Borders, Malcolm W. Browne, Herbert R. French, Paul Grimes, Michael T. Kaufman, Douglas Robinson, Gay Talese, Paul Underwood, Betsy Wade, and Bayard Webster:

At *The Richmond Times-Dispatch:* George W. Ashworth, Earle Dunford, B. William Mader, Omar Marden, and Ed Swain:

At *The Washington Post:* Ramon Geremia, Jimmy Lee Hoagland, and Thomas W. Lippman:

At *The Wall Street Journal:* Alan Adelson, Michael Gartner, A. Kent MacDougall, Richard Rustin, and Stanford Sesser.

To the following, my very special gratitude for the time, thought, and encouragement they brought to this endeavor: Richard Petrow, Chairman of the Department of Journalism at NYU; Associate Professors David Kahn and David M. Rubin and Assistant Professors Joshua Mills and Mitchell Stephens, all of our department; John Davenport, formerly of ABC radio news; David A. Duff of the law firm of Debevoise, Plimpton, Lyons & Gates; Robert Lipsyte, formerly of *The New York Times;* Richard A. Moss, Senior Deputy District Attorney, City and County of Los Angeles; Bowen Northrup of *The Wall Street Journal's* London bureau, and Richard Severo of *The New York Times.*

Finally, I would like to thank my students for their patience with "The Street Man," and for teaching him more than they can probably ever understand.

W.E.B.
New York University
October 10, 1976

# part one

# THEORY

# chapter one

# THE COMPLETE REPORTER

There is the story about the second grade teacher who asks her class whether anyone knows when bats do most of their flying. A hand shoots up in the back of the room.

"Bats do most of their flying during double-headers," answers a little boy wearing dirty sneakers, "and especially when the pitching's lousy."

I start with this story for two reasons. First, like all journalists, I want you to read what I write and you might not have gotten even this far had I opened with a quotation from Horace Greeley or, worse, with something like: "Good reporting is more important today than ever before. . . ." (As a matter of fact, good reporting is *not* more important today than ever before. It was exactly as important in 1812 as it will be in 2112, a fact Napoleon would have been the first to admit as he was being chased out of Russia by a surprisingly tenacious enemy.) So, what I want to do is "grab" you, because I know that if you don't read what I write I will have wasted my time.

Second, the story contains a message: Definitions are important. Let's spend a while, then, talking about what we're talking about.

You are already a reporter. Every time you talk to somebody or write something you are reporting. When you tell a friend that a

3

certain movie is good, a certain restaurant is terrible, an accident has happened, or that you're in a foul mood and want to be left alone, you're reporting—that is, you're conveying information to someone else. If you keep a diary or write poetry, short stories, novels, term papers, theses, book reports, or love letters, if you scrawl graffiti on walls, paint pictures, compose or perform anything from acid rock to grand opera, tell anecdotes, gossip, or act on the stage, you are reporting emotions, observations, hard facts or, as they say, all of the above. You have, in fact, been a reporter practically since you cut your first tooth and you undoubtedly will continue to be one, like it or not, until you begin that last great journey into the setting sun. So don't be needlessly intimidated (at least at this point) by something you've been doing all of your life anyway.

Professional reporters do what you do, but with three essential differences. First, they report what is judged to be newsworthy— that is, what is of interest or importance to a relatively large audience—according to generally accepted standards. Second, they do so according to generally accepted, but often flexible, rules of the craft. Finally, they get paid for what they do and, contrary to what most of them tell outsiders, many get paid quite handsomely. Reporters tend to be somewhat cynical and complaining, which is part of what makes the best of them so effective, not to mention so perversely charming.

Professional reporting—the gathering and transmitting of news— is basically a craft like cabinetmaking and, like cabinetmaking, it can be practiced badly or on the level of art. Solid reporting never comes fluttering down on the wings of divine inspiration, but neither is it reducible to tables or formulas as in mathematics or the pure sciences. The difference between the novice and the polished reporter is the difference between the apprentice and the master cabinetmaker. Just about anyone with a hammer, nails, and wood can slap together something resembling a cabinet and, likewise, just about anyone with a pad and pencil can gather some information about a tree having come down on a house and even turn that information into a story of sorts. Here is that story (or sorts):

The large maple tree in front of Mr. Knight's house fell over on it yesterday.

As in all arts and crafts, practitioners of news reporting are graded according to ability, starting with what used to be called "cubs" and progressing through various levels of competence to the point of being true and widely respected professionals. The giants get to the top in journalism, just as they do in musical composition and in cabinetmaking, because they have painstakingly followed a process having three elements and, in addition, have been blessed with a fourth that cannot be acquired. The acquirable elements are: (1) mastery of the rules and techniques; (2) constant practice; (3) the unending quest for polish and innovation. These, alone, can make an honest and conscientious reporter extremely competent. That fourth element—instinct—can make him or her great.

Master artists and craftsmen first learn the basics of their trade. They study and absorb the essential rules until they have them down cold. The rules are the foundation upon which all creativity rests, and contrary to what that inner voice may be telling you about all of your natural ability, there is no way whatever to sidestep them. Hundreds of hours of sketches and the study of anatomy are concealed under the robes of everyone attending Leonardo's *The Last Supper*. Expertise in anything rests squarely on what has come before. There are no shortcuts to professionalism, and if you are determined to think otherwise, imagine taking your broken arm to someone whose medical credentials consist entirely of having watched hospital dramas on television.

The masters also practice constantly, not because someone is pushing them, but because they are compelled to do so out of love for their work. The best of them have spent years practicing almost every day, particularly with their perceptive ability and writing technique, and still they find that they go stale when they're away from it for only a few weeks. Students occasionally come up with a thorny problem that goes something like this: "I love reporting and writing, but I find I have to drag myself to the typewriter." One young man even told me that he needed a kick in the tail to get started on assignments. I advised him in all sincerity to steer his reluctant tail to economics, romance languages, politics, or to any other discipline in which he might be more motivated. If you have to drag yourself to the typewriter, you're best advised to find another goal, because you probably don't really "love" journalism and it therefore isn't for you. That's not to say that everything you write is going to be unadulterated fun; a fair amount of it will be pure drudgery, and there's no getting away from it. But the tedious, dull, and seemingly unimportant stories have their places, too, if for no other reason than to force you to get them into the best possible shape. Competition for reporting jobs is fierce (in part because many students wander into them with the erroneous belief that journalism is glamorous and requires little more than a "way with words"), so only the most dedicated make it through that first winter or two. And from then on it's a process of elimination with possibly five or six dropping out for every one who stays in. Good reporters occasionally have to be restrained; they never have to be prodded.

With the basics learned and understood, and practice a way of life, the reporter steps up the long quest for polish, self-expression, and innovation—for his "style." That is, he gradually begins experimenting with various techniques in an effort to get his best creative ability into what he produces. This is the point (usually measured in years, *never in a blinding flash*) at which he feels sufficiently comfortable with his work so that he can begin probing for new directions, for new ways in which to approach what he does and to make it stylistically different from the styles or techniques of others. You will find if you go into reporting, or any other species of writing for that matter, that improving your technique and pushing your creative ability to the limit is often incredibly frustrating, if not actually painful, but that the triumphs—looking at what you've done and knowing down to your toes that it has been thoroughly reported and beautifully written—constitutes one of life's most exhilarating experiences. If you stick with it you will from time to time be able to read what you have produced and know deep inside that you have created something beautiful (you will by then also have learned to read what you have produced and know when it's absolute trash.) You will then be well on your way.

The last element—instinct—cannot be taught, although, up to a point, it can be acquired. But only up to a point. It is impossible to anticipate every conceivable news situation, and were it possible, the reporter's life would be pretty boring. It is the challenge of adapting the basic skills to new situations that makes life interesting and work rewarding. While the rudiments of political reporting can be taught and practiced, for example, no one can teach the ability to sense when a politician is lying. That ability comes from knowing how to do solid research, how to force yourself to think with absolute clarity and logic, and from a certain instinct. Effort and experience will do the trick most of the time, but those reporters who are right most often also have that extra sense, or what they called in the Front Page days, a "nose for news." When Bob Woodward heard a burglary suspect mention the CIA in a Washington courtroom one morning, he easily might have ignored the tidbit on the supposition that, one way or another, the intelligence community was involved in practically everything. The "third-rate burglary" would then probably have gone down in history as just that. But Woodward, who hadn't even been a reporter for very long, applied his instinct and took it from there. Likewise, you can take writing courses and practice stringing words together until your typewriter is smoking, and there will still be those around who can write better than you can: they have an instinctive ability, perfected through an understanding of the medium and constant practice, to arrange words in dynamic, beautiful, and even poignant order. Many fine news gatherers can't write worth a damn, and many excellent writers are absolutely awful at bringing in a story. Reporters who do both extremely well are in a distinct minority and what they produce, in the final analysis, is the product of training and instinct. They have that rare and wonderful combination.

So, if you really want to be a reporter, you will have to commit yourself to the proposition that mastery of the craft rests squarely on dedication and on an absolute understanding of the fundamentals. If you stick with it and keep trying, you should be rewarded with the knowledge that you're getting better all the time—that you are slowly but steadily forcing back the fright and uncertainty within your own head and replacing them with justified confidence in your ability to handle anything required of you like a professional. There's no feeling quite like it.

If you go into professional reporting you will need a great deal more than this or any single book can provide. You will need integrity, and, what is not sufficiently understood by many journalism students, you will need a lot of knowledge that goes far beyond the practice of news coverage and writing. The spittoon and suspenders days are gone forever. Reporters no longer practice their craft by acting like human vacuum cleaners, sucking up what appears to be news, and then spewing it out in some kind of hard-hitting form. That mustached, cursing, heavy-drinking "newshawk" of yesterday, a cigarette dangling from his mouth and a press card wedged into his hatband, is long finished. And good riddance.

While those characters now seem romantic, they were by and large a myopic group who, when called upon to cover anything beyond fires, robberies, and floods, were often pathetically inadequate. There were, of course, outstanding exceptions like H. L. Mencken, A. J. Liebling, Edward R. Murrow, and a scattering of others. But the ordinary member of the pack excitedly scrambled off to one war after another, adrenalin and bourbon flowing freely, without ever really comprehending—much less reporting—what was really happening around him. He wore his trench coat the way Superman wears his cape, and for the privilege of being allowed near the front lines, he dutifully obeyed even the most moronic censorship and passed on the most blatant propaganda. Without the slightest apparent qualm, he told the folks back home that the atrocities committed by their husbands and sons were necessary and heroic, while those committed by the enemy were pointless and barbaric. He time and again described the leaders of his side as beleaguered, but ingenious patriots, while portraying their opposite number as mad dogs.

At home, he often wrote admiringly of executions, gangsters, robber barons, and the slaughter of Indians, and bragged about his ignorance of science, economics, literature, and anything having to do with universities. He considered the plight of minorities, the mentally and physically ill, the aged, and the environment in which they and everyone else lived about as much as he considered making his home in some tree. Bringing in the story first—getting what was popularly referred to as a "scoop"—was everything, no matter that it was distorted or downright wrong. What that reporter *did* understand (and this has not changed) is that publishers are in the business of selling news, and the news that sells best is the news that is the most sensational and least offensive.

Such reporting is still the rule rather than the exception, but change is in the wind. It is the rule because it is still far easier to report the obvious than to pursue the obscure, easier to remain ignorant than to undertake the effort necessary to grasp hard information, and easier to pander to publishers' and network owners' desires to keep expenses down while keeping circulation or ratings up. Change has begun, though, for two essential reasons: the planet is shrinking while the communications net is tightening, and both reporters and their audiences are better educated than they used to be.

We live on a highly technologized and seriously crowded planet. The result of our cheek-by-jowl existence is that just about everyone feels the effects when someone else in the crowd sneezes, throws a temper tantrum, or drops dead from prolonged inebriation, starvation, or pollution. We now know that within a matter of weeks of the Arab oil potentates getting angry over our support of their enemy and over the price we charge them for our trucks and calculators, we can expect to see lines of cars at service stations flying green flags and sharp increases in the sale of sweaters and woollies. Had this happened in 1906, or even in 1956, we might have sent a bully little armada over there, complete with marines and reporters, and pounded the insolent blackguards into submission:

By Our Special Correspondent

TRIPOLI, June 15—An intrepid force of some 8,000 heavily armed and ready American Marines, their fixed bayonets flashing in the sun's first rays, landed at dawn here today and easily overwhelmed the city's confused and none-too-eager Muslim defenders. Amid loud huzzas from the victors, Old Glory was raised above the Royal Palace at just before noon, while the last of the enemy was fleeing its southernmost environs.

The Americans' valor and tenacity in capturing this forbidding stronghold of the eastern Maghreb can only be described as exemplary. Enemy losses during the morning's fighting numbered in excess of 2,700 killed and another 4,000 wounded. Untold thousands of Muslims, fearing the fate of their dead brethren, threw down their weapons and promptly surrendered to the advancing Marines. American casualties were described as light.

The government, headed by Sheik Abdul Benghazi, was in full retreat to the south at the moment in which the American standard first fluttered over his palace. The Marines were hard behind.

"We expect them to turn and fight at Mabruk," said the commander of the American expeditionary force, Admiral Nelson Drake. "But my orders are clear. I will regain what has been promised to us according to treaty, and if the Sheik imagines that he can disregard that treaty, he is in grave error."

Even as Admiral Drake vowed to pursue the Muslims . . .

So much for the good old days. With the complications arising, at least in part, from the fact that Libya has allies who also produce oil (not to mention a sympathizer having enough hydrogen bombs to turn the area between Washington and Boston into a moonscape), comes the necessity of having to sort out the nature of the problem and report developments in a way that is accurate, clear, and fair. That, in turn, means being able to grasp everything that contributes to the story; being able to understand why it *is* a story. The reporter covering a Libyan-American oil showdown, for example, would have to know the recent history of the area, both sides' positions and how those positions led to the conflict, and such related factors as the state of Libya's oil production and general economic and military capability, her network of relationships with friends and foes, the record of her leaders, the role of the Organization of Petroleum Exporting Countries and even of the United Nations, the increasingly important and controversial part played by the multinational oil companies and, for good measure, a few of the basics of international trade. Clearly, this is not work for anyone who is content to play poker or snooze in the press room and whose outer limit consists of describing a gangland killing while arcing wet tobacco into a brass pot.

News developments in an increasingly educated and interdependent world are too complicated to be left to reporting "machines"—even good ones—and the interests and backgrounds of the best reporters are shifting accordingly. What is needed, as it has always been needed, are reporters with solid experience and training in their craft plus wide knowledge in other areas as diverse as biology, literature, psychology, art, urban politics, and Asian affairs. Obviously, it is impossible to know everything, but the truly effective reporter understands that life is a three-dimensional process and that in order to report a single event meaningfully, he or she must in turn understand those other events that led to it or that are an integral part of it. Watergate meant nothing unless it was placed squarely within the context of the American historical and political experience. That fact became abundantly clear when Europeans reacted to the disclosures by asking what all the excitement was about. Such occurrences, they patiently explained as if to well-meaning but slightly demented American nephews, are taken for granted in Europe and in most of the rest of the world. Not understanding the rather singular nature of the American political system, then, would have meant ignoring the nature of the catastrophe. It was not ignored, though, because those who reported it understood its implications. They saw Watergate and the events surrounding it for what they were, and the reason they did so was because they understood its implications within a far broader context than the seemingly isolated events themselves.

Newspapers and radio and television stations, confronted with steadily rising costs and increasingly better educated and aware audiences, are moving quite perceptibly toward the well-rounded reporter; toward the man or woman who is solidly versed in the basic arts and sciences and who is able, without three days of heavy research, to draw freely on Dante, Thoreau, Jenner, Malthus, Hobbs, Marx, or Harry S. Truman. Editors require their reporters to have the basic journalistic skills, to be sure, but they want more than that. They want them to possess the ability to relate events and to draw on the entire historical process. The best reporters can do as much because they know that nothing—certainly no human activity—is an isolated event. Everything therefore becomes part of the professional's reservoir of knowledge, and if he doesn't know a certain fact, he at least knows where he can find it quickly.

If you think that genes are pants, that quid pro quo is an Italian seafood dish, that a peccadillo is an armor-plated mammal, that falsetto is a Shakespearian character, that Mach 2 is a men's deodorant, and that photosynthesis is made by Kodak, you are going to have trouble reporting effectively. The best advice for the aspiring reporter is therefore this: Master the skills and constantly inquire about your world because, especially as a reporter, you are going to be a key and inseparable part of it. Time permitting, go to an opera, taste a raw mushroom, watch birds, get to know the difference between pine and fir, read something about the history of Japan, think about the options on third-down situations, look at the stained glass in a cathedral, and spend some moments alone in front of a mirror. Knowledge is never wasted.

# chapter two

# SEEING IS BELIEVING (IF YOU'RE A FROG)

The sign that hung at the front of the physics room in my high school was as applicable to reporting news as it was to reporting the results of experiments with pulleys: YOU SEE, BUT DO YOU OBSERVE?

Animals believe what they see because nature never lies and only rarely deceives. A frog sitting on a lily pad has no reason to believe that the fly it sees approaching is other than the real thing, so when the insect comes within range, out goes that sticky tongue and lunch is served. The frog sees only one reality; it perceives only one truth, and that truth is absolute.

There are many truths where humans are concerned, though, because we are far more complex creatures than frogs. Not only do we perceive on many different levels, but we interpret what we perceive in vastly differing ways, according to our physical abilities, life experiences, and motivations. For people, then, a single occurrence can represent many "truths." Imagine, for example, being sent out to cover a tenement fire with Pablo Picasso (he to do the illustrations and you to do the writing). The two of you would see the same thing, but each of you would most likely observe it differently. You would have different perceptions according to your respective train-ing, interests, sensitivity, and emotions. That's challenge enough where bringing in an accurate story is concerned, but it's not the worst of it. Since news reporting has to do with people—those in-volved in the news and those who witness it—you must also cope with *their* perceptions and motives. It is axiomatic in news reporting that if a dozen persons standing at an intersection witness the same automobile accident, and each is asked to describe what happened, there will likely be a dozen different versions.

Where reporting is concerned, the area of perception takes on an added dimension, and it is this dimension that provides the re-porter's constant challenge. Just about everyone who is in a news story wants to appear in that story in the most favorable light. At best, the subjects of news stories try to convey the "truth" about themselves and what they do as favorably as possible. At worst, they lie quite deliberately and often cleverly. The stakes for doing so can be enormous.

Celebrities—movies stars, artists, athletes, politicians, authors, and everyone else in the public eye—thrive on favorable publicity the way flowers thrive on sun, soil, and water. So do businessmen, bureaucrats, union leaders, law-enforcement officials, doctors and lawyers, teachers—and journalists themselves. All know that favor-able media exposure in our society will most likely bring with it some degree of fame or fortune or both. "Good" publicity almost always translates to a better contract for the next movie or football draft, a bigger advance for the next book, election to office, promo-tion, or the selling of more automobiles, coats, phonograph records, or hamburgers. A favorable press report can make the difference between public acceptance or rejection of a municipal bond issue, school busing, or a whole war. The seasoned reporter never forgets that the person he is writing about cares just as much about himself and his product as does the reporter and *his* product.

Even the otherwise anonymous citizen who may have nothing to sell or promote almost always wants to be mentioned in an article, heard on the radio, or seen on television, since such exposure allows him to stand out in the faceless crowd and thus attain "fame," how-ever briefly. (Notice how many bystanders at street interviews or members of audiences wave at television cameras.) Being recorded in print or on tape provides even the most unassuming person with a ticket to immortality—with proof positive for all time that he existed and was considered important by his fellow creatures.

The reporter is therefore taken by almost everyone—notables and ordinary folk alike—as the great conduit for getting more than they already have. Most tend to think of the reporter as a sure vehicle for the achievement of some kind of success. Many among these deserve acclaim. Many others properly ought to be ignored. Still others deserve to be reprimanded, severely criticized, jailed, or worse. Sharp perception, based on experience and serious thought, underlies all reporting and constitutes one of your most serious challenges.

Here is a simple example. You and Picasso are sent out to cover that tenement fire. While the artist is busily sketching what both of you see, you are making notes on your trusty pad. The scene before you consists of what is left of a large brick building that has burned to the ground and is now nothing more than smoldering rubble. Firemen, doctors, and policemen are working in the debris or are watching from across the street. There is a line of bodies, each covered by a sheet, on the sidewalk in front of the building next to the one which has been destroyed. Picasso is hurriedly sketching white cubist corpses bathed in the yellow streetlight (undoubtedly with terror-filled eyes on their knees and anguished hands coming out of their ears). You have set down in writing what you see and you are now going to do something else. You are going to try to find out what happened.

During the course of an interview with a police sergeant you are told that the fire alarm was turned in by a passing patrolman who noticed thick smoke coming out of a third-floor window. There is no reason to doubt that. You next question the battalion commander whose firemen fought the blaze and, among several other details, he proudly tells you that his men were on the scene within two minutes of receiving the alarm. Taken as an isolated fact, there is no reason to doubt that statement, either. You could very easily inform perhaps a million readers, including city officials, insurance underwriters, and the relatives of the victims, that firemen were pouring water into the building and trying to rescue its occupants two minutes after the alarm was turned in. You could do that, but if you were observing as well as seeing and listening, you wouldn't. Instead, you would perceive that something didn't jell.

Given the fact that the building had been made of brick and had not been used to store TNT or aviation fuel, you would begin to wonder how it could have been so thoroughly destroyed, with so heavy a loss of life, in so short a time. Taking the sergeant's and the battalion commander's statements together and applying them to the physical evidence in front of you, you would perceive that each seemed to contradict the other.

"Something is wrong here, Pablo," you might tell the artist. "Those men are contradicting each other. Their combined account of what happened is implausible."

"Men are venal, amigo," Picasso might answer, while sketching a sorrowful teddy bear whose little owner was returning to a flaming womb. "What difference does it make? The result is the important thing, and the result here is tragic death and destruction. I must hurry to get it down." That is the truth for Pablo Picasso. But it is not the truth for you because, unlike him, the essence of your work is to find out what happened as well as to describe the result.

You would be left with these possibilities: (1) the patrolman did not turn in the alarm when the sergeant said he did; (2) the firemen did not get to the scene as quickly as their commander said they did; (3) if the firemen did get there within two minutes of the alarm, they were incompetent or negligent; or (4) both the sergeant and the battalion commander were telling the truth. You would then check police and fire department records and interview other participants and witnesses because you would know that the more "legwork" you did, the greater the probability that an accurate picture of what happened would emerge. If after checking and rechecking you decided that both men had told you the truth, you might begin to suspect that someone had deliberately turned the tenement into an inferno, perhaps after soaking the halls and stairways with gallons of gasoline.

Well before having arrived at the possibility of arson, however, you would have borne in mind that running a story in which the patrolman was pictured as being highly alert, intelligent, and energetic would mean a big brownie point for him, his sergeant, and the whole police department. Similarly, no newspaper or television account of firemen arriving at the scene of a blaze within two minutes of getting the alarm ever hurt a battalion commander's chances for promotion to chief. Any fire official who told a reporter,

"My men were actually late—I'd go so far as to say almost criminally late—because they're badly trained and mostly indifferent," would be asking for a line in *The Guiness Book of Records* and assignment to polishing hose nozzles forever. Public relations men and women are in business partly because the world is full of otherwise responsible officials (as well as many who are irresponsible) who do not know how to "deal with" the press (for "deal with" substitute "say the right thing to").

Your task, irrespective of what you are told or even what you think you see, is to get as close as possible to the truth; that is to say, as close as possible to describing the event as it happened or as it is happening. This is because, as a reporter, you are the trusted representative of the thousands—or even millions—who depend on you for an account of what actually transpired. You are in many instances their sole connection to an event in which they are interested and which may profoundly affect their lives. For them, what you say happened, *happened.* If you are lazy or imperceptive enough to feed them distortions or half-truths, you punish those who believe in you and reward those who take you for a patsy.

Irrespective of the camaraderie within journalism, journalists, if they are any good, are at bottom loners. Irrespective of the competition between newspapers, wire services, radio stations, and television networks, those who have reported the news for any length of time know that they really compete with themselves, both technically and ethically, and that they must therefore come to terms with themselves. So must the aspiring reporter. The habits learned early have a way of persisting and, in fact, of hardening as you go along. You would therefore be well advised to consider right now the sort of ethic you are prepared to bring to your work since, in the last analysis, you will have to bear the responsibility for what you do.

Some reporting assignments are what they seem to be, no more, no less. Others are in the general category of that tenement fire. Still others are vastly more complex, which is to say that the perception and energy required to cover them are greater, since the details and inconsistencies are more subtle. It is the perception of the *whole* story, of the inconsistencies and of the inconsistencies within inconsistencies, that is the hallmark of the real reporter. The flunky who takes what is handed to him obediently and unquestioningly in exchange for seeing his name in the paper or hearing it on television is scorned by the best of his fellow reporters and is usually even ridiculed in secret by those who use him. He is known in the profession as a hack.

When you can listen dispassionately to the verbiage thrown back and forth at a public hearing by those with entrenched interests, and sort out their motives, you will be well on your way. When you can come at them later with intelligent, penetrating questions designed to force their real motives to the surface, you will be still further along. And when you can take the fruits of such reporting, judge it clearly, and produce a story that is scrupulously fair and genuinely informative, you will have reached the point at which you can proudly call yourself a true professional. Frogs and hacks will never be able to do that.

# chapter three

# THE GOLDEN RULE:
# TELL THE TRUTH

Most reporters (not to mention the publishers or station owners they work for) think of libel the way people in the Middle Ages thought of the plague—as an unseen but ever-present menace that can appear out of nowhere and consume them. And they're right. The loss of a libel action can cripple or even destroy a newspaper or magazine and can effectively end a reporter's career. They worry about libel, all right, but they usually worry for the wrong reason. Reporters ought to be wary of libel, not because some judge might rule against them in court, but because lying is morally wrong. Libel is, in essence, an ethical, not a strictly legal problem. It therefore warrants discussion at the outset of instruction on reporting—well before pencil touches paper—not long afterward.

Libel is defamation in writing ("defamation of character," as some script writers insist on putting it, perhaps in the belief that it is possible to defame something else). Slander is spoken defamation, so if you write the news you do not need to worry about slander. Defamation, in turn, is taken to be any statement about an individual that exposes him to hatred, contempt, or ridicule, or that causes him to be avoided, or that tends to injure him in his occupation. Since each state has its own libel statutes, and since the United States Supreme Court decisions on the subject change every once in a while, libel can be a complicated business.

Libel laws exist to protect individuals from unfair treatment by those who write about them. If there were no such laws, many writers (reporters undoubtedly foremost among them) would use the First Amendment to the Constitution like a hunting license in a never-ending season: Here is what the First Amendment says:

> Congress shall make no law respecting an establishment of religion, or prohibiting the free exercise thereof; or abridging the freedom of speech, or of the press; or the right of the people peaceably to assemble, and to petition the Government for a redress of grievances.

Without some kind of legal restraint, that part about freedom of the press could be taken to mean that if a reporter wanted to write that you or I torture animals, steal from orphans, cheat our friends, or even commit murder, he or she could do so with impunity. If we challenged the allegations the reporter in question might very likely raise a righteous finger and, waving it under the appropriate nose, quote the First Amendment to the effect that the press is guaranteed freedom to say what it pleases. The purpose of libel law is therefore to prevent writers from writing untruths about otherwise defenseless citizens; in other words, to keep writers as honest as possible. No serious reporter, mindful of the fact that he is also an otherwise defenseless citizen, would think of objecting to the principle of libel law.

It is therefore most important for reporters to put themselves in the place of those they write about. This is not to say that they should feel especially sorry for some ne'er-do-well who clearly deserves to be poleaxed. Indeed, protecting the public from scoundrels lies at the heart of what reporters are supposed to do. But they should never lose sight of the fact that what is provable, and only what is provable, should determine who among us gets the esteem and who gets the ripe tomato full in the face. That notion forms the basis of what we like to think of as justice, not because of the threat of being sued, but because it is simply unfair to portray someone as guilty of something when he or she is innocent. In a legal sense, by the way, a lawsuit means nothing. Someone could, in theory, sue you for keeping a canary or for snoring. There is no disgrace in being sued since anyone, including the village idiot, can launch a lawsuit. The problem comes with *losing* the suit, and therefore with suffering some kind of damage, such as having to pay money, having your reputation harmed, having to go to jail, having a legal precedent established that might be detrimental to the interests of your profession, or any combination of these.

Similarly, there is a common misconception that libelous writing must be avoided at all costs. That isn't so. If reporters couldn't libel when they had to, they would be ineffective. We just said that libel is defamation. Defaming those who deserve it—exposing them to contempt, ridicule, and professional setback—is a legitimate journalistic practice. "Deserve," though, is the key word. When you report that a public official has accepted a bribe, you have libeled him, and there's no question about it. That's entirely as it should be, *provided you are right*. It comes down to a matter of Truth or Consequences.

There are two basic kinds of libel: criminal and civil. In cases of criminal libel (which are relatively rare), the government sues the person who has libeled and if it wins, the loser can be jailed or fined. Criminal libel usually relates to the defamation of groups, local government officials, or the dead, and the libeler is nothing more than a witness. The civil libel action, which is almost always the kind that stalks journalists, ends in court duels between individuals and in the payment of damages by the losers to the winners.

Civil libel, in turn, comes in two varieties: *per se* and *per quod*. Libel *per se* is libel by definition, or libel on the face of it. If you run a story accusing the mayor of having built his swimming pool with syndicate money or with public funds, you have committed libel *per se*. If the mayor thinks he can convince a court that you are wrong (irrespective of whether or not he is guilty), or if he thinks you do not have sufficient proof to justify the charge you have made, you will very likely hear from his lawyer and then become a defendant in a libel *per se* action.

Libel *per quod* is hazier because it means libel on condition, or in particular circumstances. In other words, sometimes a statement can be libelous, while at other times the same statement is not libelous. Let's say, for example, that you do a story alleging that someone used a leg trap to capture foxes during the trapping season. If there is no law against the use of that kind of trap, the judge would rule that you did not commit libel *per se*. But he might rule that you committed libel *per quod,* depending on the nature of the person you wrote about. If the fellow was known to do occasional trapping with the devices, you'd be home free. If, on the other hand, he turned out to be the president of the local humane society, you would have defamed him, and you would therefore probably get slapped with a suit charging libel *per quod*. You would then be best advised to show up in court with on-the-spot photographs of man, trap, and beast, with witnesses, and with any other foxes who happened to have been present and who were willing to testify for the defendant (you).

Journalists have three basic defenses against libel, and it pays to know them: (1) privilege; (2) fair comment; (3) truth. Again, you should familiarize yourself with the laws covering each of these defenses as they have been set down by the legislators in your state.

## Privilege.

Certain documents and proceedings in the public domain are said to be privileged, meaning that the press has the privilege of quoting them because the public has the right of access to them. If the press were unable to quote from a Senate debate, for example, the only persons who would be certain of knowing exactly what was said in the debate would be those who were present. But the press is there to provide much wider dissemination, and in order to be able to do so accurately, it must be able to quote verbatim from the official proceeding even if the statements in that proceeding are libelous. Privilege does not apply, however, to interviews, since they are not a matter of public record. Thus, if Senator Blowharde says on the floor of the Senate that a certain aircraft manufacturer produces defective airplanes, he can be quoted by the press, since the public has the right to know that he made the charge in a forum at which the public is represented. But if Blowharde tells a reporter the same thing in an interview, and the reporter quotes him as having said it, it is risky. Not only could the aircraft manufacturer sue Blowharde, it could sue the reporter. In practice, though, it would probably be the publisher or station owner who was sued, since either of them would likely have more money than Blowharde and the reporter combined.

### Fair Comment.

This defense holds that those who court publicity or who are otherwise in the public eye, and especially those who want to be mentioned in newspapers and magazines or on radio and television, must be prepared to accept criticism as well as praise, provided the criticism adheres as closely as possible to sound judgment and is given without malice. This applies to anyone who wants to be reviewed (authors, actors, politicians, directors, dancers, singers, musicans, magicans, athletes, lion tamers, and so on). The critical element in fair comment, however, is the fairness of the comment. If a theater critic pans the star of a musical by reporting that the range of her voice was not equal to the score, or that her acting was amateurish or even awful, he is absolutely within his right. But he will be judged to have been reporting with malice if he makes those assertions without having attended the performance. Furthermore, if he wrote that the actress turned in a poor performance because of her heavy drinking and carousing, he would have to be able to prove conclusively that: (1) the actress drank heavily and caroused frequently, and that (2) both of those indulgences caused her to perform badly. Even the legendary Clarence Darrow would have been hard pressed to win that one.

### Truth.

In all but a few states, the truth constitutes a complete libel defense (where it doesn't, the story must not only be proven to be true, but also to have been written without malice). In practice, though, establishing that a story is true generally has a decisive effect in any libel suit, criminal or civil, irrespective of what may have motivated the reporter. It is important to remember, though, that it is not up to the plaintiff to prove that the reporter did *not* tell the truth; it is up to the reporter to prove that he *did*. Documenary evidence—letters, canceled checks, transcripts, diaries, and the like—is generally required, as are witnesses who will testify that the defamation is true. Reporters' notes and tapes are also often admissible as evidence, which explains why most reporters hang on to them, particularly if they involve a sensitive story. After covering any story that, however remotely, might end in court, most reporters file their notebooks in chronological or subject order and keep them until mildew makes them illegible.

Probably every derogatory term in the language has at one time or another been considered for, or has actually been made the point of, a libel action. In addition to such obvious epithets as cheat, liar, murderer, thief, traitor, perjurer, informer, briber, and lunatic, impugning a woman's chastity is libelous, and so is casting doubt on someone's professional competence (and therefore, it would be charged, on his or her ability to make a living). It is libelous to call a doctor a quack, a clergyman a pagan, a lawyer an ambulance chaser, a teacher a numbskull, an airline pilot a spastic, a nurse a sadist, a policeman a crook, a soldier a coward, or a journalist a careless or malicious writer of libel. . . .

Where libel is concerned, individuals come in two types: public and private. As was mentioned in the Fair Comment defense, celebrities or anyone else courting publicity—who seek media exposure in order to enhance their livelihoods—have to be prepared to take the bad with the good unless they are treated maliciously. Where press criticism is concerned, they are considered by the courts to have walked voluntarily into a gambling casino to take their chances at the cards, and it's nobody's fault but their own if they lose.

Private citizens, however, are a far different matter. Compared to celebrities and others who get media exposure, private citizens are considered to be basically defenseless, so they get more protection. Since most private citizens do not court the media, and indeed have little or no access to it, they are far more likely to win libel suits than are those in the public eye. The courts have therefore decided that while "public" individuals must prove malice in order to win a libel suit, "private" individuals need only prove that they have been libeled through negligence or through reckless disregard of the facts. This distinction—between who is "public" and who is "private"—has been the subject of several recent court battles and is in a continuous state of redefinition. It is one of the most fundamental elements in libel law, and certainly one that should be grasped by journalists.

Further, the United States Supreme Court has ruled that even a private citizen who achieves sudden prominence by news events can successfully sue after a false and defamatory account of his role in those events has been published or broadcast. The majority opinion, written by Justice Lewis F. Powell Jr., drew a clear distinction between an ordinary citizen and "public officials [who] have voluntarily exposed themselves to increased risk of injury from defamatory falsehoods." The ordinary citizen, Justice Powell continued, "has relinquished no part of his interest in the protection of his own good name, and consequently he has a more compelling call on the courts for redress of injury inflicted by defamatory falsehoods." Again: the little guy needs more protection than the big guy.

The landmark political libel case was resolved by the Supreme Court in 1964. It came to a conclusion long held by reporters and other cynical citizens: politicians and government officials are like actors, jugglers, and magicians.

This is what happened. A civil rights group placed an advertisement in *The New York Times* accusing the Montgomery, Alabama, police of launching a "wave of terror" against black activists there. Since newspapers are legally responsible for everything they print, including letters to the editor and advertisements, L. B. Sullivan, Montgomery's Commissioner of Public Affairs, sued *The Times* for libel. Sullivan was in charge of four municipal departments (police, fire, cemetery, and scales), and although he was not named in the ad, he held that the police department had been falsely defamed and that anyone reading the ad could therefore think that *he* had been defamed, too. Sullivan was awarded $500,000 by an Alabama jury and the Alabama Supreme Court upheld the verdict. But the United States Supreme Court reversed the decision, saying: "The constitutional guarantees require, we think, a federal rule that prohibits a public official from recovering damages for a defamatory falsehood relating to his official conduct unless he proves that the statement was made with 'actual malice'—that is, with knowledge that it was false or with reckless disregard of whether it was false or not."

The effect of that decision was to provide the press with an extension of the Fair Comment defense to the political arena, and therefore to insure freer debate on issues of public importance. No longer would reporters withhold honest criticism under the threat of losing a libel action to a politician or a government official. They would have to write something really nasty, even with malice, to get into legal trouble, and no journalist would be so vindictive and unprincipled as to do that, right? Wrong.

There is a classic example of malicious political libel which, if you'll pardon my saying so, is a textbook case. It involves not only malicious libel *per se* but, in addition and more to the point, the most flagrantly unethical kind of reporting—reporting in which a target is first singled out for destruction and then "facts" are assembled to support the ax job. I refer to *Goldwater v. Ginzburg* (1969). As you read what follows, try to understand why the issue involved malicious libel, consider the quality of the reporting, and most important, put yourself in Goldwater's place.

The September-October 1964 issue of *Fact* magazine was wrapped around a heavily publicized story billed as "The Unconscious of a Conservative:  A Special Issue on the Mind of Barry Goldwater." The story's main theme was the allegation that Senator Barry M. Goldwater of Arizona, who about two months before had won the Republican presidential nomination to run against Lyndon Johnson, was paranoid and psychologically unfit for the presidency. *Fact* was owned, edited, and published by Ralph Ginzburg, a renowned gadfly in magazine publishing circles, who had a colleague named Warren Boroson.

According to court testimony (which can be cited here because it is a matter of public record and is therefore privileged), Ginzburg and Boroson decided immediately after Goldwater's nomination that they would put together a special story alerting the American people to what they saw as the danger of allowing him to become President. Boroson was given the job of gathering "every scrap of information in the public record that was relevant to the psychobiography of Goldwater," while Ginzburg polled psychiatrists across the country for their opinions on the Senator's sanity.

On July 16—the very day the idea for the story was hatched and before any polling had been done—Boroson wrote a letter to union leader Walter Reuther that clearly showed that Ginzburg and Boro-

son had already decided to skewer the Senator. Here, in part, is
what Boroson wrote: "I'm writing an article for *Fact* about an old
enemy of yours—Barry Goldwater. It's going to be a psychological
profile, and will say, basically, that Goldwater is so belligerent, suspicious, hot-tempered, and rigid because he has deep-seated doubts
about his masculinity. . . ."

While he waited for Reuther's answer (it never came), Boroson
combed newspapers, magazines, and books for material that, in his
opinion, "gave some sort of insight into . . . [Goldwater's] psychological makeup." The evidence suggests that the process was
highly selective. In several instances derogatory material was pulled
out of a paragraph that also contained complimentary references
and was printed out of context in the *Fact* article. Here, for example,
is part of an article that appeared in the June 23, 1961, issue of

While he waited for Reuther's answer (it never came), Boroson
marked it:

> Finally, the Goldwaters sent him to Virginia's strait-laced
> *Staunton Military Academy. During Barry's first year, academy
> officials repeatedly asked Baron Goldwater to take back his
> undisciplined heir.* But four years later, when Barry earned his
> diploma, he was captain of the football team, and he wore on
> his uniform the medal given to the school's outstanding cadet.

In addition to trying to squeeze Goldwater into an "Authoritarian
Personality," at least one of the drafts Boroson gave to Ginzburg
suggested that their target was a "submissive-passive-homosexual"
and that the "masculine facade that Goldwater has thrown up helps
fool many people." Further, wrote Boroson, Goldwater was suffering from "repressed homosexuality" and "fears of a homosexual
type." Portions of the draft's allegations, which were sent to Ginzburg with a magazine article on homosexuality, appeared in *Fact*.
Ginzburg eventually eliminated most of the references to an authoritarian personality and concentrated instead on the theory that Goldwater was paranoid and, in general, an all-around sickie. That's
where the well-known poll of psychiatrists came in. Having had
training in neither psychiatry nor polling, Ginzburg and Boroson
polled psychiatrists with an invitation to answer this question: "Do
you believe Barry Goldwater is psychologically fit to serve as President of the United States? (   ) No    (   ) Yes."

Here, in part, is the covering letter that went out with the questionnaire: "A recent survey by *Medical Tribune* showed that psychiatrists—in sharp contrast to all other MDs—hold Goldwater in low esteem. Among M.D.s generally, approximately two-thirds prefer Goldwater over Johnson. But among psychiatrists, the preference is for Johnson by ten to one."

After asking the recipient of the questionnaire to indicate whether Goldwater was fit to serve as president based on "public utterances, his political viewpoints, and whatever knowledge you may have of his personality and background," the letter went on to ask: "Does he seem prone to aggressive behavior and destructiveness? Does he seem callous to the downtrodden and needy? Can you offer any explanation of his public temper-tantrums and his occasional outbursts of profanity? Finally, do you think that his having had two nervous breakdowns has any bearing on his fitness to govern the country?"

It is hard to conceive of a more loaded questionnaire. Not only were the results of the *Medical Tribune* survey distorted, but the reference to the two "nervous breakdowns" was taken from articles written by Alvin Toffler and based on purported interviews with Mrs. Goldwater in which she said that her husband had suffered a nervous breakdown in 1936 or 1937 because of overwork, and that he had had a recurrence two years later. Ginzburg later admitted in court that "nervous breakdown" is an imprecise term that could mean any number of things, that he had made no effort to find out exactly what Mrs. Goldwater had meant, and that he had not thought it necessary to include any of the circumstances that preceded the "breakdowns" on his questionnaire.

According to the story that appeared in *Fact,* questionnaires were sent 12,356 psychiatrists, with 2,417 responding. Of the 2,417 returns, the article said, 571 psychiatrists explained that they did not know enough about Goldwater to answer the question; 657 said that they thought he was fit to be President; 1,189 said that they thought he was psychologically unfit for the job.

An examination of the questionnaires, however, showed that most of them were unsigned. Many of these anonymous responses were published by Ginzburg and labeled "Name withheld," followed by "M.D.," indicating that the psychiatrists had actually signed the questionnaires, but had asked that their names be omitted. In fact,

31 of the 45 letters listed by Ginzburg as "Name withheld" were anonymous. In addition, one letter criticizing the poll and that bore the signature, name, and address of the writer, was printed as "anonymous" because, Ginzburg claimed, he wanted to spare its author "embarrassment." Finally, Ginzburg admitted that he personally edited all of the published responses, with the result that statements favorable to Goldwater were taken out, while others backing *Fact*'s assertion were added. The results of the "poll" became the second part of the "Goldwater issue." The first part, which was drafted by Boroson and virtually rewritten by Ginzburg, was sprinkled with charges that the Senator was unstable and paranoid, in addition to containing the more standard political thrusts. Only that first part's last paragraph need be quoted to sum up. Emphasis is mine.

> In the context of Barry Goldwater's personality, this is not a call for an impossible victory, nor even what Senator Fulbright sarcastically termed "a bold, courageous and determined policy of coannihilation." It is a fantasy of the final conflagration, the twilight of the gods, in which he—and the whole hostile world—will heroically play out the last act of the Human Drama. *If it sounds like the death-fantasy of another paranoiac woven in Berchtesgaden and realized in a Berlin bunker not long ago, it is no surprise.*

Accustomed as he was to often vicious attacks, even Goldwater could not leave unchallenged the irresponsible and blatantly malicious accusation that he was a sexual deviate and a Hitleresque madman dedicated to turning the planet into a torch. He sued and was awarded a considerable sum in damages from Ginzburg and from Fact Magazine, Inc. The court decision was appealed but upheld, and although Ralph Ginzburg is still around, *Fact* in fact went up in a puff of legal smoke, having had its coffers emptied and reputation discredited. More important, though, is that to some degree the profession of journalism also was discredited. All of the scrupulously honest men and women who daily brought as much balance, fairness, and dedication as possible to their craft were, to some extent, tarnished along with Ginzburg.

It cannot be stressed too strongly that the best libel defense is integrity and caution, not only because of the specter of coming out on the wrong end of a court decision, but far more important, because reporters must maintain the confidence of the public they serve. The pro never forgets that it is easier to wrong rights than it is to right wrongs.

# chapter four

# WRITING IN STYLE/WRITING WITH STYLE

BUCHAREST, Romania, June 17—Dr. Gheorghe Vulpe-Sireata, the Communist Party Chief of Rumania, asserted today before a delectatious assemblage consisting of loyal Bucuresti inhabitants that the Roumanian people consider the United States to be nothing more nor less than the quintessential diabolical entity.

Vulpe-Sireata, often referred to as the "Beast of Bucherest" due to his having instigated the thorough and complete anihilation of "misanthropic" (anti-communist) elements during the revolution, exuded his customary bravado during the exceedingly dull marathon pronouncement.

Romania personifies verisimilitude, he stated to the throng of tumultuous, but spiritually moribund Slavs, while the United States epitomizes consumate hypocrisy and international lasciviousness.

Since Rumania is the land of Dracula, it was another instance of the pot calling the kettle black.

Here is a composite wretched news story. It is practically impossible to imagine a worse piece of news writing. There are so many things wrong with it that I wouldn't trust that reporter to report his own tennis score, much less a speech by a foreign leader. In fact, I find myself in sympathy with the maligned Dr. Vulpe-Sireata and those who want to read about him, and filled with contempt for the reporter who produced so much rubbish.

There are at least six major problems with the story. It is: (1) inconsistent, (2) unclear and intimidating, (3) redundant, (4) misspelled, (5) factually incorrect, and (6) blatantly biased. These are the problems that individually or in combination plague most beginning reporters. Let's take them one at a time.

### Consistency.

Most large newspapers in this country (*The New York Times* and *The Washington Post* among them) use so-called style books as guidelines to assure consistency of spelling, capitalization, punctuation, abbreviation, and meaning in their news columns. So do radio and television networks. The Associated Press and United Press International collaborate on their own style book, while book-publishing houses use the University of Chicago's *A Manual of Style* or some similar reference work. "Style" here does not mean literary style. It means, rather, a set of rules or guidelines that are followed for the sake of consistency and also to minimize editing problems. Here is what the 1962 edition (it has since been updated) of *The New York Times Style Book* said in its own justification:

"Why are rules necessary? Other things being equal, or at least in correct proportion, there is not much difference between a Martini and a martini. But a publication that capitalizes the word on one page and lower-cases it on another may lead the careful reader to believe that such untidiness extends to larger matters."

This means that a reader who notes that the capital city and the name of the country in our story are each spelled three ways may rightly suspect that whoever wrote it is sloppy in his reporting, as well as in his spelling. And once the reader suspects that, he or she will very likely become suspicious about the substance of the story.

Having noted that Romania, Rumania, and Roumanian appear in the same paragraph, even a casual reader would probably begin to wonder whether the party chief's name was correctly spelled, whether the speech was made where the story said it was, or indeed, whether the reporter was accurately passing along the substance of the speech. Experience has shown that when this happens readers go elsewhere for their news.

Whether the correct name of the country in our story is Rumania or Romania is actually secondary, where style is concerned, to picking either spelling and sticking with it. As a matter of fact, *The New York Times* and the *Encyclopaedia Britannica* use *Rumania,* while the Associated Press, *Webster's Third New International Dictionary* and, interestingly enough, *The New York Times–Times of London Atlas of the World* prefers *Romania.* Romanians also prefer the latter, perhaps because *Romans* (not Rumans) at one time occupied the land in question, because *Romania* means "land of *Rome,*" and because the national language therefore falls into the *Romance* (not Rumance) category. The debate can be left to philologists and to copy editors working the late shift. What's important is that *The Times,* having decided once upon a time that *Rumania* is correct, sticks with it. So should you. Whatever style guide you use, learn its rudiments early and refer to it as often as is necessary.

### Clarity.

Throughout your academic career, you have probably been paid by the pound for the writing you have done. Many teachers of English composition, as well as those in other humanities and in the social sciences, reward students who turn in the longest papers with the best grades. Worse, they put a premium on the number of footnotes, the length of the bibliography (which therefore tends to get heavily padded), and on words that are generally incomprehensible to anyone caught without a dictionary. The theory behind this, I suppose, is that such prose builds a massive vocabulary and sound scholarly method. But it also makes most of what is written in and for school painfully dull and unclear and, further, it produces hordes of writers who use multisyllables and grotesquely complicated phrases to conceal the fact that they, themselves, are not terribly clear about what they're doing. Universities, government agencies on every level, and corporations worldwide are loaded with theses, reports, and memorandums that are unbearably (and usually needlessly) complicated, stilted, and plain dull.

Reporters are paid in anti-pounds. That is, the shorter and clearer the writing, the better. Good reporters try to conserve space, not consume it. They understand that they can bring in the most important story in the world, but that unless people read it, all the other work is for nothing and they will have failed at their job of informing. Reporters know that most readers' attention spans are short and that prose should therefore be made as digestible as possible. The crucial difference between writing for teachers, parents, and loved ones, and writing for the public, is that the former usually have to read what you write, while the latter must want to read it. The reporter, in other words, sells his writing the way a chef sells his entrées. Both commodities must be made palatable or they will be ignored.

Therefore, always write to be understood, and understand, in turn, that even the most complicated stories can be reduced to perfect clarity with a little serious effort. And the foundation of the clear story, as opposed to the one from Bucharest, is the short word. This is not to say that there aren't some wonderful long words, or that every piece of writing you do ought to be thinned to the point of anemia. It does mean, though, that you ought to learn how to produce uncluttered prose in the beginning so you'll be able to differentiate later between long words that belong and those that don't. It's a matter of nuance. It says below, for example, that "job" is preferable to "employment." Not always. If you were to write a story about a dethroned, but proud, king who needed work, "seeking employment" might be better than "looking for a job" in trying to set the tone of the piece and portray that individual. Similarly, if our ex-monarch got a janitor's job, but didn't do well at it because he couldn't bear getting his hands soiled (as opposed to dirty), we might want to say that he was terminated (as opposed to fired). But that will come later. It is more important at this stage to develop a dependable, terse style through the use of simple, clean words. Here is a sampling of common, needlessly long or stilted words, and acceptable equivalents:

| | |
|---|---|
| altercation (argument) | conflagration (fire) |
| anticipate (expect) | employment (job) |
| assemblage (audience) | commence (begin) |
| transpire (happen) | purchase (buy) |
| sufficient (enough) | utilize (use) |
| acquire (get) | initiate (start) |
| reside at (live at) | concur (agree) |
| prior to (before) | terminate (end) |
| numerous (many) | deceased (dead) |
| exacerbate (worsen) | inundate (cover) |

Gleaning innumerable others should present no insurmountable discomfiture. . . .

You also should be aware that payment by the pound is not confined to those who write, nor even to the speech of scholars, politicians, bureaucrats, and others in the word business. Where stringing together lots of unnecessary letters and words is concerned, the rule of "mass equals class" has filtered down to the half-educated but socially aspiring man on the street who wants to show the world that his vocabulary ranks with Dr. Johnson's. Thus, you can turn on your television and listen to a bystander who has seen the result of a brutal murder say: "The perpetrator of this heinous crime should be incarcerated" (The slob who did this ought to be locked up forever).

Always try for the simplest way of describing something without sacrificing the meaning of what you're reporting.

### Succinctness.

All reporters fight two relentless enemies: time and space. Irrespective of the nature of the story, reporters work against clocks, so they must use their time with utmost care. The selling of news is a highly competitive business, since old news isn't news, it's history. Wire-service reporters (those working for the AP, UPI, Reuters, Dow Jones, Agence France-Presse, and other agencies) are in breakneck competition with one another and frequently measure their beats (the professional term for "scoop") in seconds. Furthermore, they and their brethren on newspapers, radio, and television must get to the point of the story as quickly as possible, rather than force readers or listeners to give up because they don't want to wade through excess verbiage. Professionals also know that, in large part, time and space are directly related. Given the same story, the reporter who writes "tighter" will finish first and grab the bigger audience. That's why concise writing is taken as a commandment in the news media, and why the laggard who insists on obscuring his trail with indiscriminate and unnecessary clutter is often ordered by his editor to rewrite his gem and is then warned, "We aren't putting out a weekly, Cosgrove!"

That "thorough and complete anihilation" in the Romanian story is a case in point. In fact, it's a double mistake. First, and most obviously, "thorough" and "complete" are synonymous so either could have been left out. Second, since "annihilation" means ceasing to exist, or total destruction, both "thorough" and "complete" should have been left out: something either exists or it doesn't.

Similarly, there is a long list of everyday expressions whose contents can be pared (not pared *down*) or changed in the interests of time and space. Consider "falling down," and then ask yourself, who (aside from an astronaut) falls *up*? Or: "call up" (call); "along with" (with); "end result" (result); "cheer up" (cheer); "write down" (write); "take note of" (note); "think up" (think); "hand it over" (hand to), and many others. The next time you hear someone say, "I thought to myself," consider whether it is possible to think to anyone else. Here are some other, even more cumbersome, examples:

| | |
|---|---|
| all of a sudden (suddenly) | came to a stop (stopped) |
| in the near future (soon) | went on to say (added) |
| at the present time (now) | at that time (then) |
| on the occasion of (at/when) | once in a great while (rarely) |
| a small number of (few) | is of the opinion that (believes) |
| a large number of (many) | told them that (said) |

You can also save time, space, energy, and your editor's nerves, while improving your prose, by avoiding euphemisms and clichés.

People do not "pass away"; they die. Students do not "encounter horrendous scholastic setbacks"; they fail. Ghettos do not "undergo socioeconomic deprivation"; they are ignored. Those who collect garbage are not sanitary engineers; they are garbage collectors or sanitationmen. Employees do not have their jobs "unilaterally terminated"; they are fired. Robbers are not ensnared in police nets"; they are caught. Political statements are not "inoperative"; they are untrue.

And train yourself to avoid all clichés because (1) our mother tongue is polluted enough without deliberately worsening the situation, and (2) everyone in the writing profession, plus many serious readers and listeners, knows that only lazy minds need resort to the likes of these: right as rain, good as gold; happy as a clam; kick in the teeth; slap in the face; spice of life; ups and downs; give the green light; birds of a feather; play possum; go to the dogs; eat like a horse; busy as a bee; snake in the grass; tip the scales; treat with kid gloves; give an icy stare, a cold shoulder, or a winning smile; play the game; have the roof fall in; do it all in a day's work (or in a split-second, in a month of Sundays, or once in a blue moon); take your lumps; go down swinging; rise to the occasion (in the nick of time); land on your feet (where the grass is always greener); go on the ropes; lose your shirt; remain abreast of the times; give a sigh of relief; use elbow grease (by the sweat of your brow); and on . . . and on . . . and on. . . . Remember: Don't get your back to the wall—lick the cliché habit by keeping your nose to the grindstone, your shoulder to the wheel, and maybe even your ear to the ground.

## Spelling.

Every time newspaper editors and journalism instructors discuss the state of unpreparedness of many of the young men and women who start in the profession with new diplomas and little or no experience, good grammar and sound spelling come out at the top of the Most Wanted list. "We can't spend time doing remedial work in the basics," the editors complain to the journalism instructors. And the proverbial buck doesn't stop there, either. Every time journalism instructors and high school English teachers meet (which is rare), the same thought is expressed. "We can't spend time doing remedial work in the basics," the journalism instructors complain to the English teachers. "We're doing the best we can," answer the English teachers, given budget cuts, crowded classes, a variety of social problems, and—the sorry state of primary education. . . . There is some justification for all excuses.

Unfortunately, though, national reading and writing aptitude is in a long decline. Whatever the cause of your grammatical and spelling shortcomings, you are the one who is stuck with them and, ultimately, you are the one who is going to have to correct them or face the consequences. If you aren't reasonably adept at the written form of your own language by the time you leave the university, given the competition for reporting jobs, you are going to be severely handicapped. In the case of grammar, you can take remedial composition courses or possibly work on your own with any of the good guides on the subject.

Word construction has to be treated like other facts, and for the same reason: being wrong erodes your credibility. It's a fact, for example, that contrary to what appears in the Romania story, "annihilation" takes two n's. Here are a bare few of the most commonly misspelled words in basic reporting courses:

| | |
|---|---|
| a lot (not alot) | inseparable |
| accommodate | judgment (preferred) |
| all right (not alright) | kidnap |
| commitment | likable |
| consensus | occurred |
| drunkenness (not drunkedness) | peaceable |
| fulfill | permissible |

### Facts.

True Romanians are not Slavs, but are a mixture of Roman and Dacian. Slavs, as typified by the ethnic Ukrainians in the country, are a small minority. To be honest, I don't find that fact particularly noteworthy. What is noteworthy, however, is that the reporter who covered Vulpe-Sireata's speech made a factual error. And if he made one factual error, it is entirely possible that he made others. I am suspicious. What if Vulpe-Sireata really said that the Soviet Union, not the United States, is a farce? What if those listening to his speech in Bucharest (if, indeed, it *was* Bucharest) were not loyal at all, but were openly hostile and demanding a change of government? What did that fellow miss? What else did he get wrong?

Again, the reporter is usually the only line of communication between most readers, listeners, and viewers, and the events which, however indirectly, affect their lives. If the press says that New Zealand has sunk, that Soviet submarines are painted pink, an airplane has flown backward, wheat germ causes manic depression, or Romanians are Slavs, an astoundingly large number of people who have no way of knowing better will believe it. And you're one of them. If you stop and think about how dependent you are on the "news" for information—for facts—you will see how vulnerable you are to errors and distortion. That's why, after grabbing the army and the police, dictators invariably go after the press. They do so because they want to fashion the "news" to suit their own needs; they want to distort it in order to maximize power.

Beginning reporters seldom find themselves as the link between high politics and a receptive public. They do deal with matters of fact every day, though, and their credibility depends on getting each of those little facts straight.

The serious beginner therefore accepts as gospel that for the rest of his working life all facts, no matter how seemingly trivial, will have to be checked for authenticity before being passed on. It cannot be emphasized strongly enough that no piece of information is too inconsequential to get right. If it's really unimportant it doesn't belong in the story. The rule is this: if it's worth reporting, it's worth reporting accurately. If the public ever has reason to doubt a reporter's accuracy, he's worse than useless—he's a menace.


### Objectivity.

There is no such thing. · The completely objective news story is like the utopian political system: it is a goal yet to be achieved.

Total objectivity is impossible in news reporting because, being human, we bring our emotions and prejudicies to what we perceive. Reporters have as many (if not more) ways of seeing events as others do and, in addition, they must work under the pressure of severe time and space limitations. Even a reporter who makes desperate efforts at impartiality faces two problems. First, he must not only decide which information to put in the story, but which to leave out. The part that is left out might make the story more objective but there may be no space for it. Second, he must decide which element of the story gets the most "play" (emphasis) and relegate the rest to lesser play. News judgment is the decisive factor, but even the soundest judgment does not mean that all important elements in a story will be represented in exact proportion to their real part in it.

The so-called "new journalism" (which isn't new at all) is now in vogue. It was rekindled during the highly emotional conflicts over civil rights and Vietnam in the 1960s when some reporters, rejecting the proposition that they were merely passive news gathering 'machines,' began writing as participants in the events they covered. The result was a great deal of highly subjective (and often excellent) prose by Tom Wolfe, Norman Mailer, Gay Talese, and others who injected their feelings into their reporting. Since reporters are not deaf, dumb, and blind, since they have their passions and are at least as capable as others of feeling horror and outrage, they can rightly be expected to express those feelings. But opinions should be vented in appropriate places—in certain magazine articles, in columns, and in specialized papers—not in places where they are taken as accurate and balanced accounts of what has happened. Advocacy reporting and the straight kind can exist side by side but neither should replace the other or, worse, masquerade as the other.

If people were fed only slanted news there would be no place to go for straight news and that, in turn, would mean that propaganda would be the citizen's only diet. Consider living in a society in which the only news you got came shaped according to the beliefs of the group that wrote it. The truth would be their "truth' and there would be no recourse to any other. No intelligent decision could be made on the basis of a continuous and pervasive flow of distorted or selected information. In this regard—where distortion is concerned—the far right and far left are seen by the serious journalist as posing the same problem. The radical press is the first to slash at "fascistic news distortion," while doing precisely the same thing under the banner of its own version of revealed truth. The right-wing press, for its part, is equally determined to warp and censor according to its own doctrine, and to hammer away at its left-wing rivals for *their* distortions. The reporter dedicated to passing on events as they actually occur is equally wary of both camps.

Democracy is predicated on the proposition that when citizens are given fair and balanced reporting they will make intelligent decisions about how they are governed. That has not always been the case. But such is not the reporter's primary concern when he provides the people with news. He knows that the citizens of a democracy have a perfect right to vote to go to hell in a hand basket if they want. They are, in fact, guaranteed the right to make that choice. The task of the news story is not to deliberately move the public one way or the other, but to provide it with enough balanced information so that it is able to make some knowledgeable decision on its own.

During the difficult 112-day New York newspaper strike of 1962–63, James Reston of *The New York Times* summed up the frustration he felt at being deprived of his column, and at the same time offered insight into how he saw himself, with this partly (but only partly) tongue-in-cheek question: "How do I know what to believe if I can't read what I write?"

As much should be asked on behalf of the citizens of a democracy: "How do I know what to believe if I can't believe what I read?" Yet many do not believe what they read. Indeed, the expression, "I only believe what I read in the newspaper," has come to mean the opposite; that the reader does not trust what he or she reads. And that skepticism, in part well founded, is the most dangerous thing stalking the American press.

If you want to believe in the news you write, and have others believe in it as well, you must take absolute care to report to the best of your ability what has actually happened, not what you want to have happened. Louts, liars, and laggards—stinkards of all stripes —who are accurately portrayed and precisely quoted in free and open forum, will either hang themselves or provoke others to do it for them. You need not use the news columns to do the job and, in fact, you will very likely bring them sympathy they don't deserve if you try. More important, even louts, liars, and laggards are entitled to fair and impartial reporting, since one person's liar is another person's sage. Your morality is not necessarily more valid or compelling than the next person's. To believe otherwise is to be the sort of person you would probably be the first to condemn. An unquestioned reputation for fairness is the sure mark of True Style.

# part two

# PRACTICE

# chapter five

# FORMAT

News writers are generally required to prepare copy (what they write) in a form prescribed by the organization for which they work. That form varies slightly from one news operation to another, but in general, the rules in this section should see you through any news-writing situation.

You must prepare copy the way your teacher or editor wants it prepared. This doesn't mean that your creative instinct is going to be squelched. It does mean, though, that you have to make a distinction right now between substance and form. Varying creative styles make the newsroom the vibrant and interesting place it ought to be. But varying form, when several editors and others must work on your copy and speed it along, makes for chaos. Chaos tends to annoy teachers and has been known to cause chair-throwing, fist-fights, and probably at least one duel in some newspaper office at deadline time.

The following rules for news-copy format have evolved out of the need for speed and efficiency. You should get them down as quickly as possible and know them so cold that they can be followed without serious thought, since your serious thoughts are going to be needed for the content of your stories.

1. Set the margins on your typewriter for a 60-stroke line and keep the left-hand margin wider than the right for editorial marks and comments (an inch-and-a-half is about right).

2. Type on one side of the page only, and indent all paragraphs ("grafs") at least five spaces. Double- or triple-space every line, no matter what you write or are quoting, so that changes can be made on any of them without turning the copy into something that looks like a cross between Arabic and Sanskrit.

3. Put the story's "slug" (the word that identifies it) on the upper left-hand corner of the page, about half an inch from the top and even with the left-hand margin. Slugs are critical to news flow because they quickly identify a particular story and its consecutive pages ("takes"). For this reason, no two slugs are ever the same in one newsroom on any given day. Slugs are usually, but not always, written all upper case: COUNCIL. Also, they are generally only one word and are as descriptive as possible of the story. A story about a bank robbery might therefore be slugged ROBBERY or even BANK-JOB; one about the President would be slugged PRESIDENT or, better, would be given his last name; one about Hurricane Betsy could be slugged either HURRICANE or BETSY (most likely the former). Repeat the slug in the same place on each consecutive take, followed by a dash and the appropriate number of the take. Thus: COUNCIL on the first take, COUNCIL—2 on the second take, COUNCIL—3 on the third take, and so on. Since slugs are sometimes accidentally printed, never use vulgar, tasteless, or inappropriate ones. You wouldn't want to see SPIC, KRAUT, JAP, WOP, or KIKE gracing the top of something you got in print, and you may be sure that most of your readers wouldn't want to, either. Also, never use KILL, which is used by an editor to tell a printer not to set a story in type, or MUST, which tells the printer the opposite. Use SLAY, MURDER, HOMICIDE, or something similar in place of KILL.

4. Your name goes under the slug and is lower-cased: hodgson. Unless there are two reporters with the same last name working in the same office, the last name is usually enough. Furthermore, some editors think that when you use your full name you're trying to remind them that you want a byline, which is considered presumptu-

ous. And since you probably *do* want a byline, why take a chance of putting your editor in a spiteful mood? Some news organizations want your name under (or occasionally over) the slug on every take, while others want it only on the first. You'll be told which during your first hour on the premises.

5. Begin all stories at least halfway down the take, but only on the first take, so the editor can write a headline ("head") on top of the story if it's a short one, or typesetting instructions no matter what its length (heads for longer stories are written on separate pieces of paper).

6. End each take with a complete graf, begin each take with a new graf, and never break a word with a hyphen at the end of a line unless the hyphen belongs in the word anyway. Since each take begins with a graf, it stands to reason that each take must end with a complete graf. Never start a graf at the bottom of one take and run it onto another. Make each take a series of complete grafs even if that means chopping the last graf in half and using the second half as the first graf of the following take. Also, your English papers were probably not written to be set in type; your news stories will be. Printed words do not correspond to their positions on the typed page. Therefore, if you write *care-* at the end of a line and *lessly* at the beginning of the next line, you might see *care-lessly* in the middle of the line when it is printed (unless the editor manages to undo the damage beforehand). Exceptions are words and compounds that take hyphens: After accepting the award for her deep-dish pie, the 17-year-old reemphasized her love of Southern cooking.

7. If the story continues to another take, write (MORE) at the bottom of the take, either centered or in the right-hand corner. Do this every time you continue to another take. Obviously, this tells the editor that (MORE) is coming and that the story is therefore open and running.

8. Grafs must be as tight as possible. Try to hold your grafs to four lines and consider six to be the maximum. Deathless though your prose may be, readers tend to get bored and stop reading when you force them to struggle through seemingly interminable para-

graphs. Further, many long grafs on a newspaper page make it look too gray, which is not esthetically pleasing. Four short grafs are better than two long ones.

9. Never touch a pen to copy. In the first place, it's next to impossible to cleanly undo a change in ink after you see that you shouldn't have made it, or when you want to modify it. Second, your story might have to be photocopied, and there are machines that don't do justice to ballpoint. Whenever you're going to write anything, and particularly news, show up armed with a good dark pencil and an equally good eraser.

10. Do not write perpendicularly in the margins when making pencil corrections or additions to a story. Put the changes right above where they belong in the typed line, and print them neatly; don't scribble. Remember that the pencil changes are going to have to be read and understood by an editor. If a letter is upper case, indicate as much by using the appropriate symbol, and press on the pencil. (See the sample story below for format and for examples of the correct way to make changes.)

11. Never type over a letter since e+o=ø, and who can figure that out? X-out the mistake and type the correct letter directly over it.

12. If you decide that the graf order is wrong, neatly cut out the grafs and rearrange them with paste or tape, either on the take itself, or on a separate sheet of paper. If you use tape that cannot be written on, apply it to the back of the paper so your story can be edited. Never put numbers beside grafs and never use arrows. Takes with penciled-in numbers and arrows look like invasion maps and are as difficult to follow.

13. Put an end-of-story symbol at the end of every story (even a one-graf story) so those processing it will not sit there, waiting in vain, for (MORE). END, ENDIT, FINIS, ###, or the traditional —— 30 —— are equally acceptable. Take your pick. If you're writing on deadline, put the time you finish the story directly under the symbol, using p for p.m. and a for a.m. So:

ENDIT
5:45p

14. Always read your completed story before handing it in. Check for errors of fact, awkward writing, wrong graf order, and typographical errors ("typos"). Double-check all factual information—names, titles, addresses, ranks, ages, and so on—for accuracy. Putting a small check above those kinds of facts will help you to remember that they have to be confirmed. Your goal is to produce stories that are ready for publication when they leave your hands; all errors are yours, not the copy editor's.

And speaking of copy editors . . . . The surest way to raise a journalism instructor's blood pressure or cause a working editor's knuckles to whiten is to defer the checking of spelling and supportive facts to the copy editor. It happens too often. The beginner turns in a story saying that the first ship went through the Panama Canal on August 15, 1944. The instructor or editor points out that it was 1914, not 1944, and is answered with a shrug and this line: "Well, that's what copy editors are there for."

The clear inference is that the reporter has been mandated by God to joust with the enemies of mankind in the true Arthurian tradition, while the copy editor remains behind, rubbing leather, pounding the dents out of the armor, sharpening the lance, and sweeping the stable. This is not only sheer nonsense, but an annoying manifestation of laziness and lack of responsibility. Copy editors have clearly defined roles in the newsroom, none of which include doing the work that the reporter is supposed to do. Copy editors are supposed to raise (and usually answer) good questions about the story, make sure that it's in logical order and is factually correct, slice off excess words, and put on a head that will summarize the story in a way that is not only clear, but interesting. That's work enough for anyone but, unlike most reporters, most copy editors handle from three to ten stories a day, depending on their length and difficulty. They therefore resent having to place the second "m" in accommodate, wrap commas around dependent clauses, capitalize Communist Party, change Rumania to Romania, and prevent readers from being informed that polio is a game played on horseback.

When copy editors must work at those things in order to keep a resident knight in the saddle, they talk about it at lunch and after hours, and before long sarcastic jokes are spreading all over the castle. It is then a matter of time before the knight turns into a jester and someone with more responsibility is brought in for the serious assignments. Those who work under extreme pressure—and newsmen and -women are certainly among them—deeply resent having to carry lazy or incompetent colleagues. You are responsible for what you do.

Again, and this cannot be emphasized too strongly, learn the format rules right now and practice them until they come automatically. It will save you grief later. Here is a story written in the format. It isn't important that you pay particular attention to the content of the story, but it *is* important that you understand the way in which it is laid out.

SHARK

brown

Two Portland teen-agers were critically injured in

shallow water off Old Orchard Beach yesterday when they

were attacked by a large shark.

Stephen Marsh, 16, of 48 Neal Street, had his left

leg amputated last night at the Maine Medical Center. The

other victim, Harrison Goodman, 15, of 95 West Street, may

lose his right arm, according to doctors. Both boys were

listed in critical condition.

(MORE)

SHARK — 2


The area where the attack occurred, just off Pine
Point, was put off limits for swimming immediately after
the attack and will remain so until further notice, a
police spokesman said.

Marsh and Goodman are friends and students at Deering
High School.  They were cutting classes and had decided to
go swimming, according to Larry Newcombe, 15, another Deering
student who was in the water with them when the shark
attacked.

Newcombe described the shark as being 12 feet long,
light gray or blue, and "absolutely voracious." He trembled
as he described the attack.

"We were just standing around and I wasn't paying too
much attention.  Then, suddenly, I heard this scream and I
saw a great big thing right under the surface," said Newcombe.
"There was a lot of splashing and yelling, and when I saw
what it was, I got out of there as fast as I could."

Newcombe's description of the shark, as well as
descriptions by others nearby, led authorities to speculate
that the fish was either a small white shark or a full-grown
mako.  Both are considered man-eaters and are known to
prowl shallow water in search of food.


                                        (MORE)

SHARK -- 3


    Yesterday's attack was the first off the coast of Maine

since October 1956, when Leslie Crockett, a skin diver, was

killed near Christmas Cove.

                                        ENDIT
                                        6:25p


This is the way in which a typical news story is arranged. Again,
notice that: writing on the first take begins halfway down the page;
takes are slugged and consecutively numbered; no word or graf is
broken; no graf is longer than six lines; (MORE) appears at the bottom of the first take and the last is tied off with ENDIT and the time
at which the story was completed.

Now, let's suppose changes are needed. In the course of double-
checking your notes you find that some facts are wrong. Furthermore, your editor tells you that the story has to be cut a bit because
it is too long. There is a list of editing symbols at the back of this
book and you should familiarize yourself with them as quickly as
possible. For the moment, though, you ought to understand what
has been done to the following grafs. And remember that all editing
is done *in pencil only*.

The first two grafs are nice and tight and they are correct, so they
can be left as they are. We therefore begin surgery on the third graf:


    The area where the attack occurred, just off Pine
    (immediately)
Point, was put off limits for swimming immediately after
the attack and will remain so until further notice, a
police spokesman said.

    Marsh and Goodman are friends and students at Deering

High School. They were cutting classes and had decided to
                                    H
go swimming, according to Larry Newcombe, 15, another Deering

student who was in the water with them when the shark

attacked.

SHARK -- 2

Newcombe described the shark as being (about) 12 feet long,
light gray or blue, and "absolutely voracious." ~~He trembled~~ ℓ
~~as he described the attack.~~

"We were just standing around and I wasn't paying too
much attention. Then, suddenly, I heard this (horrible) scream and I
saw a great big thing right under the surface," said Newcombe.
"There was a lot of splashing and yelling, and when I saw
what it was, I got out of there as fast as I could."

~~Newcombe's description of the shark, as well as~~
~~descriptions by others nearby, led~~ authorities ~~to~~ speculate
that the fish was either a small white shark or a full-grown

stet    mako. ~~Both are considered man-eaters and are known to~~
~~prowl shallow water in search of food.~~

~~Yesterday's attack was the first off the coast of Maine~~
~~since October 1956, when Leslie Crockett, a skin diver, was~~
~~killed near Christmas Cove.~~

ENDIT

6:25p

The task in editing copy is not only to make the necessary
changes, but to make them in such a way so they are easily understood by everyone. Although no one expects reporters working on
deadline to turn in copy, edited or otherwise, that looks as though
it has already been printed, editors do expect reasonably clean work.
Turning in sloppy copy, full of unintelligible scrawling, will probably alienate whoever has to work on it and, worse, will defeat your
purpose: to get the story processed as quickly as possible. Every
pencil mark on those six grafs has as its purpose not only a necessary
change, but the clearest possible change.

Sentences or ends of sentences are taken out by running solid
lines through them. The editor's attention is drawn to these deletions
by the use of a curlicue, acting as a flag, in the margins. A sentence
that begins on one line, has a chunk taken out of its middle, and

ends on another line is rejoined or "closed" by connecting either end with a pencil line that can be followed like a trail. That's also why words that are eliminated in one line only are not just blocked out, but are turned into arrows that point the way to where the live copy picks up. Similarly, the last graf was killed by being boldly blocked out, x'd, and then flagged so the editor has no doubt about its destiny. Notice, too, that changed or added words and letters are set in eye-catching funnels to help the editor see that they're there and show him precisely where they belong. If you have time to type the changes or additions, so much the better; if not, be scrupulously neat with your pencil.

If you make a correction and then change your mind about it, you need not waste time erasing: write STET in the margin beside whatever is to be restored.

Now is the time to go over that list of copy editing symbols at the back of the book. Pay particular attention to the following, which ought to be memorized: graf mark, period, comma, quotation mark, delete mark, capitalization and lower-case symbols, close-up and open-up symbols, and letter- and word-transposition marks.

again it's important for that you learn editing marks

(as) quickly (possible as), since you're going two need them them

from now on.

That way, you'll be off to a good start.

# chapter six

# THE LEAD

The lead (sometimes spelled lede to distinguish it from the metal used to make type) is the first graf, or occasionally, two or more grafs, of a story. It's worth a whole chapter because it's the single most important part of the story.

Readers shop for stories in newspapers and magazines the way they shop for vegetables in markets. Like the produce man who puts his best lettuce on top of the pile so shoppers will buy it, the reporter puts his best graf on top, and for the same reason. With the exception of the head, readers read the lead before they read anything else, and they wander elsewhere if they don't like what they see. It's a serious sales job.

"Hey," shouts the reporter to those browsing around his and competitive stalls, "come over here and take a look at my fine, crisp lettuce. Pick one off the top. It's delicious. Taste it and you'll want all the others I've got today."

Go into any newsroom at or near deadline and you'll probably see some reporters seated at their desks and either staring into some great void, biting their lower lips, drumming their fingers on the sides of their typewriters, or all three. They will probably be reporters—good, old hands as well as beginners—who are trying to find their leads. It has been known to take sensitive writers three days or more to find a lead they liked for a particular, noncompetitive, story—a beginning that best set its unique tone or meaning. It is said that the back of the story is broken once the right lead has been found; that the rest of the story unfolds, as if by magic, once the lead is on paper. Sometimes.

Although there are variations, leads come in three basic forms. Let's call them: (1) the immediate single; (2) the immediate dual; and (3) the anecdotal. Each, however, shares the same basic function: to begin the story in the most accurate and interesting way.

Both immediate leads—single and dual—are used, appropriately enough, for immediate, or "hard," news stories. Immediate news is, in turn, news that is highly competitive and perishable. That is to say, immediate news stories are useless unless they are printed or aired right away. If the Empire State Building blows up, it will generate immediate news, with many reporters competing to get the story to the public first and most comprehensively. The reporters would lead their stories straight-on because the news—what happened—would be immediately compelling. After readers had been told about the explosion, it would no longer be news to them, but history. An immediate lead is therefore used to get the news out as quickly as possible.

The immediate single lead is used to get the single most important element of the story on top, and since one such element can be isolated in most stories, the immediate single is by far the most used lead.

The immediate dual is used when the reporter feels that two separate facts or events of equal or near equal importance have to be put in the first graf or two.

Anecdotal leads, on the other hand, generally begin stories that are less immediate (though not necessarily less important) and are used mostly to tease readers into wanting more information, rather than shoving the news right at them. Anecdotal leads get the reader into the story more slowly than do the immediate kind, but their redeeming quality is that they occasionally begin stories that amount to serious literature. They are used mostly for feature stories (which are generally noncompetitive), or for sidebars, which are separate stories that accompany and supplement important major stories.

Let's blow up the Empire State Building and try each of our three leads (in their most basic forms) on the event.

## IMMEDIATE SINGLE

The Empire State Building blew up yesterday.

## IMMEDIATE DUAL

The Empire State Building blew up yesterday, killing nearly 500 persons.

## ANECDOTAL

Henry Snodgrass was sitting at his desk in the Empire State Building yesterday when he heard the explosion.

The immediate single informed us only that the building blew up. The immediate dual added the fact that nearly 500 persons were killed. The anecdotal tried to make us want to find out what happened to Henry Snodgrass.

Some beginners are still told by some teachers that a sound lead should contain the so-called "Five Ws and H"—Who, What, Where When, Why, and How. It's a pity that whoever invented that formula couldn't come up with another W to substitute for that poor, lonely H. The formula is fine in theory because it gets plenty of information into the lead. In practice, though, it can make a lead so cumbersome and awkward that the reader is discouraged from wanting to push on for more information.

Instead of the "Five Ws and H," I would like to suggest, in the manner of everyone who invents catchy little formulas, the application of J+SDS. (No, that's not a call for journalism students to join their radical colleagues in raising the barricades and liberating the dean's cigars.) It stands for the use of Judgment and the Short Declarative Sentence.

Some scholars (not to mention politicians) tend to think of the short declarative sentence the way dog-show judges think of dachshunds with spots or collies with heads like dalmations—as an evil detrimental to sound breeding and vaguely distasteful. You have been taught writing by expository writers of one sort of another and, as has been mentioned, they have probably paid you by the pound. Now you must learn to write, not with brain-busting complication, but with absolute simplicity and clarity. Don't be fooled: it's not easy. You can only simplify what you do after you've mastered it. If there is one trait common to all beginning reporters, it's the tendency to overcomplicate what they write, and especially their leads. They crowd their leads with trivia because, being unsure of the real news element in a story, they feel they can best cover themselves by tossing in everything. They clutter their leads because they clutter their heads.

When asked to turn a simple statement, such as "The apple is red," into a lead, at least one student, and usually several, produce something like this:

> Standing before a crowded classroom full of journalism students who were watching him with great interest, Associate Professor George Hotchkiss of the Department of Journalism and Mass Communication at State University, smiled whimsically and, with his hands in his jacket pockets, made this statement yesterday: "The apple is red."

(One exuberant young man, having finished such a lead, couldn't resist adding: "The apple had no comment.") The point is that you have to cut through the clutter and ask yourself, "Exactly what happened?" What happened, most basically, is that Hotchkiss said, "The apple is red." *That's* what happened. That is the news, and when it is clearly perceived, it can be sweated down to this immediate single lead:

> Associate Professor George Hotchkiss said yesterday, "The apple is red."

Secondary information goes into the second and subsequent grafs:

> Hotchkiss, who teaches journalism at State University, made the statement to a class full of students. They watched him with great interest.

An immediate dual lead, based on two equally important bits of news, would go something like this:

> Associate Professor George Hotchkiss said yesterday, "The apple is red." Four students immediately challenged the statement.

Here, the reporter made a judgment. He decided that the statement made by the teacher and the response it drew from the four students were equally important, and he therefore decided to pair them. Dual leads, by the way, do not have to be written in two sentences. Single sentences, provided they are not too long, are preferable, as was the case with the nearly 500 persons who died when the Empire State Building blew up. Having decided that the death toll and the building's blowing up were equally important, the writer blended both pieces of information into a short, smooth, dual lead.

Getting back to our friend Hotchkiss and his apple, here is the anecdotal approach:

> Associate Professor George Hotchkiss likes to tell his journalism students about apples.

This kind of lead would be used to arouse the curiosity of the reader, who is supposed to wonder why a journalism teacher tells his students about apples. If after reading such a lead, the person who is supposed to be made curious isn't the slightest bit curious, the game is lost. That's why reporters who doubt the effectiveness of such straight anecdotal leads are often tempted to make them cute, super-cute, or downright unbearable:

> Associate Professor George Hotchkiss looked at an apple yesterday and saw red.

George Hotchkiss, a professor of journalism at State University, thinks of leads as the apples of his eye.

Associate Professor George Hotchkiss is not one to compare apples and oranges.

An apple a day keeps journalism students attentive, or so thinks Associate Professor George Hotchkiss.

Associate Professor George Hotchkiss is, in his own way, a real apple-polisher.

Where Associate Professor George Hotchkiss is concerned, A does not stand for excellent, it stands for Apple.

Beware of overly cute leads, and especially of those wrapped around puns or clichés, since they stand for C (corn) and show the world that you're so unoriginal that you're forced to take refuge behind someone else's invention. That doesn't mean you shouldn't try to turn a nice phrase when the opportunity arises. By all means, use your imagination, and explore the possibilities for interesting and clever leads. It *does* mean, though, that you shouldn't strain (or "reach," as they say in the profession) for phraseology that is distorted, abrasive, or tasteless. With experience comes the ability to tell whether your leads are effective or not. Everyone who has ever reported has produced his share of bummers, but the best reporters try to learn from their mistakes and improve. In the great majority of cases, improvement comes with playing the lead more conservatively, not with juicing it up. All else aside, the lead is supposed to accurately summarize the story and provide it with appropriate flavor, no more and no less. When in doubt about the kind of lead to use, play it safe by using the most immediate one you can.

## RULES FOR LEADS

1. Avoid overly sensational or equivocal leads from which you will have to back off when you get deeper into the story. In other

words, never try to hawk your lettuce under false pretenses, which is called "hyping." Here are examples:

> Mayor Thomas Finletter's record on ghetto issues is so abysmal that he will not get a single vote from the poor in the coming election.
> That, at least, is the opinion of Lawrence B. Davis, a grocer in the blighted Chelsea area.
> Elmer Musgrove, a Chelsea dentist, thinks differently, however. . . .

or

> Two cars filled with vacationing families slammed into each other on Rt. 84 outside of Atlanta last night, killing everyone in both vehicles.
> That, at least, is what state trooper Melvin Boyd thought as he approached the wreckage. But Boyd was wrong.

Neither of those leads summarizes what follows and, in fact, they distort. Every lead has to be fully supportable by what follows it, and every fact in a lead ought to be documented and treated in detail in the body of the story.

2. Do not lead with a direct quotation ("quote") unless it is practically mind-boggling for its importance, or interest, or both. First, the odds are overwhelming that you can summarize the most important element of the story better in your own words than you can by using someone else's. Second, phrasing the lead yourself should make it clearer and will probably allow you to get in more information. Third, leading with a quote tells your editor and your best readers that you were too lazy or incompetent to fashion your own words.

> "If we are unable to establish an accord with our allies on the matter of nuclear reactor safety, we shall be forced to severely curtail the amount of fissionable material we supply to them," Secretary of State Harlow Laswell warned last night.

Either of the following is better. Think about the reason:

> If the United States cannot reach agreement with its allies on nuclear reactor safety, it will sharply reduce the amount of nuclear fuel it sells to them, Secretary of State Harlow Laswell warned last night.

or

> The United States intends to get a nuclear reactor safety agreement with its allies or they are going to get much less American nuclear fuel, Secretary of State Harlow Laswell warned last night.

Partial quotes, or the lifting of key words or phrases out of the rest of the statement, are all right, provided: (1) they don't begin the lead; (2) they're smoothly blended into what goes around them; (3) they in no way distort what they're meant to represent:

> If the United States cannot reach agreement with its allies on nuclear reactor safety, it will "severely curtail" the amount of nuclear fuel it sells to them, Secretary of State Harlow Laswell warned last night.

As should be clear from this lead, the partial quote is used for explicit emphasis—to get the key word or phrase on the record precisely as it was spoken because of its importance.

3. References to persons in immediate leads should include their titles or occupations, since what they do is usually justification for writing about them. Titles, particularly of politicians and bureaucrats, generally go immediately before their names. Also, use the full name in the lead unless the person you're writing about is so well known that doing so borders on being insulting to the reader (mayors, better-known cabinet members, and Presidents of the United States are in that category; congressmen are not). So: Mayor Thomas Finletter or Mayor Finletter (not Thomas Finletter, the mayor); Secretary of State Harlow Laswell or Secretary of State Laswell (not Harlow Laswell, the Secretary of State); Chief Justice Benjamin Weinberg (not Benjamin Weinberg, the Chief Justice).

4. Do not use a time frame (Yesterday, Today, Tomorrow, Last

Week, On June 21) as the first word or words in a lead, since doing so practically guarantees that the result will look more a diary entry than a news story. What happened is generally much more important than when it happened, so get right to the event and slip in when it happened a bit farther on.

> The British heavy cruiser H.M.S. Vulnerable sank in the North Atlantic yesterday after hitting a large iceberg.

> not

> Yesterday, the British heavy cruiser H.M.S. Vulnerable sank in the North Atlantic after hitting a large iceberg.

The first sounds like a news story. The second sounds like a yarn spun on a cracker barrel when there was nothing else to talk about. "Today" is used by afternoon and evening papers, whose reporters start work early enough so they can get that day's news in that day's paper. "Yesterday" is used by morning papers, whose reporters usually work from mid-morning to early evening for the next day's paper. The result is that the evening paper gets the afternoon explosion first, while the paper that comes out the following morning probably has a more accurate and comprehensive account. The morning paper gets the evening explosion first, while the paper that comes out the following afternoon or evening probably has a more accurate and comprehensive account (all things being equal, which is never the case).

5. Datelines (LOS ANGELES, June 21—) are never used by serious newspapers in the leads of local stories. It is universally understood that stories without datelines concern events taking place in the city served by the newspaper. Use "here" to emphasize that a local story is local, and use the name of a neighborhood, section, or borough to pinpoint where something happened for local and other interested readers:

> Dulles International Airport is the safest airport in the United States, the president of the Airline Pilots Association said here today.

or

A gas main exploded in the Flatbush section of Brooklyn yesterday, injuring three persons, one of them seriously.

Never use a dateline unless you are where the dateline says you are when you write the story. The dateline tells readers that you were there—in person—covering the news and writing it where it happened. If you were to cover a story in London and write it in New York for a Chicago newspaper, the story would have a New York dateline even if it was about the Prime Minister barricading himself in the Tower of London. If you wrote the same story in Chicago, it wouldn't take a dateline. Datelines are indented. The name of the city or locality is all upper case and is followed by: the state or country capitalized normally, a comma, the date (abbreviated if possible), and a dash. Put in the state or country only if leaving it out would confuse the reader, and also abbreviate the state if possible. It is obviously unnecessary to write France after PARIS, Spain after BARCELONA, Kenya after NAIROBI, Fla. after MIAMI, Ariz. after PHOENIX, or Ill. after CHICAGO. But if you ever do a story in STINKING WATER, put it in Neb., where it belongs. Remember, too, that two or more places can have the same name. There are towns named Lima, for example, in Paraguay and Sweden, as well as in several U.S. states. If you're reporting from Lima, Ohio, you ought to get both into the dateline so as to avoid confusion. Finally, since a dateline contains a date, the time frame is always that day (today, this morning, this afternoon, this evening) provided the event happens then.

The lead, like every other element in a piece of writing, is ultimately flexible. It should bend as the situation requires. As was said, a lead can run two or more grafs, particularly when it is updated (see New Lead). It can be written in anecdotal form to begin an immediate story. It can be very short ("Pssst." is probably the record) or quite long. The variations, happily, are as infinite as the writer's skill and imagination. The great joy of writing—all writing —lies in its infinite flexibility.

In the beginning, though, it is best to stick with one-graf versions of the three basic types of lead (and particularly the immediate ones) until they are mastered. When you are able to pick out the most important element in a news story, and write it with accuracy and brevity every time, you will be ready to start exploring some of the wonderful variations.

Irrespective of their structure, the best leads (to borrow a slogan from a brewer), have purity, body, and flavor. They almost invariably lead to superior stories.

# chapter seven

# THE BODY

The body of a news story is the part—all of it—that comes after the lead. When properly written, bodies flow smoothly and logically from their leads and with them, form complete stories.

As traditionally taught, bodies come in three basic structures, all of which seem to have been named by a professor of architecture at the Aswan Institute of Technology sometime around 300 B.C. They are: the inverted pyramid, the pyramid, and chronological. The inverted pyramid structure is supposed to begin with the most important news element and have what follows diminish in news value until you get to nothing, which, I take it, is where the story ends. My problem stems from the fact that pyramids come to *points* (and so should news stories), so if the most important news element is on top (and is therefore the *point* of the story), why isn't this variety called the pyramid? Why, in fact, have we been left with this analogy at all? Why not triangles and inverted triangles, cones and inverted cones, or funnels and inverted funnels?

I prefer (respectively): (1) most important news first; (2) most important news last; and (mindful that conventional wisdom cannot be dismissed entirely) (3) chronological. Memorizing all this is very possibly the least important thing you could ever do. You should understand, however, how each structure is used. You should also know that, like football's classic T-formation, each has variations which sometimes overlap. And some stories have the most important news right in the middle—a situation that does not easily lend itself to the pyramid approach (unless there are pyramids, or perhaps obelisks, that bulge in the middle).

The three basic structures, as well as most of their variations, have two rules in common: they must be as complete as possible and as tight as possible.

News stories should be relatively complete (there's no such thing as being, well, *completely* complete) because the essence of the service performed by reporters is to supply all relevant information. As they say in the newsroom, "Leave no questions unanswered." That doesn't mean you are expected to know the color of the police commissioner's underwear. It does mean, though, that any question likely to be raised by a careful reader ought to be anticipated and answered. Obviously, you can't raise and answer a question unless it has occurred to you. This is one of the most difficult aspects of the profession. When the treasurer of a company embezzles money, investors and most others who are interested in the event want to know how much he took, what he did with it, whether it can be recovered, and all other very important information. Given little time for an interview, the reporter who neglects such questions in favor of, "How does it feel to go to jail at your age?" and "Would you do it again?" is doing a disservice to his serious readers. All reporters ask questions; the trick is to ask excellent questions. The excellent question is the core of the excellent interview. That's why solid reporting is built on knowledge, curiosity, and alertness. You will not know what to ask if you're uninformed, and you will not want to ask if you're not interested.

News stories should provide information in the shortest possible space or time, (1) because you don't want to lose your audience, which tends to be busy, fickle, or easily bored; (2) because, where publishers and station owners are concerned, time and space are money; and (3) because carefully used words, rather than a deluge of weak ones, are the basis for effective writing. Good, tight prose— making every word count for something special—is very hard to come by. Marie de Rabutin-Chantal, the Marquise de Sévigné, put it nicely in the 17th Century when she apologized to a friend for having written a long letter, but went on to explain that she hadn't had time to write a short one. In this regard, the best writers are invariably good editors, and editing begins in the mind—before pencil touches paper. It is the process by which you decide not only what should go into the story, but what should not go into it. You then write in the most economical way while saying what needs to be said. Finally, if there is time, you apply the pencil to your words the way a butcher applies the knife to fatty meat.

The most-important-news-first story has the most important information in the beginning. The importance of the information—its news value—decreases as the story progresses. As you would expect, this kind of story is always topped with an immediate lead.

There are two advantages and one disadvantage to this approach. The most obvious advantage is that the reader gets the most important aspect of the story right away, thereby not only helping him to quickly grasp what it's about, but also grabbing his attention. The other advantage has to do with editing. Harassed copy editors who have to make space cuts—who have to squeeze a story into a smaller news "hole" than it was meant for—tend to start chopping at the end of story and work their way up, or toward its beginning. (In fairness to copy editors, it should be pointed out that they do this mostly on stories which lend themselves to it; that is, to this kind of story.) Nevertheless, pruning a word here, a clause there, and perhaps an unnecessary sentence somewhere else, is a seldom realized ideal under deadline pressure. It is simply easier to delete the last three or four grafs and move on to the next story.

Every time you write a news-first story, then, you ought to ask yourself this question: "If half of it ends in the wastebasket or on the spike, which half do I want that to be, and which half do I want to see in print?" For example:

> Yesterday was one of those lovely spring days on Park Avenue, with strollers casually inspecting shop windows, and businessmen happily setting out for leisurely lunches in cool cellars or at bright sidewalk cafés.
>
> The mood was broken only by the robbery of the Chase Manhattan Bank branch at Park and 55th St., where four gunmen made off with almost $1 million after killing a teller, a guard, and two customers.

The problem, as this should show, is that it's impossible to structure such a story unless you can recognize what belongs at the beginning, what should come after it, and what ought to be left out altogether. News judgment has to tell you.

There are many who would not hesitate to say that the loveliness of Park Avenue in spring—the bright flowers in the medians and the faces of people just emerging from their long bout with dirty slush and bitter cold—is far more important than yet another group of ferocious gunmen knocking off some bank. The world would be in a sorry state without such people, but they are not the souls we want to depend on for information with which to decide whether we are sufficiently protected against crime. Furthermore, Park Avenue in spring is an annual and relatively long occurrence, while a bank robbery in which four persons are killed and nearly $1 million is taken is rare and immediately important. Finally, anyone interested in seeing Park Avenue during spring can come to look at it (from as far as Hong Kong if they care enough). They don't need your account. They cannot have the robbery reenacted, however, so those who are interested need to be told about it.

The news-first style therefore requires that critical judgment be used in deciding what the most important news element is before the story can be structured. This isn't to say that news judgment isn't necessary for every kind of story, but only that this kind requires an especially sharp focus, and one which usually has to be brought to bear quickly. Reporters develop the ability to make such quick evaluations and to structure their stories accordingly by studying what the best in their profession do, and by practicing constantly. Reporters think about what news is, and what it is not, practically all the time. They think and talk about it whether they're working or not. One tells another over lunch (or at the beach, or while mountain climbing, or . . .) that his Aunt Mildred's plane had to return to Lisbon after making it almost halfway across the Atlantic because it lost two engines. "Hey," says the second reporter, "that's a good story." Not only is it a "good story," it's a story whose structure immediately begins to form in the light mist somewhere between his conscious and subconscious:

A New York-bound airliner carrying 175 passengers and a crew of 12 had to turn back near mid-Atlantic and return to

Lisbon yesterday after two of its four engines overheated and were turned off.

The plane, an Air-India 747, landed safely at Lisbon. There were no reported injuries and passengers were put on another jet two hours later.

The first indication of trouble came as the giant airliner approached the so-called "point of no return," or the position over mid-ocean at which it is safer to go on than to go back.

As the plane neared that point, flight engineer R. A. Thomas saw that the dials monitoring the right inboard and left outboard engines' temperatures showed that both were dangerously overheating. Thomas told pilot Robert Conrad.

"There's always the possibility that the dials, not the engines, are malfunctioning," Conrad said later. "But you don't take chances. I turned back and, as it happens, that was a wise precaution."

This story is written with the most important fact—that an airliner developed serious engine trouble far over the ocean—in its lead. This is its news "peg," or the reason for doing the story in the first place. An infinitely greater number of readers would be interested in this fact, and ought to know about it, than would be interested in knowing that Aunt Mildred got so nervous that she asked for a second glass of sherry and made several mistakes in her needlepoint.

The lead clearly explains why the situation was serious: *187 human beings were in an airplane that was flying on half-power, a dangerous thing to do.* The lead also tells the reader (1) when the event happened; (2) where the plane was bound for; (3) where it had taken off from (hence "return to Lisbon"); and (4) that it landed safely. It is presumed that the plane landed safely because, had it crashed, the news would have been different and so, therefore, would the lead and the rest of the story:

> At least 100 persons were killed and 40 injured yesterday when a crippled New York-bound airliner returned to Lisbon and crashed while trying to land.

Getting back to the first version, the information in its lead—all of it—is contained in only 36 words. Further, if the rest of the story had to be killed, the lead would be able to stand alone as a one-graf news item.

The second graf, while also containing important information, is a bit softer than the lead. It reinforces the fact that the plane landed safely and that no one was reported hurt, and also tells the reader (1) the name of the airline; (2) the kind of plane it was, and (3) that the airline managed to get the passengers on another plane two hours later. This information, besides being germane, provides a public service, since many readers also purchase airline tickets and have a right to know about the safety record, efficiency, and helpfulness of the companies they may be thinking about choosing.

Having used 61 words to supply nine very important facts (or 6.77 words per fact, if you like such statistics), our reporter begins to explain what happened in greater detail in the third graf. Remember, though, that the first 61 words could also stand as a self-contained story.

The third graf is softer still. It tells, quite simply, when the trouble started. But it does more than that. It says that the trouble began near the midpoint of a long flight over the ocean—specifically, near the "point of no return." And having decided to use that technical term because it is accurate, visually helpful, and suitably dramatic, the reporter smoothes the way for the reader (instead of making him feel ignorant and frustrated) by explaining simply and concisely what "point of no return" means. He defines it so smoothly, in fact, that even a reader who has never been up in an elevator, much less an airplane, may think he knew it all the time.

The fourth graf introduces the first person in the story, tells who he is and what he does, explains his role in the drama, and even mentions which of the four engines ran fevers. News stories are about people, so people ought to be in them, and Thomas is a logical first choice. The person the reader would probably be most interested in, of course, is the able fellow who managed to get the thing safely back to earth—the pilot. A mechanic at the Lisbon airport or even a stewardess on the plane would not do as nicely as pilot Conrad, since he's the one most qualified to explain what happened and was the most important participant (assuming that the President of the United States wasn't sitting somewhere back in the economy section). Always try for the most knowledgeable or prominent source.

The fifth graf has Conrad talking. It is a good, selective, quote that allows the pilot to summarize in his own words the decision he had to make and the fact that it turned out to be a wise one. Quotes, as we will see in some detail, get the human element into the story in the most direct—and often the most interesting—way by letting people speak for themselves. They also nicely break up graf after graf of often tiresome description.

Now, consider how few words you had to read in that story before you got a grip on what it was about. Then, imagine that you are the copy editor who has to trim the story by about 50 words while maintaining its integrity. Which 50 would you take out? Suppose you had to remove 100 words and still retain the most important elements of the story. Which would you "go with" and which would you "hang up" (slap on the spike used in newsroom to hold discarded copy)?

The most common problem beginning reporters have when they try to set up a news-first story is that of confusing an event's framework with the sharpness of its key element. Being unsure of their news judgment they seek safety, or what they perceive as safety, in the catch-all lead and story. Instead of taking a chance on sharply focusing their reporting and writing, they blur their work in the apparent hope that at least some of it will be acceptable. Many, sent out to cover the issuance of the Emancipation Proclamation, would begin their stories like this:

President Lincoln today issued a proclamation about slaves.

Of course he did. But he did a great deal more than that: he *freed* them. The most important fact in the story is not that the proclamation generally concerns slavery, but, more specifically, that it *ends it*. That is the news:

WASHINGTON, Sept. 22—President Lincoln issued a proclamation here today which will free the slaves.

The preliminary Emancipation Proclamation, as it is called, will take effect on January 1 in all states, including those now in rebellion.

It is the first time that a federal official of any kind has sought to legally ban slavery.

Should the South lose the war, which is expected, Lincoln's proclamation will have serious effects on an agricultural economy geared to the use of slave labor. It will also have profound social effects.

In an attempt to strengthen the document, which claims to make all slaves "forever free," the President has stipulated that their freedom will be guaranteed by the Union's full civil and military power.

Lincoln presented the proclamation to the Cabinet this morning. No Cabinet member was available for comment. Reactions elsewhere were mixed, however, and were occasionally critical.

"It's another cheap political trick," said a congressional source who asked not be be identified.

"He's doing this because Lee and Jackson are pushing us all over Virginia and the British are thinking about tilting toward the other side," he said.

"How are we supposed to enforce emancipation in Louisiana when we can't even hold Manassas? I like Abe, but he's a headline-grabber."

Again, think about trimming this. You would probably want to get in at least one of those quotes, but you couldn't sacrifice much of the material above them, and certainly not the first four grafs.

The disadvantage of the news-first approach is that it tends to be predictable and, almost irrespective of its content, seems to have been stamped out of the same mold as all of the other stories in its class. Many reporters have for this reason begun edging away from the most-important-news-first format toward less formularized variations, some of which have been spectacularly innovative and interesting.

Still, the news-first story remains the standard (and once it's mastered, the easiest) vehicle for getting competitive news to the reader most quickly and intelligibly. Since it's the one you will be using most of the time, it's the one you ought to learn first and work at hardest. Reading the newspaper, and particularly page-one stories, will help greatly. Read them for construction, as well as for content, and ask yourself why they have been put together as they have.

The most-important-news-last story, appropriately, is the opposite of the news-first variety. Here, the information gets more important as the story progresses, drawing the reader ever deeper out of curiosity, the way he might be drawn into a Conan Doyle mystery. Irresistible (it is hoped) morsels of information are carefully dropped, like so much birdseed, in front of the ravenous reader. The anecdotal lead is the first seed:

> Mrs. Mildred Fenwick had just finished lunch and was about to get back to her needlepoint when the pilot's voice came over the loudspeaker. It was her first indication of trouble.

or

> Robert Conrad, an Air-India pilot, has often wondered what it would be like to fly a plane full of passengers with two of four engines gone. Yesterday, he found out.

or

> The engines on a Boeing 747 jetliner are like people in at least one regard: they stop working when they overheat. That is what happened yesterday 31,000 feet over the Atlantic.

Imagination plays a greater role in the news-last piece than it does when many of the most important news elements are crowded in and near the top of a story. It is said that such stories require more "writing" than do the others, meaning more use of the reporter's creative ability. True. But beware of three factors. First, you must know when the news-last approach can be used, and when it can't be. This hinges on how competitive, or perishable a story is, and also on its content. News-last stories lend themselves most easily to features, not to breaking news, and especially not to sudden tragedies, such as transportation accidents in which there is loss of life, or to fires, murders, riots, natural disasters, and the like. Second, the important news elements are there, but they are arranged in a different order. Doing a news-last piece is not license to disregard facts when reporting or to discard them when writing. You must always be able to support what you write with liberal doses of factual material. Third, the price you pay for being able to get less information and more "creation" into the top of the story is having to use taste, a devilishly difficult commodity to come by. The following, for example, wouldn't do:

> Mrs. Mildred Fenwick gasped when she heard the pilot's words.

or

> Pilot Robert Conrad, his mouth contorted and sweat pouring from his forehead, knew that he was going to have to turn off two of the four engines or the airliner would never make it to New York.

or

> If the 747's engines had not been turned off, they probably would have exploded, sending 187 persons plummeting into the Atlantic.

All three are overly dramatic and at least two of them are specious. They are badly overwritten. Let's get back to Lincoln.

> WASHINGTON, Sept. 22—Few who were present at today's Cabinet meeting expected President Lincoln to show up with a document that is as historic as it is difficult to enforce.
> Secretary of War Stanton, mindful of recent military gains by Lee and Jackson in Virginia, and also aware of possible British entry into the war on the side of the Confederacy, assumed that Lincoln had called the meeting to announce a new strategy. Stanton was wrong.
> Edward Bates, on the other hand, knew better. As Attorney General, Bates has been working on the preliminary Emancipation Proclamation since at least July. Bates therefore knew that Lincoln had come with a major proclamation about slavery.
> That is exactly what happened. Before a mostly surprised and not altogether happy Cabinet, Lincoln presented what he called the Emancipation Proclamation, setting all slaves "forever free" in those states still in rebellion on January 1.

The "nut graf," or the one about which the story revolves, is the last. But the writer has tried to draw the reader to it with a series of calculated teases: (1) the lead not only mentions some historic document, but also notes that even high-ranking government officials were surprised by it; (2) the second graf says that no less a notable than the Secretary of War has not guessed what Lincoln was going to do (and since secretaries of war know a lot more than you and I, this must really have been secret); (3) the third graf lets out a little more—a "major" proclamation about slavery—but still does not get to the heart of the matter; (4) the last graf unwraps the news, but notice, too, that it uses "not altogether happy Cabinet" to tease the reader—to make him wonder why the document is controversial.

It's important to explain here that news-last doesn't necessarily mean that the most important news should always be saved for the end of the story. Such is occasionally the case with this kind of story, but more often, news elements are let out, a little at a time, much in the manner of telling a story with a punchline, but giving the punch line somewhere near the middle, and then going on to explain it. This form, in fact, was in vogue throughout the 18th and part of the 19th centuries, when reporters wrote news in exactly the same way that their readers gossiped: "An interesting event occurred in Dale Brand's barn on Thursday last. . . ." But the technique was finally abandoned with the development of the highly competitive reporting of the late 19th and early 20th centuries. Sensationalist "yellow" journalism, the emergence of fiercely competitive wire services in the 1930s and '40s, and finally the development of radio and television, got readers and listeners used to wanting their news first (and fast), so they lost patience with being teased.

Now, though, the news-last structure is making a strong comeback, ironically, *because of* radio and television. Since no newspaper can match radio and television in speed of news delivery, they are increasingly trying to present what they carry in as interesting a way as possible. Whereas readers once had to go to them because they were the only game in town, newspapers now see themselves as being forced to make their product as lively and entertaining as possible to keep their readership, and this means more feature stories, more of the kind of offbeat coverage that television doesn't have time for, more pictures, and more "writing" (as opposed to relatively dry, news-first reporting).

Chronological stories are what their name says they are. They are stories structured in the approximate sequence in which the event happened. This does not necessarily mean a minute-by-minute description, but it does mean that you have to follow the same "script" as the players about whom you are writing. Here's the Proclamation story in straight chronological form:

WASHINGTON, Sept. 22—President Lincoln, his face drawn from fatigue, had a light breakfast this morning and then took his Emancipation Proclamation to the Cabinet.

He left his bedroom (and a plate of half-eaten eggs) at 8:15 and, the historic document clutched in his right hand, walked slowly to the Cabinet room. The Cabinet had been waiting there since 7:30: waiting and mostly wondering.

When the door opened and the President walked in, everyone around the oval table stood, but he quickly motioned for them to be seated with the hand that held the most important document he had written while in office.

Abraham Lincoln then sank into his chair at the head of the table, smiled faintly, and carefully laid the papers in front of him. He stared at them for a few moments. Then he looked up, searching the expectant faces.

"Gentlemen," the President of the United States said at last, "we are going to proclaim to God and to the world that slavery in the United States—*all* of the United States—is abolished."

Secretary of the Treasury Salmon Chase, who had been doodling various types of naval artillery, dropped his quill and groaned.

Sidebars (of which this Proclamation piece is an example) are stories written to supplement main news stories when the main stories can't contain all related events, either because of space limitations or, more usually, because the events are distinct enough to warrant separate stories. The chronological structure is used mostly in sidebars.

Say an ocean liner sinks. An editor would obviously assign one or more reporters to cover the fact of the sinking, and they would produce a news-first account of the event. But other reporters might be asked to write sidebars about events related to the sinking: biographical sketches of the ship's captain and the most prominent passengers; a history of the ship that would include any other trouble it had had; a recounting of similar disasters; a description of how coast guardsmen and other rescuers handled the situation; and a chronological account, by the minute or hour, of what happened, starting with the collision (or explosion, or arrival of the tidal wave, or whatever) and progressing through its listing to starboard, lifeboats being lowered, the arrival of the first rescuers, the removal of passengers and crew, and finally, its slipping under the surface.

This kind of sidebar is often used to accompany stories about terrorists holding hostages, police staging major raids, soldiers seizing or withdrawing from vital positions, and for the itineraries of heads of state and other politicians making important trips.

Less frequently, the chronological approach is used for self-sustained stories, but only when they are relatively soft, or non-perishable. The typical-day-in-the-life-of athletes, beauty contest winners, movie stars, policemen and firemen, models, test pilots, ambassadors (and their wives), and others whose daily routines are considered to be of interest to readers, lend themselves to the chronological narrative.

The various kinds of leads and bodies are to the reporter what the various kinds of carpentry tools are to the cabinetmaker. Each produces the best possible product by using the right tool for a particular job. Each matches the tool to the task. Progressive levels of experience should warn you of likely mismatches before they happen. Eventually, you should reach the point at which choosing the story structure for a particular news event becomes second nature, and you then will begin concentrating increasingly on the more creative and experimental aspects of writing.

# chapter eight

# THE WORD

During the social and political turmoil of the 1960s and early '70s, some reporters who were covering the activities of the young people spearheading change noticed an interesting, and perfectly logical phenomenon. Not only did the rebels reject the "establishment," but they rejected the establishment's language, as well. If it was necessary to be articulate and have an extensive vocabulary in order to move up the traditional ladder, the members of the counter-culture seemed to think, then they would go the other route. They would reduce speech to its lowest possible denominator. Thus, everyone—man, woman, and child, young and old, the exalted and the lowly—was referred to simply as "man," which is not only a very short noun, but one which stresses the sameness of all people as being the race of man. "Change is in the wind in this country, man," male students would warn their college presidents, tell their fathers, and remind their girl friends.

At the same time, the all-purpose response to just about everything was, "Oh, wow." Depending on pauses and inflection, "Oh, wow" could be used to express anything from deep sorrow to total exhilaration.

REPORTER:    Four students were killed at Kent State University to-
             day.
STUDENT:     Oh . . . wow . . .
REPORTER:    How do you think other students will react to that?
STUDENT:     Oh, . . . WOW.
REPORTER:    Do you think there'll be a protest here because of the
             killings?
STUDENT:     OH . . . *WOW*!

This is not to criticize that generation's speech. Anyone who has
ever used the real McCoy, the cat's pajamas, the living end, George
all the way, cool, wild, crazy, or far-out, would be on shaky ground
in doing so. It is only to show that fads apply to language as surely
as they apply to clothing, hair styles, automobiles, and popular
literature.

Consider writing the following, not as a quote, but as straight
descriptive narrative for a *general* readership:

> The fuzz really laid it on last night by busting the Brass Cat
> and doing a number on the boss guru.

Although this kind of writing may reflect its user's speech, there
are two problems with it: (1) it will probably have to be deciphered
by anyone using it for research after it has been replaced by new
slang, and (2) it is unintelligible to the majority of general readers.

Reporters, like other writers, are in the business of communicating. That is to say, they sell information to their audience, and they
do so in a way that is the easiest to understand without insulting
their audience's intelligence. It is just as senseless and self-defeating
to write stories that people can't understand as it is to make shoes
they can't wear.

Languages, like the societies they serve and reflect, are constantly
changing. And as is the case with society, there are those who want
to turn language inside-out to suit their own needs and purposes, and
others who would leave it unchanged until it atrophies and, if necessary, disintegrates. The former constitute the great majority. Either
out of convenience or necessity, they bend the language or practically change it entirely, so that it is often unrecognizable to outsiders. But relative to any single group or profession, everyone else

is an outsider, and is therefore capable of being confused. Reporters who work for general interest, or nontechnical news organizations, must always communicate with the outsider. They are therefore codebreakers.

All professionals use code for specific communication. We will look more closely at this in Part 3, and especially in science reporting, but it is important to note here that the scientists aren't the only ones who use code. Just about everyone uses it, from prostitutes (who "turn tricks"), to policemen (who "make collars"), to pilots (who "rotate"). They use code because it is easier, quicker, and often clearer to others in their profession than laying out the whole situation in standard English. The pilot of a bomber rolling down a runway at 155 miles an hour finds it easier and just as accurate to tell his crew that they are leaving the ground by saying "rotate," than by saying, "We have achieved sufficient speed to become airborne, so I am now easing back on the control column in order to initiate flight."

Semiprofessional code, though it exists everywhere, has its greatest bastion in Washington, where alternatives are "viable" (as opposed to workable), files are made "secure" (as opposed to locked), and generals at Senate hearings answer "in the affirmative" (as opposed to saying yes). Washington is also the acknowledged home of the acronym. It is not uncommon for Department of Defense (DOD) personnel to say things like, "We're requesting SHAFE and NATO to send a CO and two ADCs to SALT." Other memorable acronyms include: HUD, COPE, CORE, CENTO, SEATO, SHAPE, CREEP, ERTS, TACAN, LORAN, ECOSOC, and WHO. I have a theory about acronyms. I think that all of them are invented in one small government office hidden deep in the basement of an otherwise innocuous-looking federal building. There, an 86-year-old man wearing a green eye shade and a Phi Beta Kappa key turns out acronyms for all authorized personnel who need them. "I represent an Indian civil rights group which needs something really catchy," says a visitor. "AIM," answers the old man. "The American Indian Movement. It's viable because it hints of perfectly directed arrows with very sharp points." If there is such a place, I'm sure it's called the Federal Office of Unintelligible Language (FOUL) and is part of the Official Bureaucratic System for Creating Unintelligible and Risky Enterprises (OBSCURE).

Acronyms also need definition unless they are so widely understood that further explanation is unnecessary: FBI, CIA, and UN
are cases in point. NATO, however, is not widely known, or at
least not widely enough so that it can stand as is. There are at least
three ways in which to unobtrusively tell readers what NATO stands
for, and all of them belong in the first reference, so the confusion
will not go on for longer than necessary. You can write: the North
Atlantic Treaty Organization (NATO); the North Atlantic Treaty
Organization, or NATO; or you can get NATO so close to North
Atlantic Treaty Organization in the narrative that there is no mis-
taking their relationship:

> The navies of six North Atlantic Treaty Organization mem-
> bers held maneuvers in the Mediterranean last week, while other
> NATO ships gathered in the Baltic.

When you have to use professional or bureaucratic code in news
stories, break it into plain English if there is any possibility that your
readers will not understand it as is. All code, including Greek, Latin,
and stilted English, should be broken for the sake of clarity.

You would not use "rotate" in an aviation story unless you were
directly quoting someone who used it. You could handle it like this:

> "I had maybe 200 yards of runway left," he said, "so it came
> down to rotating or going through the barrier." Rotation is the
> moment at which a plane leaves the ground.

If you were describing such a scene without having to quote
someone, you would avoid the word altogether:

> Leverett said that the runway ended only about 200 yards
> ahead, so it was a matter of either taking off at that moment
> or crashing into the barrier.

Doctors, lawyers, and scientists are the heaviest users of code.
Usually, but not always, it is through necessity. "Injunction," for
example, is a perfectly good word that also happens to be legal code.
So are subpoena, writ, summons, and warrant. But "predecease,"
which appears in my will, is on the other side of the line. It is stilted
and wholly unnecessary jargon meaning, simply, to die first. If you

can't figure out for yourself the meaning of a code word, always ask its user for a translation, and put that in the story.

Codebreaking is not confined to technical jargon, but applies to all words and expressions that are either the slang of the hour, or are just plain ostentatious. The suffix "-wise," as in promotionwise, qualitywise, mediawise, or (groan) contrarywise, gets decoded: "Where promotion is concerned. . . ." So does that species of slang that is used by all who are "with it" today, but who will wake up tomorrow to discover that it's no longer their "bag." "Split," "rap," and "rip-off" are three of the more obvious examples.

Here, in no particular order, are other basic problems:

### Overstatement (hyperbole).

It is better to understate than to overstate. Travel writers and some of their brethren who cover sports probably lead the kill-a-fly-with-an-anvil crowd:

> The Olympus restaurant is truly fit for the gods. The over-stuffed chairs in the foyer will make you think you're perched on a creamy cloud floating just above heaven; the palest of pale blue walls, set off by white Grecian molding, infinitely accentuates the lofty effect. And the food!!! Zeus himself would be honored to grope for the grape here. . . .

or

> Bunim is a southpaw with an arm like a cannon and a brain like a computer. His eyes are everywhere. The hand that holds the apple ought to be registered as a lethal weapon. . . .

Read that kind of thing for too long (60 seconds is my limit) and you either go to sleep or to the medicine chest. Overuse of adjectives and metaphors not only fatigues any reader with sensibility, but also erodes your credibility, since it makes you seem glib and emotionally untrustworthy. Avoid: "The room looked like a cyclone had hit it," "Her brain felt like a bomb had gone off inside it," and the rest.

### Redundancy.

The person who complains that he or she doesn't "need to be told twice" speaks for all attentive readers. Most adverbs and adjectives are unnecessary in news stories and are annoyingly redundant when used to modify verbs or nouns that are perfectly capable of standing on their own. The next time you're tempted to write "grinned happily," ask yourself whether it is possible to grin unhappily. For "screamed loudly," consider the possibility of screaming softly. Also, the state of being happy, miserable, healthy, eager, cunning, brave, afraid or delighted, to list a few, is like the state of being alive— either you are, or you aren't. So "thoroughly happy," "completely healthy," and "very much afraid" are *absolutely awful*. . . . Finally, there is no need to tell readers that wheat is yellow, grass is green, snow is white, rubies are red, violence is physical, tornadoes are powerful, crashes are sudden, killers are dangerous or flowers are in bloom, unless you are also prepared to tell them that fish swim, organists play organs, and reporters report.

### Tenses.

News stories can be written in any of the three basic verb tenses— past, present, and future—or variations of them.

Since news happens before it is written about, most news stories come in the past definite, a nice, simple, unoffensive tense:

> Yale University yesterday graduated the largest senior class in its history.

The virtue of the past tense is that it describes an event that is concluded; one that is over and that has already taken its place in history. I think, but I cannot prove, that readers find this satisfying in the same way they are satisfied when they finish a book and close it. But that strength is also the tense's unavoidable weakness: it lacks immediacy.

In the same way that sports fans are more interested in a game being played as they watch than they are in one that is over (all things being equal), readers are more interested in current events than they are in past ones. The present tense—what's happening now—increases the reader's involvement because it helps him to feel as though he and the event are existing simultaneously:

> Bicycle riding may be a source of relaxation for most people, but not for Harry Stevens, who races them—six days at a time.

A close look at this lead will tell you that it belongs either to a feature story about bicycle racing or to a profile of the racer, neither of which would be perishable news. The present tense is usually, though not always, used for features or for noncompetitive ("exclusive") news stories:

> Dr. Bertram Prince operates 15 nursing homes in Georgia which have been described by state authorities as "inhumane." Now, a source in the Attorney General's Office says, there is enough evidence against Prince to put him out of business and behind bars.

Because of its liveliness and immediacy, the present is finding increasing favor with reporters who are able to use it. You could say that the present tense has a perfect future. Like the others, however, it also has a built-in problem: events can easily overtake it. Here is a competitive story that should illustrate the problem:

> "Bold Venture," the gas balloon that left Cape Cod early Friday with France as its destination, is only 150 miles from Brest, according to its captain.

This looks fine. It's possible, though, that by the time the story hits the newsstands, "Bold Venture's" crew will have been staining the ocean yellow and firing rescue flares for 24 hours or more. If your competition reports that the intrepid balloonists are bailing water, while you still have them riding the jetstream, you're embarrassingly late with the news—you're saying they're in the air when they're not. You can protect yourself against such a situation only by dropping back a tense and establishing when the balloon's captain made his report: ". . . was only 150 miles from Brest last night, according to its captain." This way, you're not telling the world that "Bold Venture" *is* airborne; you're saying that it *was* air-

borne at last report. The competition may come out with news of
the ditching before you do, but that would only make you late, not
wrong.

If the present tense plays on immediacy to stimulate reader interest, the future tense goes it one better—it plays on anticipation:

> More than 300 Iroquois Indians will perform tribal dances
> and hold a crafts show Thursday at the Harrison County Fair
> Ground outside Windsor.

Since news reporting is based on reporting events, what could be
better than writing about an event that hasn't even happened yet?
Nothing, that's what. But here, too, there is a specter that haunts
newsmen and -women: what if the dances and craft show don't
happen as reported? What if all 300-plus Iroquois follow the wrong
trail and wind up in Albany? What if they all get sick Thursday
morning, or go on strike, or get caught in a blizzard? Then you will
have said unequivocally and for the record that something which
never happened was going to happen. This is a recurring problem
with politicians who "will not seek office." "I will not seek office"
usually means "I don't think I can make it, but if the picture changes,
I will assuredly run." If you report that Mayor Smiley will not run,
and he changes his mind, it is you who get credited with the error.
You can protect yourself from that possibility by appropriate hedg-
ing or attribution or both:

> More than 300 Iroquois Indians are scheduled to perform
> tribal dances and hold a crafts show Thursday at the Harrison
> County Fair Ground outside Windsor.

and

> Mayor Smiley said yesterday that he will not seek reelection
> in November.

If the Harrison County Fair Ground goes up in smoke just before
the first hoop dance, and Smiley wakes up one morning to find that
both parties will back him, you still will not have been wrong—you
will have reported what was *scheduled* to happen and what was
*said*.

### Transitions.

Smooth transitions, from one sentence to the next and from graf to graf, make the difference between a story that moves along evenly and interestingly and one that can read as though it were pounded out in Morse Code:

> Seven firemen were injured fighting a fire at Jackson's Department Store yesterday. One fireman was injured seriously. It was a big fire. It started before dawn. It was extinguished at 11:15 a.m.
> Eight pieces of fire-fighting equipment and 60 firemen were there. They came from Henderson and Endover Falls.
> All of the injured firemen were taken to Our Lady of Mercy Hospital. Six firemen were treated and released. The seventh fireman is still in the hospital.
> The seventh fireman's name is Roy Rutledge. He is 24 years old. He was struck by a falling beam inside Jackson's. The beam hit him on the head. Rutledge has a fractured skull. He is the father of two. No one else was injured.
> Fire inspectors said they suspect arson. The owner of Jackson's said he has no idea how the fire started.

Just about all of the elements that need to go into a news story are in this one, yet it doesn't "hang together" and is irritating to read. To a reasonably studious reader (let alone to a writer), it becomes a series of dots and dashes saying: t h i s　i s　r a g g e d　a n d　t i r i n g　s t o p　a n d　m o v e　o n.

Transitions link otherwise self-contained groups of words so they form flowing stories—ones which move smoothly in a direction. You can improve your transitions this way: (1) remember that it is easier to link similar or related thoughts than it is to link greatly differing ones, so lay out the story so that it progresses from one related thought or event to another, rather than having it bounce back and forth; (2) either turn clusters of short sentences that deal with the same subject and that begin with the definite article (the) or a personal pronoun (he, she, it, they) into longer sentences held together by a dependent clause or, better, knock out the pronouns and periods and pull the whole business together to form a straight declarative sentence. Here, respectively, are the three approaches:

It was a big fire. It started before dawn. It was extinguished at 11:15 a.m.

The big fire, which started before dawn, was extinguished at 11:15 a.m.

The big fire started before dawn and was extinguished at 11:15 a.m.

The same applies to the next graf:

Eight pieces of fire-fighting equipment and 60 firemen were there. They came from Henderson and Endover Falls.

Of course the firemen and vehicles were *there*—where else would they have been if they put out the fire? You would do better to replace *there* with some nice verb that will go out and work for you. Also, since firemen don't fight fires with garden tools or movie cameras, it is implicit that they used fire-fighting equipment. Either say what kind (pumpers, hook-and-ladders, cherry-pickers, or whatever) or let "equipment" stand alone:

Sixty firemen and eight pieces of equipment from Henderson and Endover Falls battled the blaze.

You would now be able to consolidate the two tightened grafs into a single one having good transition. Here they are, before and after surgery:

It was a big fire. It started before dawn. It was extinguished at 11:15 a.m.
Eight pieces of fire-fighting equipment and 60 firemen were there. They came from Henderson and Endover Falls.

The big fire started before dawn and was extinguished at 11:15 a.m. Sixty firemen and eight pieces of equipment from Henderson and Endover Falls battled the blaze.

This, in admittedly drawn-out form, is the process by which writers make smooth, tight transitions. The only difference between the beginner and the accomplished writer is one of speed. The professional automatically works transitions into the sentences and grafs that come together in his mind. But he started just like this. Then came all the practice.

# chapter nine

# QUOTE
# AND UNQUOTE

If, as they say, the eyes are the windows of the soul, then the mouth is the door of the mind. People constantly say things. Some of what they say is important, much of it is trivial, but most of it indicates what they're thinking.

Reporters not only look for the "good quote," they often push hard for it. As has been said, since quotes directly represent what people actually say, they liven copy—they make it more interesting because, more than anything else, they represent the human element. Good quotes should summarize what the subject has on his mind. One of the differences between the good reporter and the poor one is that the latter is content to bring back stories that seem to have happened, including quotes that seem to represent what people think, while the former works to pull away the veils and get at the truth of the situation.

The good reporter and the not-so-good one, both sent out to learn what the fabled "man on the street" thinks about graffiti, will come back with very different stories. Both will open with a general question and then get a bit more specific:

*"How do you feel about graffiti?"*

"Oh, I think it's all right. It's the only way those kids in the ghetto can express themselves artistically. Maybe someday one of them will be a great artist."

*"You don't mind seeing all those splotches and dirty words on buses and trains, on walls in subways, and on the sides of buildings?"*

"Well, I'm not crazy about it, but kids will be kids. I don't think their expression ought to be stifled. Besides, it adds color to this drab city."

Here is where the hack, his notebook holding a couple of fair quotes, leaves to write a story saying that the man on the street is tolerant of graffiti. And, of course, that is precisely what perhaps half a million readers will learn. But they will be misinformed. The other reporter will push harder and will probably be rewarded with the truth:

*"Then how would you feel—what would you do—if you saw them painting graffiti on your house?"*

"On *my* house? If I saw some punk using a spray can on *my* house, I'd break his neck."

Through the process of closing in on the true nature of the situation, of working to narrow the focus of the questions and to sharpen them, the better reporter has gotten his subject to admit that either he doesn't really approve of graffiti, or that he has a double standard. This is not to say that the man on the street is a liar. Often, he simply hasn't thought the matter through. Carefully directed questions help him think it through, though, and therefore provide readers with a story that is closer to the truth. Further questioning (*"You think that graffiti is all right on public property, then, but not on yours?"*) will probably establish exactly what he does think.

Like almost everything else in reporting, or so it seems, quotes come in three varieties: direct, partial, and indirect.

*Direct quotes,* which are set between quotation marks, are verbatim accounts of what was said or written. They are usually a minimum of one sentence long and a maximum of two consecutive grafs (they can go on for longer, but that is generally done only when they are taken from major speeches or from documents in which continuity of quotation is important. Here is typical direct-quote construction taken from the body of a story:

"If the mayor doesn't come to terms by midnight," warned the union leader, "there won't be a train or a bus moving in this city when the sun comes up."

*Partial quotes* are what they sound like they are—key words or phrases lifted out of a sentence, written verbatim, and also set between quotation marks. Use the partial quote to accurately summarize an important point when the sentence from which it comes is either unwieldly or extraneous. As with everything else you write, make sure it fits smoothly into the sentence structure:

The mayor answered by saying that he was "appalled by the union leader's insensitivity" to the commuting public.

An ellipsis (. . .) is used to tighten direct or partial quotes and show the reader that one or more words have been omitted. "Considering the state of the nation, which I have to do, I think tax reform is a priority item," said the President. Since "which I have to do" doesn't contribute much to the quote, it can be removed by substituting an ellipsis: "Considering the state of the nation . . . I think tax reform is a priority item." Make certain, when you use an ellipsis, that it in no way distorts the meaning of the quote.

*Indirect quotes* are not verbatim reproductions of what has been said or written so they do not take quotation marks. They *do* closely paraphrase it, though, and they must therefore be true to the meaning of the original statement. Indirect quotes are used to clarify complicated or very ungrammatical language, to filter unprintable language, to abbreviate long statements, or because the reporter didn't get the quote as it was given.

One angry commuter, waving his martini like a battle flag, said that the mayor and the union leader are both self-serving scoundrels who deserve to be driven from office.

Here is the beginning of that story (probably slugged STRIKE). Notice the way each kind of quote is used and how it is fitted into the story to make it flow smoothly:

United Transportation Workers president Simon Allen warned

yesterday that no city bus or train will move tomorrow unless there is a contract settlement tonight.

He made the remark after another angry, but apparently fruitless, negotiating session wtih Mayor Burnside and other city leaders.

"If the mayor doesn't come to terms by midnight," warned the union leader, "there won't be a train or a bus moving in this city when the sun comes up."

Allen had no sooner issued the warning to reporters gathered outside the negotiating room when Mayor Burnside emerged, heard what the union leader said, and made his way into the group.

The mayor answered by saying that he was "appalled by the union leader's insensitivity" to the commuting public.

City Hall was not the only place where tempers were flaring, though. Commuters waiting for their trains in Union Station generally expressed anger and frustration over the progress of the contract talks.

One angry commuter, waving his martini like a battle flag, said that the mayor and the union leader are both self-serving scoundrels who deserve to be driven from office.

Each quote has been set up—its way has been prepared—by the graf or sentence before it. This, again, makes for smooth transitions. Beginning reporters often find that outlining a story, including placement of quotes, helps the transition process quite a bit. Experienced reporters can outline even "spreads" of 500 words or more (as opposed to "shorts" consisting of a few grafs) in their heads. Here is the way that story might have been outlined:

1. Allen warns strike if no contract by tonight.
2. Says so after apparently fruitless session.
3. "Won't be a train or a bus moving" tomorrow.
4. Burnside comes over (angry).
5. Burnside "appalled" by insensitivity.
6. Commuters unhappy at Union Station.
7. Martini guy's "scoundrel" quote.

### "Good" quotes.

"Good" quotes not only reflect what the source believes, thinks he believes, or wants on the record, but they are incisive, illuminating, interesting, or all three. The criteria for this formidable cluster of qualities are the source, the nature of the story, and their relationship. Take this quote, for example: "I don't know." It's hardly scintillating. Or is it? Compare the questions as they relate to the answer:

> Rex Proudfoot, the NASA official who heads the program, was asked what he will do after the current manned flight to Mars is over.
> "I don't know," he answered.

> Rex Proudfoot, the NASA official who heads the program, was asked whether the four astronauts now approaching Mars will ever return safely to Earth.
> "I don't know," he answered.

The ramifications of the answer to the first question concern moving to another NASA project, finding a job outside NASA, or retiring. The ramifications of the answer to the second question concern the lives of four men, perhaps the future of a multibillion-dollar program, and national prestige. Proudfoot's job situation is not unique, but his job is. He knows more about the Mars mission than anyone else, including the astronauts, and if he isn't sure whether they are going to make it back to Earth in one piece, something is dangerously wrong. That is of considerable importance. The first quote is nothing special; the second is very special.

The answer to that second question, of course, would bring a follow-up question: *Why* doesn't he know? Here's the way Proudfoot's follow-up answer might appear in the reporter's notes:

> "I don't know because there has been a communications problem between the ship and Mission Control for two days, and right before it developed, the crew told us that they had picked up a meteor shower moving their way. We're still tracking the ship—we have it—but we don't know about its condition. We don't know about the crew's condition."

The most important elements in those notes are: (1) no communication for two days; (2) the approaching meteor shower; (3)

uncertainty about the ship's and crew's condition. The best quotes must come from some or all of those elements:

> Rex Proudfoot, the NASA official who heads the program, was asked whether the four astronauts now approaching Mars will ever return safely to Earth.
> "I don't know," he said.
> Mission Control has had a communications problem with the space ship for two days, Proudfoot explained, and before it started, the crew reported a meteor shower "moving their way."
> "We're still tracking the ship," Zeus VII's project manager added, "but we don't know about its condition. We don't know about the crew's condition."

The quote in the last graf sums up the situation in Proudfoot's own words. It could have been quoted indirectly, but it wasn't, since his own words lent justified drama to the situation. Notice, too, that "—we have it—" was dropped because it was redundant. Proudfoot was called "Zeus VII's project manager because: (1) three references to Proudfoot's name in four grafs are excessive, and (2) substituting mention of Zeus VII unobtrusively gets in new information or reinforces a previous reference to the name of the space ship. Finally, notice that three attributive verbs were used (said, explained, and added), and that Proudfoot's job—his reason for being important enough to write about—was given in the first reference.

### Attributive verbs.

If someone says something, have him or her *say* it, or use a substitute verb that will accurately set the quote in context without being overdramatic or stilted. "Said" is short, clear, and faultlessly accurate. The only problem is that it gets tiresome when repeated without a break: he said, he said, he said, she said, he said, she said, she said. You can therefore alternate it with any of the following, provided they accurately describe what happened:

| added | explained | complained |
|-----------|-----------|------------|
| continued | warned | cautioned |
| went on | recalled | charged |
| insisted | maintained | predicted |

But remember: people don't "insist" that the sun come out or "charge" that oak is a hard wood. Use "explain" only when the subject is really explaining something, "warn" when a dire prediction is being made, "recall" when a recollection is involved, and so on. Here is the beginner's enemies list:

| | | |
|---|---|---|
| avowed | averred | asserted |
| propounded | exclaimed | snapped |
| snickered | pointed out | quipped |
| remarked | chuckled | chortled |
| allowed | declared | stated |

Beginners who want to lend a certain majesty to their prose almost invariably reach for "pointed out," "declared," or "stated." The first is fatuous, the second is overly dramatic, and the third (and most popular) is plain dull. Use "declared" only if a war has been formally announced, and "stated" only if you're quoting someone who is reading from a scroll.

Attributive verbs usually go between clauses or at the ends of sentences. "It's a false charge," she insisted, "and I'll fight it." Or, "It's a false charge, and I'll fight it," she insisted. "Insisted" smacks of determination—it nicely flavors the quote without getting in the way. The goal is to use attributive verbs like salt and pepper—to enhance flavor, not to destroy it.

### First reference.

On first reference (the first time someone is mentioned in a story), sources take as complete a description as is necessary to identify them for everyone who doesn't know who they are. This, in turn, depends on the audience. If that strike story was getting only local coverage, it would be all right to use Mayor Burnside in first reference, since just about everyone in the community would know that his first name is Julius. But if you were writing the same story on a statewide or a national basis, first reference would require his full name plus, of course, the name of the city. This does not mean that the man and the city have to go back-to-back (Mayor Julius Burnside of Chicago), but only that it should be clear that he is the mayor of the city in question. The same holds for Simon Allen, the union president:

> None of Chicago's buses and trains will move tomorrow unless there is a contract settlement tonight, United Transportation Workers president Simon Allen warned today.

Having said in the lead that the story is about Chicago, it follows that Burnside is the mayor of that city, not of Detroit, so the locale would not have to be repeated when referring to him. If, on the other hand, the lead was about the mayor, his title, name, and the city would have to be linked so that readers far away would understand who he is and where the news is happening: Chicago's Mayor Julius Burnside; Julius Burnside, the mayor of Chicago; Mayor Julius Burnside said today that Chicago. . . . When the title or occupation comes after the name it is set off between commas: Simon Allen, president of the United Transportation Workers, said today that. . . . When the title or occupation comes before the name, though, commas are unnecessary: United Transportation Workers president Simon Allen said today that. . . . Because the commas tend to slow the flow of the sentence, most reporters lean toward using the title immediately before the name.

Title and last name, or last name only (depending on the style of the news organization) are used in the second and all subsequent references. Doing otherwise is awkward and space-consuming. So after the first reference, it's Mayor Burnside, Mr. Burnside, or simply Burnside.

Note: Unless you're (1) writing a particularly intimate feature story, or (2) reporting on your fifth grade class activities, *never use first names only*. First, most adults who are named in print or on the air are offended by such familiarity, and second, news organizations are the keepers of the record, and those who are interested in that record want the full and correct name of the person in the news. Usually, then, it's Elizabeth, not Liz or Betty, and Robert, not Bob or Bobby. The rule can be broken only by the person named, since he or she has a right to whatever name they choose ("Ike" Eisenhower, "Betty" Ford, "Teddy" Kennedy). Be as careful with first names as with last names. If someone tells you his name is Jimmy don't jump to the conclusion that it's really James—ask, since

Jimmy is a common proper name in the South. Harry S. Truman wasn't really a Harold, either.

### No name/no comment.

For whatever reason, many persons don't want their names in the news and don't want to talk to reporters. That is their privilege. But you can unfairly slant a story by the way you phrase a person's not wanting to appear in the news. "He refused comment" or "refused to give his name" has stubborn, if not nasty, connotations. It's better to say: "declined to coment" or "declined to give his name"; "did not wish to be identified"; "preferred" or "asked to be anonymous."

### Talking bad English.

In the same vein, you can malign or unnecessarily cause to be ridiculed someone whose English is poor by quoting him verbatim phonetically. Taste and good judgment should prevail. You can often get charming, colorful quotes from someone whose English is faulty and use them to come up with a flavorful, more realistic story. Or you can make them appear to be unnecessarily ignorant or mean:

> "Cheez," Isaacs complained, "dis jernt is fulla pigs an' creep judges. I ain't gonna get no fair trial in dis place."

Since it's also unfair to the reader to make it seem as though Isaacs holds a chair at Cambridge, you would have to quote him indirectly:

> Isaacs, looking warily at the police and judges, said that he did not think he was going to get a fair trial in that court.

### Contractions.

Although change is in the wind, most newspapers and magazines still prefer complete words, not contractions, when the writer is

using his own prose. (Books like this one allow more flexibility.)
Direct and partial quotes, however, are a different matter. Very few
people would say, "I do not think that it is going to rain today."
If you listen closely, you'll notice that they are more likely to say,
"I don't think it's going to rain today." Quote them accordingly,
since doing so makes them sound more like humans than machines.
(If you ever have to quote a machine, the same rule applies—write
it the way you hear it  . . .).

### The third-man theme.

Mayor Burnside says that he wants Simon Allen to go to jail. It's
news and it's a good quote. But here is what many beginners would
do with it: Mayor Burnside added that he "wants Simon Allen to
go to jail." For such a quote to be accurate, Burnside would have
had to have said, "I *wants* Simon Allen to go to jail." This is the
third-person trap. If Burnside really talks like that he isn't fit to be
the mayor of Dogpatch. Or maybe he is. Anyway, either directly
quote the entire sentence or quote it indirectly, but don't quote
partially if it means making the subject, or yourself, seem semi-
literate.

### The anvil chorus.

Another trap for the novice. Unless you're quoting the West
Point Glee Club in action, don't attribute direct or partial quotes to
more than one person at a time, even if the pronoun is plural: "We'll
go to prison rather than give in," they said. If they really talk in
such close harmony the other prisoners should find them very
entertaining.

### Piping.

This means: to make up quotes. Next to fabricating an entire
story, the "piped" quote is the greatest sin a reporter can commit.
And like most other sins, it's tempting to the weak. "He would have

said it, anyway," or "That's what he meant," is the way the piper usually rationalizes what he has done to his victim. The real explanation is that the reporter either couldn't find the right person to interview, or couldn't get him to say anything "quotable." Piping is therefore an admission of failure—of incompetence. It is also morally unfair to readers as well as to the person being misquoted. Further, it is factually inaccurate, legally dangerous, and, like other crutches, habit-forming. Having been complimented by an editor or other reporters for his "good quote," the piper has to do it again for fear of seeming to lose his ability. Inevitably, the piped quotes from the relatively lowly produce such good stories that the reporter is sent out to cover bigger stuff, like the state assembly. Since he wants to get sent to Paris, though, he keeps piping. But state assemblymen and little old ladies who have 33 cats are very different articles. The reckoning comes. It comes.

# chapter ten

# SEARCH
# AND RESEARCH

Professional intelligence officers know that 10 percent or less of information gathering is done by the cloak and dagger types who skulk around with miniature cameras, forged passports, and knives hidden in their socks or bras. The rest comes from people who look like you and me, and who work in libraries, radio monitoring studios, computer rooms, and photo interpretation departments. Analysts in the CIA and its foreign counterparts spend their days poring over transcripts of foreign broadcasts, satellite pictures, military academy yearbooks, tractor-production charts, weather maps, literary magazines, rates of exchange, accounts of speeches, crime statistics, and piles of other material that, taken by itself, may mean little or nothing but which, when fitted into the bigger picture, may mean a great deal.

Professional intelligence officers and seasoned journalists know that the world is practically glutted with information waiting to be gathered and used.

I. F. Stone, the liberal muckraker who founded and for several years published *I. F. Stone's Weekly,* maintained that his considerable success as a ferreter of rascals in Washington rested for the most part on voracious reading and then applying serious thought to what he had read. Stone was not referring to leaked testimony and secret documents. He was talking about *Congressional Quarterly,* the *Congressional Record,* publicity releases, reference books, and every serious newspaper and magazine he could lay his hands on. The simple combination of reading and thinking, he explained, was usually enough to allow him to flush out large quantities of impacted political dirt.

Reporters research for one of two reasons: to provide important background material or additional information for a story they have, or to develop the story in the first place.

The "morgue"—the place near the newsroom where "clips" are kept—is almost always the starting point.

Every professional newspaper and magazine in the country, as well as many of the better college publications, keeps some sort of record of what appears in its columns. A few newspapers, such as *The New York Times,* use computers to retrieve isolated bits of information: a coded query is punched in and specific data (not an entire story, or even chunks of it) come back almost instantly. Computers don't look like they are going to replace the trusty clip file, though, because editors and reporters need to see entire stories in order to best use their contents for ongoing developments. Newspapers therefore still use the traditional method of cutting out every story (often in quadruplicate) they run and cross-filing them in alphabetically arranged folders or heavy-duty envelopes. The editor or reporter who needs to know whether a story has already appeared (there is an understandable aversion to running the same story twice), or who wants background information, almost always goes to the clips first.

Say a reporter is writing a story about Caesar T. Rosenberg, the famous chef, who has come to town to peddle his latest book, *The Benign Beet,* and to demonstrate the preparation of a few of his creations at the better of the two department stores. Before he goes out to watch Caesar autograph cookbooks and combine beets with white onions in a light cream sauce, our reporter goes to the clips and pulls the folder labeled: Rosenberg, Caesar T. (chef). The maestro also might be mentioned or featured in clips inside the folders labeled: Beets, Chefs, Cooking, Cuisine, Gastronomy,

Gourmets, or Vegetables. But Rosenberg's own folder is obviously the best place to start. There are, let us say, seven clips. Together, they provide a reasonably clear picture of who Caesar T. Rosenberg is—his age, origins, education, professional experience, and specialty, all of which give the reporter the benefit of knowing something about the subject of his story before he goes out to cover him.

Among other things, one clip makes brief reference to Caesar's having won the coveted *Prix Mondial de Lyon* for his *potage bortsch à la russe*. Having once had three years of French our reporter knows that the subject of his story won the World Prize of Lyon for his Russian bortsch recipe. This, seemingly Caesar T. Rosenberg's chief claim to fame, should go in the story. The problem is that our reporter doesn't know how to fry an egg, much less understand what "bortsch" is. But it has to be defined for the benefit of any reader who is as ignorant as he is. He goes to the dictionary and learns that bortsch is beet soup, which figures, since Caesar is a beet specialist. He also notes that his *Webster's Third New International Dictionary* (unabridged) gives these spellings: borsch, borscht, borsht, bortsch, and borshch. In other circumstances, our reporter would use the first spelling, which is always the preferred one in dictionaries. But not this time. Since the chef calls his creation "bortsch," and it was "bortsch" that took highest honors at Lyon, it gets written that way. If the reporter wanted to learn more about *potage bortsch à la russe,* he would head straight for the office library and turn to page 920 of the *Larousse Gastronomique,* where he would find its ingredients and method of preparation. But he wouldn't put either in the story until he had interviewed Rosenberg because even someone who doesn't know how to fry an egg knows that chefs don't win awards for other people's recipes. *Voilà.*

Research for possible story development requires more thought and initiative than are necessary to fill small holes in existing stories. It also requires imagination and a fair amount of general knowledge.

Let us pretend, for example, that the President has just appointed Lieut. Gen. Rockingham Smedley, a retired Army officer, to head the Environmental Protection Agency, and our reporter is going to write the story. Besides going to the clips, he picks up *Who's Who in America,* considered to be the standard source on important living Americans. There, he finds a fact-packed biographical sketch of General Smedley, including when and where he was born, his education, service record, awards and citations, immediate ancestry, and a bit of material on Mrs. Smedley and the two younger Smedleys. In addition to some other commands, the sketch says, Smedley spent his last six years in the military as chief of the Army Corps of Engineers.

Since our reporter is reasonably knowledgeable, he knows that the Army Corps of Engineers is not the grown-up equivalent of the Corps of Cadets. It is responsible for building dams, diverting streams and rivers, clearing and dredging channels and harbors, and otherwise adjusting the landscape to suit man's needs, or what the Corps thinks are his needs. If the reporter knows that much, he likely also knows that most environmentalists think of the Corps of Engineers the way a mongoose thinks of a cobra. This, in turn, raises a few serious questions:

1. Why has the President appointed a former member of the Corps of Engineers to head an agency that is supposed to protect and purify the environment, not move it around?
2. What kind of a job can Rockingham Smedley be expected to do at the Environmental Protection Agency, given his background, experience, and probable loyalties?
3. How will environmental groups react to the appointment?

Assuming that there was nothing improper about Smedley's appointment, answering these questions will produce a better, fuller, more balanced story. If there *was* something improper, answering them will produce a first-rate investigative piece. Either way, the genesis will have been, as it always is, the fusion of knowledge, imagination, and sound research.

The essential purpose of a university education, according to the old (and valid) saying, is not to fill students' heads with all the knowledge in the world, but to whet their appetites for learning and to teach them how to acquire it on their own. This applies as well to journalists. No editor or reporter has ever faced execution (at least in the United States) for not knowing every word of the national anthem and its history. But they *are* expected to know where they can quickly find that information.* The reporter who is familiar

* *The World Almanac & Book of Facts.*

with a wide variety of basic source material and who feels comfortable in a library will do an infinitely better job than the one who flounders in what seems to him to be nothing more than a morass of meaningless paper.

There are literally thousands of reference books and specialty magazines covering every conceivable subject. You should be aware of the fact that the major ones are stocked in most libraries and you ought to know how to find them there or, failing that, how to find the librarian.

You should own the first three of the books listed below and know about the others.

### A good paperback dictionary.

Keep this on your desk. Having it next to the typewriter will save you time because you won't have to keep referring to the unabridged monster at the front of the room.

### An up-to-date almanac.

Almanacs are loaded with trivia that have a way of becoming crucial at deadline time: the date the first Sputnik went up; Canadian egg production; the capital of Outer Mongolia; Mississippi River bridges; politicians' terms of office; and a million or more other details. The *Information Please Almanac* and the *World Almanac & Book of Facts* are the best in their class.

### A style book.

As mentioned earlier, some publications have their own, while others rely on someone else's. *The Associated Press Stylebook,* published in collaboration with United Press International, is popular and inexpensive. *The New York Times Manual of Style and Usage* is more comprehensive and interesting than the AP book, but it is also many times as expensive.

You might also want *The Elements of Style* by William Strunk Jr.

and E. B. White. It's a concise and witty general guide to American English usage.

## A thesaurus.

I am squarely in the use-only-the-words-in-your-head school of reporting for three reasons: (1) looking up substitutes is time-consuming; (2) you usually end up with a longer word, which defeats the purpose of trying to write clearly; (3) the smoothness of your prose can suffer when you use alien words. If you must, though, *Roget's International Thesaurus* lists 250,000 words and phrases that are indexed and easy to locate.

## Unabridged dictionaries.

*Webster's* Second International (for purists) or Third (for the avant-garde) are standard. The 12-volume (plus supplement) *Oxford English Dictionary on Historical Principles* is lexicography's most ambitious and probably its finest undertaking. Leave it alone unless you have an hour to kill.

## Atlases and maps.

You have to know where places are. If the Russians and Chinese start shooting at each other near Oblast, and you think that's where Englishmen go to curse, you're in trouble. Similarly, if either or both start shooting at Americans at the intersection of Prospect and Decatur, you will need to know either how to get there as quickly as possible or, if you *are* there, you may well want to know the fastest route in the other direction. *The London Times Atlas of the World,* first published in 1895, is still about the best around. The *Encyclopedia Britannica World Atlas International* is in serious contention. The *Columbia Lippincott Gazetteer of the World,* which lists about 130,000 place names and geographical features, plus populations, resources, industries, and other information, is also useful. The major oil companies provide free state and regional maps, and city maps can be bought relatively cheaply in most stationery and department stores.

### General encyclopedias.

Except for using their bibliographies, serious students tend to stay away from these because they have at least one disadvantage, and occasionally, two. First, they become outdated relatively quickly, and the yearbook supplements don't help much. Second, some of their material is occasionally a little short of being completely objective. Britannica's 14th edition, for example, had an article on the FBI signed "J.E.H." Although no one would challenge J. Edgar Hoover's knowledge of his bureau, his perspective can be questioned. Similarly, a piece on Congressman Sam Rayburn was signed "L.B.J." The 15th edition has articles on Soviet republics that allegedly were prepared with the cooperation of the Soviet government. That's a little like allowing a movie star to review his own films. The rule on using general encyclopedias for quick reference is to be very selective. They do splendidly for the Magna Carta, early American flags, the atomic structure of emeralds, a sketch of Thomas A. Edison, and other areas that are complete. Using them for the latest developments in rocket technology, cancer research, or the theater, for the latest rules in professional football, or for contemporary politics, is probably a serious mistake.

### Media news indexes.

First and foremost is *The New York Times Index,* which comes out twice a month with a comprehensive list of that newspaper's contents arranged by subject. You go from the appropriate volume to a microfilm machine. *The Wall Street Journal* provides a similar service. The *Reader's Guide to Periodical Literature,* which is also published biweekly, (except in July and August) does the same thing for more than 100 general magazines. Its following calls it the *Reader's Guide. Television News Index and Abstracts,* put out by the Vanderbilt University libraries, is a comprehensive guide to the evening news broadcasts of the three major networks. Tapes of all broadcasts are stored in the Television News Archive for retrieval as needed. Since the original material is generally not available to the public except in special circumstances, this service is particularly valuable.

### Biographical material.

The *Who's Who* group dominates. The original *Who's Who*, which started in 1849, has sprouted others, including the *International Who's Who, Who's Who in the East, Who's Who in Finance and Industry,* and many others. *Current Biography,* a monthly, concentrates on those who are prominent in the news. It is put together in annual volumes. The *Dictionary of American Biography,* which is some 20 volumes long (not counting supplements) and is indexed, pulls together everyone who (1) is judged to have made a significant contribution in his or her field, and (2) is dead. *The New York Times Obituaries Index* is what it says it is.

Following is a very short list of other reference books in specialized fields.*

### Art.

*American Art Directory* (catalogues museums, schools, associations, publications, and other information for the U.S. and Canada); *Encyclopedia of World Art* (7,000 pages of plates and text covering the visual arts from their beginnings).

### Aviation.

*Jane's All The World's Aircraft* (a widely respected annual compendium of military and civilian planes, missiles, and engines of all nations, together with photographs, drawings, and performance charts).

---

* Most of them have their own bibliographies.

### Biology.

*Encyclopedia of the Biological Sciences* (covers the whole biological spectrum for the layman); *Larousse Encyclopedia of Animal Life* (more than 600 pages of text and illustrations covering everything from protozoans to us, plus a glossary and classification table).

### Chemistry.

The *Condensed Chemical Dictionary* (lists names, properties, grades, derivation, uses, and formulas); *Handbook of Chemistry* (general reference volume for chemical and physical data).

### Economics.

*The McGraw-Hill Dictionary of Modern Economics* (defines about 1,300 terms, some with graphs and charts, and lists 200-or-so private and public agencies); *Encyclopedia of Banking and Finance* (covers about all the bases, including banking theory and practice, money and credit, and securities trading); *Moody's Manual of Investments* and *Poor's Register of Corporations, Directors and Executives* (the daily working tools of business and finance reporters who need current information on companies and those who run them).

### Education.

*Digest of Educational Statistics* (current information on school enrollments, finances, educational levels, teachers, programs, and more, courtesy of the federal government); *American Universities and Colleges* (a wide-ranging survey of American higher education, including an extensive list of colleges and universities and data on them); *Encyclopedia of Education* (10 volumes with more than 1,000 articles, plus bibliographies on American and foreign education).

## Law.

*Black's Law Dictionary* (this one can send you to the aspirin bottle, but it's the standard for law students and lawyers who need definitions, historical evolution, and *stare decisis* . . . precedent).

## Medicine.

*Stedman's Medical Dictionary* (edited by Isaac Asimov and others, this one defines medical and related terminology in comprehensible fashion); *American Medical Directory* (registry of American physicians and their specialties); *Gray's Anatomy* and *Morris' Anatomy* (illustrated catalogues of the human body for medical students, physicians, and exceptionally knowledgeable laymen).

## Physical sciences.

*Van Nostrand's Scientific Encyclopedia* (more than 16,000 scientific, engineering, mathematical, and medical terms are explained for laymen and scientists); *The McGraw-Hill Encyclopedia of Science and Technology* (a 15-volume, 7,000-article work giving comprehensive coverage to natural, physical, and applied sciences).

## Political science.

*The American Political Dictionary* (term definitions in 18 categories, plus material on statutes, cases, and agencies); *Municipal Year Book* (tightly written directory of officials, political units, finance, welfare programs, and other information about 10,000 American cities); *Yearbook of International Organizations* (directory of active international bodies, including their purposes, officials, financing, publications, and activities); *Statesman's Yearbook* (a concise annual with data on governments of the world, including their political systems, economic and diplomatic activities, defense programs, and educational levels); *Congressional Directory* (*the* source on congressmen, including biographical sketches, political profiles, and committee assignments); *U.S. Government Organizational Manual* (the executive branch's equivalent of the *Congressional Directory,* covering all departments); *Congressional Quarterly Weekly Report* (loaded with information on bills, voting records, and other relevant matters); *Congressional Record* (a daily record of Senate and House debates, speeches, and related subjects).

### Psychology.

The *Encyclopedia of Psychology* (more than 5,000 authoritative entries and bibliographical data make it the best general source).

### Psychiatry.

*Psychiatric Dictionary* (ample coverage of terminology, including that used in social services and occupational therapy).

### Social sciences.

*A Dictionary of the Social Sciences* (UN-sponsored dictionary of political and social science, terms, plus history and usage); *International Encyclopedia of the Social Sciences* (17-volume study of theoretical and comparative social sciences, and 600-or-so biographical sketches); the *Encyclopedia of Associations* and *The Foundation Directory* (these list, respectively, details about more than 12,000 organizations and 7,000 nonprofit foundations).

### Sociology.

*A Modern Dictionary of Sociology* (defines sociological, psychological, philosophical, anthropological, and a lot of other "-ical" material with emphasis on current usage). There are also several good source books (and a slew of rotten, semihysterical ones) on blacks, Indians, Chicanos, and all religious groups, which can be found by category.

### Sports.

Library shelves are groaning under sports material. The *Encyclopedia of Sports* (1,100 pages of history, rules, records, teams, stadium capacities, and more on just about all sports); *Baseball Record Book* (the sports writer's choice for obscure statistical information); The *Football Register* (another annual loaded with statistics on players and coaches).

This is only a smattering of the good reference books that are available to help find facts fast. In addition, there are literally thousands of magazines and journals in just about every field imaginable, from breeding Arabian horses to general zoology. They come with titles like: *Dance Magazine, Aviation Week and Space Technology, American Economic Review, New England Journal of Medicine, Journal of Jewish Studies, Journal of Applied Psychology, Journal of Organic Chemistry, Annals of Physics, Journal of Higher Education, American Political Science Review, Harvard Law Review, American Anthropologist, American Historical Review,* and *Modern Fiction Studies.* The great advantage of the magazines and journals is their currency. In fact, many of them are used more as sources for general-interest news stories than as references for checking facts. Reporters on the science or medical beat, for example, often turn the most important articles in *Science, New England Journal of Medicine,* or *Journal of the American Medical Association* (JAMA) into feature stories for the general audience.

Be wary of magazines for automobile, boat, and airplane enthusiasts, as well as those written for people who buy farm machinery, clothing, and appliances like phonographs and sound systems. Most such magazines (*Consumer Reports* is an exception) depend on advertising to survive. The editorial policies of many of them are therefore set by the advertising staff, not by the editors and writers. This means that if the *Weekend Aviator* runs an article reporting that Munster Aviation's new Super Canary has an engine that tends to stop at altitudes above 15,000 feet, it can expect to see perhaps $100,000 in Munster Aviation advertising revenue stop faster than the Super Canary's engine. Since that would mean the end of the *Weekend Aviator,* too, the review has to say that the Super Canary's optimal altitude is 10,500 feet. Period. The rule for most popular consumer hardware magazines was set years ago by a songwriter: Accentuate the positive, eliminate the negative, and don't mess with Mr. In-between.

Those who put together corporate annual reports and government budgets on all levels are sometimes tempted to flirt with distortion, too, but they have a harder time because it is illegal to do so. You are not supposed to lie in records that the public uses as guidance for investing or to see where its tax money is going. An oil company that slips the Emir of Hadibu $1 million extra for an offshore concession has got to account for that money or the books won't balance. Since such bribery irritates many stockholders and the government, though, the accountants account for it by burying it in "operating expenses," "equipment replacement," or simply as an "adjustment." Likewise, the American public does not mandate its intelligence services to equip and pay small bands of insurgents in enemy countries or spies on campuses at home. The funds for such operations are therefore siphoned from similar innocuous accounts. In each case, and not to mention day-in, day-out municipal, state, and federal book-juggling, the story is there in black and white; it's a matter of pursuing the numbers to their real meaning. Reporters are tantalized by the notion that within the $4,323,615 listed by a corporation for foreign "public relations," there could be $250,000 that went into a pocket that entered a Swiss bank that paid for a chateau in Geneva that the shareholders neither enjoy nor approve of. Here—in black and white—is where the story begins for the good reporter.

# chapter eleven

# INTERVIEWING

It should be said here that, contrary to what most beginners seem to think, interviewing is not the heart of reporting: research is. Research can be more important than interviewing because it's often more dependable—people are almost always more thoughtful when they write than they are when they talk. But most students have a tendency to dismiss research as being boring, vaguely academic, and almost superfluous, while at the same time approaching the specter of an interview with something like partial paralysis: "Oh, my God, *then* what do I ask?"

Interviewing, like every other element of reporting, is a tool. It has its place, no more, no less, and should be used in conjunction with the other tools, including careful research. There is no such thing as a story wrapped only around an interview, or if there is, it has to be awful. Good interviews come from good questions. Good questions come from good research. There's no way around it.

Interviewing—getting people to give you information of some sort—is a kind of competitive game like poker. And like poker, it can be played by novices and masters, often against each other. It is a game in which the "players" confront each other by consent, have at least some idea of the rules, occasionally bluff, and always want to win. Good interviewing is, above all, a game of control in which the ante is steadily raised.

Winning the game means getting the "truth" to the public. It is a contest of often competing truths. And as has been said, truth is—again—a matter of perception. For the politician, the truth is that he is better suited for office, or is more knowledgeable about a piece of legislation, than his opponent. For the movie star, the truth is that he is very talented and is therefore deserving of recognition. For the public utility executive, the truth is that power reactors offer our best hope for limitless energy. These truths, and an infinite number of others, derive from some form of self-interest: money, power, fame, sincere belief, or any combination of them. The person who is willing to be interviewed—who, in most cases, wants to be interviewed—does so because he or she wants to get a particular truth to the public. (There is no such thing as a forced interview in journalism; forced interviews are conducted by interrogators, not reporters.) Those who allow interviews, or who agree or consent to them (don't use "grant" unless you're interviewing the Emperor), do so because their interests can best be served with public recognition or support. Obviously, I don't mean the folks on the street who are asked to say a few words about the heat. Nor do I mean only the rapacious and evil among us. There are a great many dedicated politicians, honest and brave policemen, altruistic bureaucrats, genuinely talented and deserving artists and athletes, and countless ordinary citizens who say things with the most laudible of motives. But whatever their motives, they almost always think of the public as a bottomless well of supportive energy waiting to be drawn upon and used. And they think of the reporter as their bucket.

Played at its best, the interviewing game becomes an intensely interesting clash of "truths"—a test of competing awareness, resources, and intelligence. Reporters who are skilled interviewers almost always have the respect, however begrudging, of even those of their subjects who are most opposed to them. Reporters who allow themselves to be used as ever-available and compliant buckets are thought of and treated accordingly, particularly in their own organizations.

**Equipment.**

Although an increasing number of reporters are using tape recorders for interviews, most still depend on the traditional notebook.
Recorders have two advantages over notebooks: they get what is
said verbatim, and they allow the reporter time to collect his
thoughts and therefore, in theory, to ask better questions. But they
also have three disadvantages. First, most newspapers and magazines don't pay for tapes because they are relatively expensive, so
storing interviews, either for later reference or because they may be
necessary for use in a libel case, is prohibitive. Second, there is always the possibility that the thing will have a heart attack and, early
on, it will begin picking up nothing more than the sounds of its own
wheezing and panting. You then return from the interview with an
empty basket. The result of this on your nerves and your editor's
blood pressure is easily imagined. Third, there are many individuals
who either cannot, or will not, talk to a microphone. Some simply
don't want a verbatim recording, clearly in their own voices, of
what they tell reporters. They are afraid that they may somehow be
held accountable for what they say and, particularly in court, tapes
can be devastating when used as evidence. Others are intimidated
by the gadgets. They look at one, stammer, and practically go
speechless. It then becomes harder to get information than it is
when using a notebook.

If you use a recorder, check it carefully before each interview:
batteries charging, recording volume preset, and all necessary buttons, switches, and dials working.

Set the microphone so that it will pick up your voice, as well as
the subject's, so the questions as well as the answers will come over
on play-back. Place the machine near enough to you so that you
can monitor the little needle that registers sound input as the interview progresses. You don't have to stare at the needle, but it's wise
to look at it every once in a while. Start each interview by recording
the date, place, and name and title of the person you're interviewing.
Then play it back. Your subject may think you have the most
orderly mind outside the Library of Congress when, in fact, you're
mostly trying to find out whether the machine is working or whether
you should start looking for a pencil sharpener.

Notebooks are still the surest tools for coming back with what you go out to get. Assuming that you do not have shorthand (and it would be better if you did), you can help yourself most by developing an abbreviated note-taking technique similar, perhaps, to the ones taught commercially. "With" becomes "w," "this," "the," "that," "those," "them," and the others become "ths," "th," "tht," "thm," and so on, "complete" becomes "cmplt," "professional" becomes "prfsnl" or simply "pro." If y cn rd ths y cn lrn t b a rprtr n lss thn 10 yrs. . . .

If you try to take down every word that is said in an interview, you will not only be too busy to ask any but the shallowest questions, but you'll probably begin popping circuits within a matter of minutes. The warning signals, in approximate order, are: cramped thumb and forefinger, teeth pressing hard on the tongue, sweaty hand, lip-biting, and desperate longing to get out of the room. Solution: take selective notes. You don't have to write everything that is said. Take only those comments that seem to be the most important and necessary to the thrust of the story, especially if it's one covering immediate news, and leave the rest alone. Also, never be embarrassed about asking your subject to repeat anything important that you miss (but don't overdo it).

Some reporters use recorders and notebooks in combination. They jot down important material for emphasis or to refresh their memories while the tape goes round and round, picking up every inflection. This is insurance. They know they will return to the newsroom with something even if a mechanical malfunction turns that verbatim tape into a pile of linguine. *

### Types of interviews.

There are three types (not counting formal polling) with a variation: (1) the short "man on the street," or reaction interview, in which witnesses to news events are asked for comment; (2) the standard interview, in which a person involved in the news is asked fairly extensive questions about the event being covered; and (3) the inclusive interview, which concerns the person being questioned, rather than an event of which he is a part. The variation is conducting the first two by telephone.

## The short interview.

These are done mostly to sample public reaction to news events (questioning 30 or 40 commuters for their reactions to a bus drivers' strike that has just stranded them), or to provide first-hand accounts of news events (witnesses to a plane crash or survivors of a fire).

Since short interviews generally mean questioning several persons in a relatively short time, you have to get to the point quickly. But that's not hard to do. Unlike the longer interviews, in which the questions become sharper or more detailed as they progress because of the more complex nature of the subject, "react/witness" interviews usually require no more than two or three obvious questions. The nature of the questions is dictated by the nature of the story. And as with all interviews, the first question usually sets off the others.

In the case of that bus drivers' strike, you would be dealing with an emotional situation, so the first thing you would want to know is how the stranded commuters felt about the strike and about being stranded. You might therefore walk up to one, identify yourself, and pose this obvious question:

"How do you feel about the strike and about being stranded here?"

You would assuredly get a reaction. If experience is any guide, most of the commuters would be frustrated and angry because of the inconvenience, a few would take the side of the strikers, and there would be at least one buoyant soul who would find the whole business interesting, if not actually fun. That one question would probably give you the information you were after:

"I think it's disgusting. The public is always the scapegoat in situations like this. Fares keep going up, service keeps getting worse, and then there are strikes like this, to boot."

If you wanted to pursue the matter, appropos of the graffiti exchange in Chapter 9, you might follow up with:

"But the bus drivers say they're severely underpaid. How would you feel if you were one of them?" This is a question calculated to draw a quick and truthful answer because it stimulates the subject's emotions much more so than, "Is your wife going to hold dinner?"

The first question to be asked of a witness, obviously, is "What happened?" You want to find out what the witness saw or heard and that, in turn, will lead to the next question:

"I heard an explosion right overhead, looked up, and saw the plane falling."

"Did any part of it seem to be on fire, or smoking?"

"Yeah. The engine on the left wing was burning and the plane started spinning like a leaf."

Remember: get to the point quickly. And don't forget to get the witness's full name and, if appropriate, age, address, and occupation, every time.

Standard and inclusive interviews are a different proposition. Since you are questioning a newsmaker—someone with a personal and serious interest in what the public is told—there will almost always be a clash of truths. Here are some suggestions:

### Be prepared.

If depth interviewing is a game of control, it follows that you can't control what you don't understand. Either you are going to whittle an ever-sharper point to your questions based on knowledge of the subject, or the person you are questioning is going to lead you down whatever path he or she chooses, camouflaging as necessary along the way. Start with the clips and then, if necessary, go to the books. For interviews with persons who are interesting, but who are virtually unknown, brief yourself on what they do. A couple of hours of research will tell you enough about hockey so you can get something interesting out of a hockey player. Put yourself in his place. How would you feel if a reporter showed up for an interview and led off with something like: "Does hockey require a lot of stamina?" or "What's the name of the little thing you try to get into the net?" Questions like these will lead the hockey player to suspect that the interviewer isn't taking him or his profession seriously. From that point the air hangs heavy with scorn and aloofness.

### Don't wear a "uniform."

The person you interview has his or her own sensibilities and perceptions and, providing he or she is not demented, they will be brought to bear, first on how you look, and second, on how you act. Common sense prevails—you are there to get information from your subject. Bank presidents are not amused by reporters who show up for interviews in jeans, sneakers, and "Don't Rot: Smoke Pot" buttons. Similarly, ghetto reporting doesn't call for tie and tails. As a general rule, dress on the conservative side and make certain that you are decently groomed. There's nothing wrong with a beard (if you're male), but a three-day stubble is offensive. Above all, never wear "advertising" that could be interpreted as meaning that you are not objective or that you are scatterbrained. That means no political candidate's button, party button, peace button, war button, liberation button, religious button, conservation button, or cute button ("Kiss Me, I'm Tibetan," and so on). Vote as you please, but stay out of uniform.

**Attitude.**

Be calm and confident. Be polite. The fictitious television series reporter who exudes righteousness, oneupmanship, and the power of Zeus, and who comes to an interview clearly prepared to pelt his victim with barbed arrows shot from under the glorious mantle of the Fourth Estate, would get his nose caught in a slammed door in real life. Personality is a major element in interviewing because it establishes the rapport necessary to get the subject to say something (as opposed to merely talking). Be quietly confident and, if appropriate, be soothing or cheerful. Be pleasant. Time and your subject permitting, open with small talk (but not with the weather unless it's 108° in the shade or people are building arks) until you both have settled down. The best interviewers are part actor, part psychologist. They learn through experience to size up the person they are interviewing within minutes, and to shape their approach accordingly. The best reporters are virtually Oscar caliber: they can use sympathy, compassion, flattery, surprise, bewilderment, ignorance, disdain, revulsion, thinly veiled threats, or any combination of them to keep things moving. Never lose sight of the fact that you are there to get information, and that anything you do that prevents you from getting it, defeats the purpose of the interview. Never try to bully or intimidate.

Here are some general rules:

1. Come prepared with a few key questions. Write them in your notebook or on an index card and arrange them so they get harder as they progress. Don't come with the fabled 20 questions. The person you interview will occasionally go off on tangents that are worth pursuing, so you may end up ignoring three-quarters of your prepared questions anyway. At the same time, don't let him wander too far off the track: When the conversation goes too far afield, gently steer it back to where you want it.

2. Remember that you are there mostly to listen and get information, not to filibuster. Don't talk more than you have to. Further, you want to leave with the information you came for, not with a lifelong friendship or a feud. Though you should appear interested and concerned, keep your personal feelings out of the interview as much as possible.

3. Be positive, not defeatist. Here is the way one television newsman put a question about the CIA to the subject of an interview: "I would assume if I tried to get the details, you'd refuse to talk to me, but I'll try anyway." He tried. The subject refused. Why would anyone answer a question knowing that the reporter didn't really expect an answer? Look as though you've come to be reckoned with, not ignored.

4. Avoid questions that can be answered with a yes or no. Shape them to be specific and provocative: "What does that mean?" "How did that come about?" "What will happen next?" "Don't you think there's another side to it?" Tell subjects what their opponents or enemies have said and push for serious and detailed rebuttal.

5. If you think that the person you're interviewing has said something that isn't true, attack the point from a different angle— rephrase the same question three or four times if necessary:
"Did you kill Mrs. Thorndike?"
"No."
"Who else would have had a motive?"
"I don't know."

"Would you say that you had a motive?"

"No, I didn't have a motive. I didn't do it."

"But didn't they find your gun nearby?"

Notice, too, that the exchange goes from the general to the specific.

6. Never tell the person you're interviewing that you're going to write the story a certain way. In the first place, it shows a moral commitment that erodes the appearance of objectivity. In the second place, you might change your mind when you start writing (or have it changed for you by an editor), thereby violating your promise.

7. Never agree to show your story to the person you interview before it is printed. The odds are high that he or she will find something in it that is personally objectionable (as opposed to inaccurate): "You can't run a story saying that my office is shabby! I'll sue." Some people will go to almost any length to prevent a story from appearing if they don't like the way they're portrayed in it; they can get amazingly finicky, not only about what they're quoted as having said, but about the color of their hair, the quality of their clothing, or their job description. But the odds are equally high that you won't get hassled after the story has been printed and done with. If your subject asks to see your story before it runs—even at the outset of the interview—say with mild astonishment that just about everyone knows that it is against universally accepted rules to do so. If the interview is conditional on handing over the story before publication, there can be no interview.

8. Stimulate responses, when necessary, by setting up conflict questions. This is a little like being the matador who shakes his muleta more vigorously when the bull refuses to charge. Like that matador, your performance depends on getting a good response, and you should be able to do that with the right question, even if it has to be slightly barbed. Here, again, is where research comes in: "How do you reconcile your probusing stand with the fact that your own children are in private schools?" It's impossible to respond to such a question with a yes or no answer, and it's most unlikely to draw a "no comment" reply.

9. If your subject declines to answer a particularly important question, especially one having two sides, gently explain that you need the answer for balance and fairness. Say that if you cannot get his or her side you will have no alternative but to go with the other side only. Rather than see the opposition win the day, the subject usually comes around.

10. Interrupt only when when it is absolutely necessary. There are few things more annoying than that of trying to make a point or explain something while being repeatedly interrupted. It has the effect of irritating your subject and then making him spiteful enough to not want to participate in the discussion. The interviewer is engaged in a lopsided conversation, but a conversation nonetheless. When the person being interviewed raises a point worth pursuing, pursue it gently, getting your follow-up question in during the first pause. Points that don't have to be pursued immediately can either be written in the margin of your notebook, or the relevant notes themselves can be bracketed or otherwise marked to remind you to get back to them later.

11. The last question in an interview should be: "Is there anything else you would like to say that we haven't covered?"

### Phone interviews.

They usually require an extra measure of politeness because of your obvious psychological disadvantage: you can get hung up (in both senses of the word). Since you don't generally make appointments for phone calls, assume that the person you're talking to was doing something important when the phone rang. Identify yourself immediately and explain why you're calling. If he or she wants to talk, get to the heart of the matter quickly, particularly if you don't know the person. Also: (1) give a number at which you can be reached in case the person you interview thinks of something to add an hour later; (2) never make long-distance calls collect, even if you're calling the president of General Motors, first because you're not supposed to work with other people's money, and second, because it creates a bad impression.

**Not for publication.**

You can be walking around with the biggest story since Moses got the Ten Commandments, but if it's not for publication, you have nothing. Journalists are supposed to sell news, so their accepting information provided it is not published or aired is like a grocer's accepting 1,000 cans of peas provided he does not sell them. It makes the whole business pointless. Most of those who deal with the press with any kind of regularity know that what they say is for publication unless there is an agreement to the contrary. Such agreements are rare because reporters know that they allow sources to act irresponsibly. Character assassination is but one manifestation of the problem. "This isn't for publication, but Oliver Smelts over at Applied Chemical once spent a year in prison for check forging." More often, however, it goes something like this: "I don't want this printed, but we're going to more than double our profits in the third quarter." What, exactly, can you do with such information if you can't report it? Nothing. At best, it's just useless; at worst, it's information designed to make you eternally grateful to the person who gave it to you. Tell him that if it isn't for publication, you don't want to hear about it.

**Sourcing.**

This is stickier. Here, too, there is a tendency to take reckless potshots at opponents, test public opinion on controversial issues (known as sending up "trial balloons"), or enhance without foundation a person, company, agency, or some other body behind the safe veil of anonymity. Many people are tempted to tell reporters that so-and-so is a nincompoop or a scoundrel when they can do so anonymously. They think twice, though, when they know that their names will appear next to the allegation. For this reason, reporters don't like their sources to hide behind the veil.

Occasionally, however, the veil is used because it is the only way to get the news (particularly in Washington and in other places where bureaucrats feel compelled to keep their tracks covered). There are two basic criteria used to determine whether news can be reported without direct attribution: (1) it must be relatively important and appear to the reporter to be true, a factor that usually can be double-checked by going to a second source; (2) the "source" must be someone who would either be in great professional trouble, or whose life would actually be in danger, if his or her name appeared in the story.

So-called "backgrounders" and "deep backgrounders" make the veil even more opaque. If the Secretary of State does not wish direct attribution, he may tell reporters as much, and the resulting story will be pinned to a "highly informed State Department source." Information given in a backgrounder, however, separates him from what he says just a little more: "A State Department *official* said yesterday that . . ." There are far fewer highly informed sources in the State Department than there are officials, so by being labeled an official, he is that much more protected. A deep backgrounder is the ultimate in this kind of camouflaging and is used only on the highest levels of government and industry. Here, the reporter cannot even refer to an official's having supplied the information. It therefore seems to come from the reporter himself. "The Air Force will send four squadrons of fighters to South Korea tomorrow as part of a sharp military build-up there." The Secretary of Defense, or whoever put that information into a deep backgrounder, would likely have done so (1) to warn the North Koreans and others that the United States is prepared to meet force with counter-force, and (2) to avoid being attacked by opponents of the operation at home, be they others in the executive branch, congressmen, or peace groups. The danger here is that the reporter, not the Secretary of Defense, takes responsibility for the story. If it is wrong, it is the reporter who is left holding the proverbial bag, not the official.

Ground rules for attribution are generally set between reporters and their sources before interviews and backgrounders take place so there is no confusion. The reporter has the option at that moment of either going along with the "off the record" unattributed story or of declining the information that is to be offered. If the person giving the interview does not bring up the matter, it is taken for granted that what is said is on the record for direct attribution. If the person you are interviewing doesn't mention attribution, don't you, either.

Reporters and their sources use each other, often in very serious circumstances, and they must therefore coexist. During a reporter's first weeks on a beat, he and his sources feel one another out for personal compatibility and professional reliability. Within professional boundaries, they do each other favors, such as swapping information. The relationship between reporters and their sources is generally built on mutual trust based on experience. Sources rarely lie to reporters because the best of them understand that, where the newsman is concerned, the first lie has to be the last. Having tricked the reporter once, they can no longer remain sources, "reliable" or otherwise. For their part, reporters who agree not to name those who give them information stick to the agreement even if doing so means going to jail (which has sometimes happened). Word of a reporter who reveals sources gets around quickly. The result is that the big mouth is soon shut out of the information system and finds it more and more difficult to get inside news. In the relationship he has with his sources, no less than in the relationship he has with his readers or listeners, the "sourcerer" is only as good as his word. That word has to be protected at all costs.

# chapter twelve

# FEATURES

Features differ from immediate news stories mainly in the fact that they are usually noncompetitive. To squeeze even more juice out of an already limp piece of journalistic jargon, they are exclusive. They are used by both newspapers and the electronic media either to supplement immediate news stories or to provide a pleasant or informative alternative to them.

Feature articles are being used increasingly by newspapers as competitive weapons against television. As just about any television news executive will admit, entertainment is a fundamental component of news programming. One network official went so far as to say that "the line between news and theatrics is a thin one." So radio and television are (or can be) very entertaining. Furthermore, both are quick to deliver "breaking" news when they have to be. Not only do we have all-news radio stations throughout the country that stay on several stories as they are developing, but any radio or television program can be interrupted for an important "bulletin." No newspaper, locked as it is into appearing only in the afternoon or in the morning, can match that. Time is the great ally of radio and television and the enemy of the print media in this contest. But, newspaper editors and publishers have come to realize, they have an ally, too. It is space. They have column upon column of space to fill, and if they can't match radio and television in being first with the news, many have decided, they must provide more depth and variety in what they cover. A newspaper's space advantage rests on the fact that it can run perhaps 100 stories a day, while its television news competitors can air only one at a time, and those have to be relatively brief or there would be all-news television.

With larger news "holes," the need to entertain, and an audience that is increasingly better educated and has more leisure time for hobbies and other interests, newspapers are turning more and more to the feature article (so much so, in some cases, that immediate news has practically disappeared). There are features about antiques, gardening, architecture, home repair, stamps and coins, art, cooking, wine, photography, fashion, theater, restaurants, ballet, and boxing. There are features about bird-watching clubs, women who set preserves, men who grow champion-size tomatoes or breed beagles, skin-diving and sky-diving groups, children who are chemistry wizards or who are batting .450 in Little League, and many more designed to attract readers who want an alternative to war, terrorism, revolution, murder, municipal budget battles, highway tragedies, and campaign rhetoric.

But all features are not just diversionary fluff. Many supplement immediate news or provide depth coverage of important, but otherwise neglected individuals, groups, or developments. A feature about an extremely talented but unknown musician, a species of bird that is close to extinction, or a historic landmark in danger of being destroyed, can arouse public support and thereby reverse the situation. One portraying conditions in a ghetto or a prison can stimulate enough change so that the bloodshed that would have led to an explosive page-one news story never happens.

Features are both a pleasure and a problem for good reporters. They are a pleasure because they allow "real" writing. They are a problem because they *demand* "real" writing.

Most reporters can write Councilman So-and-So-said-yesterday stories in their sleep by their third year on the job. Having learned the lead and body formulas and absorbed the necessary style, they can apply them to any immediate news story, and while the finished copy may not be in the award category, it at least gets the news out in acceptable fashion. But in addition to considering themselves news gatherers, reporters also see themselves as writers (for "writers," read "artists"). While the thrill of putting together a breaking story never diminishes, they feel increasingly compelled to *write* whenever they can, rather than simply string grafs together by formula. Serious features allow them to do that and also to undertake depth coverage of things that are interesting, though not necessarily newsworthy in the deadline sense.

The problem is that there are no inflexible rules on features: they depend entirely on the reporter's information-gathering technique, imagination, and writing ability. It is not terribly hard for a decent reporter to get his audience to read a story about a father going berserk and killing his wife and five children, for example, but getting people to read about how a nuclear reactor works (a more important story in the long run) is quite another matter.

Features ought to be approached with some sort of central concept, but that concept doesn't necessarily have to include the hardest element in the story. In other words, the most interesting element in the story doesn't have to be the one that most clearly meets the eye. You see a ghetto, for example, and you translate that to a community of poverty and crime. That's the big picture. You are going to write a story about a poor and crime-ridden neighborhood. Such a story could be structured around a general description of the area and interviews with dozens of families, several merchants and professional people, and some policemen. You might interview a total of 100 persons. You might, but the story probably wouldn't be terribly effective because, given space limitations, it could end up reading like a poll.

Zeroing in on one family, one shopkeeper, or even one child, and using that element as a vehicle with which to portray the bigger picture, though, would probably be more effective because it gets the immediate human dimension across, and quickly. Furthermore, you don't have to lead with great immediacy. Teasing is usually more effective and is always more fun.

Say you decide to do such a story and pick for a vehicle a grocer who has been held up and robbed nine times in six months. You could start this way:

> Victor Lopez, a grocer on Fox Street, has been held up and robbed nine times in six months.

There are two drawbacks to this lead: (1) Victor Lopez comes across as being a name, not a person, and (2) it tells so much that unless the reader has a special interest in the subject, he probably would not be inclined to go deeper into the story. Since you want to inject life into Victor Lopez and make the reader want to share that life, you tease:

> Victor Lopez keeps the best stocked grocery store on Fox Street. He has canned goods, detergents, fresh bread and rolls, fine cold cuts and cheese, and a .12-gauge shotgun.

The idea is to arouse curiosity. That shotgun, placed at the very end of a list of otherwise innocuous grocery items, does the job. The reader goes into such a lead wondering why anyone would print a story about some grocer and his mundane wares and is caught, finally, by the shotgun. What is Lopez doing with a shotgun? The answer—that nine robberies in six months have driven him to the point of arming himself—will be held, like a full house in a game of poker, until the last possible moment:

> Lopez, a devout Catholic and the father of four, calls himself a peace-loving man whose only wish is to be able to provide for his family. A crucifix hangs on the wall behind the counter where the shotgun is hidden.
>
> In a way, the crucifix and the shotgun symbolize life in this city's Hispanic community. Lopez has been to church 24 times in the last six months. He has been robbed at gunpoint nine times during the same period.

You have now explained what you're doing. The situation has been established and the reader already knows several things about Victor Lopez. The grocer should speak for himself about here. Notice how his physical description is slipped in and his state of mind is indicated:

> "I'm afraid of guns," says the slightly-built grocer, his somber eyes darting toward everyone who enters the store, "but I've found that I'm more afraid when they're pointing at me than when I'm doing the pointing. If I don't do this, they will destroy me."

"They" are the holdup men, mostly drug addicts, who have been plundering neighborhood merchants for years. Most of the shopkeepers and others in the area say, however, that the robberies are increasing and becoming more brutal.

On July 8, two gunmen pistol-whipped Angela Lopez, the grocer's oldest daughter, because she did not hand over $52 fast enough. The 16-year-old spent two weeks in the hospital.

"I will surely kill the next one," warns her father. "I will kill him or he will kill me."

There have been 68 robberies on Fox Street so far this year, according to police, or nearly twice as many as during the same period last year. The number of murder victims jumped from three to eight in the same period. That is why Victor Lopez is not the only man in the neighborhood who is angry enough to fight back.

Carlos Rodriguez, who owns a luncheonette . . .

This story goes from the specific (Lopez) to the general (68 robberies and eight murders) and then back again (Rodriguez). In doing so, it manages to portray the desperate problems of the people in the area by mixing their own words with vivid description. It also contains a good deal of hard information that doesn't interrupt the flow of the story. "She spent two weeks in the hospital," for example, doesn't say as much as "The 16-year-old spent two weeks in the hospital." The latter most obviously supplies the girl's age. But it does more than that: it says that she isn't a full-grown and probably strong woman, but a young girl. This kind of detail, as well as .12-gauge shotgun, July 8, $52, and the area's robbery and murder rates, makes the story more credible. So, of course, does the crucifix and its juxtaposition with the shotgun. Good feature writers have eyes for that kind of detail. First they perceive. Then they let their imaginations work with what they perceive.

A "snapper" is a surprising or ironic story ending that is supposed to provide the reader with a little more to think about. It is a flourish —a tie-off—that shows alert and appreciative readers that the writer didn't just keep typing until he ran out of words. It shows that the story was written by a craftsman who maintained control until the last period. Having gone through perhaps 30 grafs describing the plight of Lopez and his neighbors, the last graf might look like this as a snapper:

Victor Lopez has actually fired a gun only once. It was at a fiesta in San Juan when he was 19. He fired the gun for about half an hour, he recalls, but he could not hit the target even though it was less than 30 feet away.

Many beginners, however subconsciously, equate feature writing with fiction writing. Nothing could be further from the truth. There is considerable information in the Lopez story, all of it true, and all of it the result of a great deal of "legwork" and questioning. In the first place, Lopez had to be found, and that very well might have meant talking to a dozen or more other merchants first. Sure, most of them have guns, but that may be about all. So you spend all day talking to them and come back with relatively little. But the last says, "Why don't you talk to Lopez, the grocer? He got hit nine times, and his daughter went to the hospital all smashed up."

Not only does the reporter talk to three or more times the number of persons he can use for the story, he saturates them with questions and pursues the answers. The answer to one question leads to another: "Do you really know how to use that shotgun?" Don't take it for granted that he does know, especially after he says that he's afraid of it—ask, and keep asking, as you would with any story.

The key to approaching any feature is to loosen up before and during the early stages of the reporting so your mind is agile enough to consider more than one angle. It is natural for inexperienced reporters, and particularly those under time pressure, to construct leads or even entire stories in their heads before coverage actually begins. This is usually futile and always dangerous. Since preconception and reality rarely merge in a feature, it is a waste of time to plan how to do the story before you know what's involved. Chances are that timeless, Hemingwayesque lead you developed at breakfast will have to be discarded within an hour of your starting to make notes, so why burn all that energy for nothing? Worse, preconceived approaches are dangerous because they limit your vision: you won't want to look around if you're already focusing hard on a single element. The reporter who walked into that grocery store wanted to find out what the owner's life was like, and he did so with his perception idling in neutral. The general then led to the specific: the number of robberies and the beaten girl led to the ineffectiveness of the police and that, in turn, led to the purchase of the shotgun.

The best feature material is usually found in areas unknown to the general public, but those which nonetheless affect it, however obscurely.  People tend to be curious, if not downright nosy, about what other people do and about the peculiar things happening around them.  The story possibilities are virtually limitless and run the full range from the bizarre to the uproarious.

Be funny if you can.  There is a widespread notion among the overeducated and underendowed that humor, like caviar, becomes tasteless in large quantities.  Nonsense.  The writers who most scorn the light story as being unsophisticated are usually the ones who are taken like warm milk before bedtime, and for the same reason—to induce sleep. Mark Twain, H. L. Mencken, Robert Benchley, James Thurber, Ogden Nash, S. J. Perelman, E. B. White, Alva Johnston, Ambrose Bierce, Ring Lardner, Cornelia Otis Skinner, and scores of others of our finest humorists were not known for mental deficiency.  They have been cherished for generations by readers who have appreciated their enduring wit.  Look for light approaches and, when you can use them tastefully, do it.  Is there anything humorous about a malpractice suit?  It depends on who the defendant is:

> Along with most other surgeons in this country, the specter
> of a malpractice suit has got Samuel Cowan out on a limb.
> Cowan's case is different, though.  He is a tree surgeon.

Taste is the operative word for light writing.  It applies in two ways.  First, there is nothing funny about death, pain, destruction, mental suffering or anguish, or other serious problems, so never approach them that way.  Second, there is a line separating the laugh from the laff:  bring wit to what you write, not slapstick.

Unfortunately, the feature is irresistible to the heavy-handed because it permits more time for writing and is as close to "literature" as most reporters get.  There is a temptation to spend hours, if necessary, groping for the precise word or phrase that will immortalize it.  The result is often a story so loaded with gunk that it can't float.  Here is a lead that took a couple of hours to put together.  It was one of my first, and undoubtedly, one of my worst:

> The jet fighter, its black pointed nose glistening in the sun-
> shine and its powerful engine whining loudly, rolled quickly out
> of the dark hangar like an animal charging out of its lair.

Given the fact that I was capable of writing such trash, I'm relieved that I didn't describe the engine as roaring like a lion or screeching like a banshee. But it's bad enough. Had there been 15 minutes in which to get that story moving, rather than all afternoon in which to indulge my senses with every metaphor I could think of, the lead would have had to go something like this:

> Richmond will soon have its own contingent of supersonic fighters.

or

> The first of four supersonic F-106 "Dart" fighters to be stationed at Byrd Field took off from there yesterday for a practice run over the Atlantic.

Neither of those would have been a candidate for an anthology of great reporting, but either would have spared me the contemptuous looks of my colleagues after the story appeared. Play it straight when you can't come up with something clever.

Another common problem is that of trying to squeeze size 12EEE words into a size 6A shoe:

> "I would vote for you for President of the United States," she extolled with aplomb.
> "And I, madam, would be forever honored," came the rejoinder. He then departed the auditorium with great haste.
> The applause was rampant. Courtly politicians are popular here, and so are peripatetic ones.

What you write should not have to be studied like Urdu, but easily read and enjoyed. SIMPLIFY.

Avoid the first person (singular or plural). Because television is an entertainment medium, television reporters and anchormen and –women are being cast increasingly as personalities in their own right while on camera. Not only do they report the news, but they often take part in it, and sometimes even make it. The idea is to show the audience that they're not just journalistic automatons, but flesh-and-blood human beings worthy of empathy. This, the producers figure, should get them loyal followings (and higher ratings) in Hollywood's Doris Day-loves-kids tradition. It is the cult of personality in full bloom. But it has no business in news columns because: (1) nobody who reads what you write cares whether you have a pretty face and a lovable personality; (2) it by definition subjectifies what you report; (3) it gets in the way of the news flow; and (4) it tends to make your story read like a diary entry (when done with consummate tastelessness it can make your story read like a diary entry in a bad novel):

> We had no way of knowing that evening as we rolled into Tangier that two of us would be in the hospital the next morning.
> I had never been afraid of snakes, poisonous or otherwise, and certainly had no reason to believe they would be in a city the size of Tangier. How wrong can you be?

That kind of stuff is all right for the Sunday travel section or for a magazine article, but it doesn't belong in serious news stories, feature or otherwise. There are two situations in which the rule can be broken, but both take the third person, not the first. If you have a long and important interview or press conference, and you don't want the story to read as though the subject was talking to a wall, you can slip in either "told a reporter" (or reporters), or "told a visitor" (or visitors). The second, and far less common situation, is the one in which you are unavoidably caught in the action. Being one of two persons wounded in a holdup or injured in a major accident comes to mind. Then, it is: "A policeman and a reporter were wounded by stray bullets." Never (*never*) use "this reporter," the clear inference of which is that you are the sole, indispensable, and ordained link between the reader and the rest of the world.

Profiles are an important subcategory of features. When properly done, they are as close to high art as a reporter is likely to come, given time and space limitations. A good profile paints an accurate, though possibly highly stylized, portrait of someone who is interesting.

"Interesting" is the key word, but don't be put off by it; *you* are interesting. In most cases, again, unknowns turn out to be far better candidates for profiles than do celebrities just by virtue of the fact that what they do is little known. While the big names are irresistible to many readers, which accounts for the success of fan magazines and the "people" sections of the news weeklies, profiles of them are for the most part uninformed, unimaginative, and untruthful. Show-business personalities and politicians are among the most difficult to accurately profile because the nature of what they do depends on favorable exposure in the media and they react to questions accordingly. Actors and actresses, in particular, can stage virtually any appearance or reaction and they seldom let their guard down when a reporter is around. Remember that acting is by definition not real life, but a replica of it, and that those who act do not do so exclusively on stages or in front of cameras. Most celebrities feel they have to fool reporters as a matter of practical necessity; many actors and actresses do so as a matter of professional pride. The resulting profiles are inescapably pure pap.

The better profiles come from unsuccessful artists, minor inventors, lobstermen, steeplejacks, forest rangers, lion tamers, state troopers, blacksmiths, coopers, wagonmakers, and all of the others who do interesting, but not well understood, things. Profiles of successful athletes are abundant and are not terribly interesting. Bush-league baseball players, football players who didn't make the draft or who were so badly hurt they had to quit the game, and the swimmer who placed last in the Olympic free-style, are good candidates for profiles. What is the anguish of coming in last in the Olympics, and what lessons can be learned from it and applied, not only to sports, but to all of life? We lionize winners and ignore losers. It should not be so. The losers can tell us more about ourselves than can the winners, since they represent the majority.

The good profiler probes beyond the obvious and seeks the subtle shades of meaning that make human beings multidimensional. Look closely at Goya's *The Family of Charles IV,* and particularly at the startling contrast between the angelic Doña Maria Isabel and her fat, vulgar, seemingly dull-witted mother, Queen Maria Luisa. The Queen often bragged about her fine, plump arms: the painter rendered them fat to the point of being gross because, irrespective of what she said, that is the way he perceived them. Goya was never again asked to paint a portrait of the royal family. There is no evidence that he cared.

Goya, Van Gogh, Gauguin, and expressionists like Edvard Munch and Emil Nolde have a great deal to teach us about portraiture—in every instance, about what is happening *behind* a face, not necessarily on it. The superior writer of profiles, no less than the superior painter of portraits, should capture the true essence of the subject and the situation. The same questions, repeated, run through their minds: Who are you, *really*, and what do you do?

In 1969, I did a profile of Tempest Storm, the stripper, for *The Wall Street Journal.* I spent the first of three days watching her perform four times. I watched while standing at the rear of the theater, while sitting up front in the audience, and twice from backstage. It occurred to me after a while that the curtain separated two very different worlds as effectively as if it had been a brick wall. On one side, there was a beautiful and apparently glamorous woman bathed in a spotlight and holding the undivided attention of almost 300 persons. When she left them and came out on the other side of that curtain, however, she became a lonely, unattended, tired woman who had come to New York alone on a bus and who was picking up the fake fur and other clothing she had just taken off. The contrast would not have come to mind had I not seen the show from both sides of the curtain, and it was a contrast which, to me, marked her life and the lives of others in show business.

I opened the story with four grafs, set in the present, that described in some detail what the audience saw and heard—the white negligee slipping off, three musicians grinding out her theme song, the attentive audience, and the rest. But the space separating the fourth and fifth grafs, I knew, had to be that curtain. Here is the fifth graf. It is the one that set the true tone for the rest of the profile:

> Then Tempest Storm, the reigning queen of a dying art, picks up her clothes, climbs to a small, electric blue and white room, and drops onto a folding bed whose soiled sheet is marked with a predecessor's lipstick. She uses a tissue to mop the perspiration from her face and from under her long, red hair, while a single fan tries to dislodge thick dust and push around hot, stale air.

I never heard from Tempest Storm after that story appeared. There is no evidence that I cared.

# chapter thirteen
# INVESTIGATION

While generally feeling pride in the role the press had in unseating the Watergate crowd, exposing My Lai and other massacres, and other monumental pieces of "investigative" reporting, many thoughtful journalists are worried that such stories, and the glamour associated with them by the uninitiated, have produced a grossly distorted picture of what so-called investigative reporting is all about. They are concerned that the apparent glamour is attracting a legion of young people who, far from believing that the pen is mightier than the sword, want to turn the pen into a sword with which to slash their way to fame and power. Consciously or otherwise, novices tend to see investigative reporting as a sure path to glory and self-promotion. They are deceived.

To the extent that all serious reporting requires the asking of questions and the putting together of facts, virtually all of it is investigative. When you call the transportation authority to find out why a bus route has been canceled, ask an agriculturalist why the price of peaches is going up, or interview an old woman who lives alone and who is afraid, you are investigating things. You are trying to find out what happened, why it happened, and what the likely effects are going to be. In that sense, then, almost every story a reporter does is investigative. Striking down rogues and rascals is only the tip of the proverbial iceberg.

Investigative reporting, as it is understood by the uninitiated, has no resemblance to the real world. Ask anyone who has done it to capsulize it, and you will hear: "dull," "monotonous," "excruciating boredom," or "exhausting." The average serious investigative story consumes hundreds of hours of poring over bank statements, court records, police files, speeches, or testimony, and many more hours of pounding pavements at odd hours and in all kinds of weather, of dialing telephones until blisters form, of studying and restudying clips until the eyes burn, and of swallowing more coffee or booze than the body can safely cope with. Marriages have ended (or have failed to start) because of investigative reporting. Investigative reporters (or, more usually, reporters who are investigating something), tend to show nerves, argue a lot with editors and other colleagues, and speak in tones louder than normal. Their common denominator is an abiding cynicism. Occasionally, one gets badly hurt or, as was the case with Don Bolles of *The Arizona Republic,* is murdered. Bolles's car was bombed on June 2, 1976, while he was working on a story about organized crime. He died 11 days later, after both of his legs and an arm had been amputated. Although the result of Bolles's effort was tragic, not just frustrating, it dramatized the other side of investigative reporting: the hero lost.

Be under no delusions, then. In nine cases out of 10, the end result of all the drudgery, legwork, and aggravation is to nail some water commissioner in a town of 100,000 who has improperly given a pipe contract to a second cousin. You do that to serve the public, not yourself.

All investigative stories start in one of two ways: either through a reporter's initiative (reading court testimony or an annual report and realizing that $2+2=3\frac{1}{2}$), or because of the so-called "tip." The latter probably occurs more frequently by a factor of 10. Thinking, after all, is very hard work.

Tips, in turn, come from three basic kinds of sources: (1) those who are frustrated by their working conditions, employer, salary, or whatever, and who therefore hold a personal grudge; (2) those who are altruistic, who think they see evil, and who want it exposed; (3) those who want to enhance their own competitive position by undermining the opposition. Those who tip the press are often motivated by an combination of these, so the lines can be blurred.

The first rule for dealing with tips is therefore not to pursue them immediately and unquestioningly, but to examine the person who is doing the tipping, and to try to understand his motives. You can best do that by questioning him closely (always face-to-face) and probing to get a clear fix on his personality, intelligence, sanity, and personal interest in the story. The first question that should occur to you is "*Why* is he telling me this? What, exactly, is in it for him?" Assuming that you don't want to be used as the henchman for some irresponsible lout, you will need to satisfy yourself that your informant is giving you a legitimate story. This isn't to say that his motives aren't sinister, anyway, but only that the tale might nonetheless be worth pursuing:

HE:    Senator Blowharde got a kickback for pushing through the Lake Apache Reservoir legislation.

YOU:   How do you know that?

HE:    I work in his office. I'm a speechwriter.

YOU:   Can you prove he got a kickback?

HE:    Several people know about it.

YOU:   That's not proof.

HE:    I have a photocopy of the canceled check and other things.

YOU:   How much was kicked back?

HE:    $20,000.

YOU:   Why are you coming to me with this?

HE:    Blowharde is a crook. He ought to be exposed for what he is.

YOU:   That legislation went through last year, didn't it?

HE:    Right.

YOU:   How come you waited so long before saying something?

HE:    I wasn't sure for a long time that I ought to say anything. But now, I've convinced myself that it's the only thing to do.

YOU:   How many speechwriters does Blowharde have?

HE:    Three.

YOU:   Who's the head of the team?

HE:    Ron Meyers.

YOU:   Who's next?

HE:    Nancy Turino. She came a year ago from a public relations
       job at Bancroft Industries. She's real good.
YOU:   How long have you been speech-writing for Blowharde?
HE:    Four years . . .

It is conceivable that HE: (1) is angry at having been passed over
by a newcomer (and particularly by a woman) and is therefore trying to get even by planting a malicious and unfounded story about
his boss; (2) is angry at having been passed over and has therefore
decided to get even by bringing YOU a true story; (3) isn't angry at
all, but has decided that he can't abide by Blowharde's dishonesty;
(4) is or isn't angry, but has been paid handsomely by one of Blowharde's enemies to discredit him; (5) has made an honest mistake;
(6) is motivated by some combination of these or by some other
reason. You must find out before you go any further, but you know
at least one thing: Since no politician would leave a $20,000 can-
celed kickback check lying around, HE likely went to some trouble
to find it and photocopy it if it's the real thing. Whatever his
motives, then, they are strong.

If you decide to follow up, you will want preliminary corroboration of at least part of what you have been told, and certainly about
your source himself. Beat reporters, who generate the most investigative stories, are usually well acquainted with their sources, so
fixing motives and levels of reliability is less a problem. Discreet
inquiries can be made among the source's friends or associates and,
of course, the clips and other research material can be checked. In
most cases, however, there is little or no need for this, since the reporter is already on fairly good terms with the source (which is why
the source feels comfortable enough to come to the reporter in the
first place).

There is no rule for determining whether a given story is worth
pursuit but, again, the problem is usually moot when the reporter
is well acquainted with his or her beat. He or she understands fairly
quickly whether the source is nothing more than a disgruntled em-
ployee or a nasty competitor bearing nothing but bile, or whether
there's a story in the revelation. The difficulty lies in the fact that
even the most personally embittered and spiteful persons can bring
solid material to reporters. That's what makes the sorting of motive
and material so important.

To the extent that there are accessible records (annual reports, crime statistics, budgets, court transcripts, voting records, committee minutes, published articles, and so on), these ought to be checked. Municipal, county, state, and federal expenditures are always recorded somewhere. If public funds are involved, the hall of records, accounting office, bureau of the budget, or whatever it's called, would be among your first stops. Where records are not open to the public, you have every right to ask your source to bring them to you, either in the original, or as copies. Never ask someone you don't know, or who isn't directly involved, for corroborating documents. Telling them what you need is telling them what you're working on, and that could not only send the story up in smoke, but it could very likely jeopardize your original source. The targets of investigative stories have a way of trying to cover their tracks as soon as they learn that a reporter is snooping around. You and I probably would, too.

Where there is no official record, or where a record is inaccessible (graft payments are usually recorded in the legendary "little black book," if they are recorded at all), ask your source for the name or names of others who would be willing to corroborate the accusation. Besides making your reportorial position stronger, a second or third source will usually be able to add dimensions to what you have been given by the first, since no two persons see things exactly alike. Although everything Frank Serpico told *The New York Times* about police corruption in that city proved to be correct, his offbeat manner and appearance (including a thick beard and a ring in his ear) unnerved at least one reporter. The corroboration of Serpico's friend and colleague, Sergeant David Durk, helped convince *The Times* that it had a major story, and added elements to it that Serpico couldn't provide alone.

Don't talk about what you're working on except to those who need to know. Your editor needs to know, and probably, so do a few colleagues who might be able to supply their own knowledge. But most of your colleagues don't need to know, and neither do relatives, friends, or acquaintances. Even the most important investigative piece you ever do will be just one of thousands of stories you work on during your career. Where your target is concerned, however, that single story could mean the destruction of a lifetime endeavor or even a jail term. It's important to you, but it may mean life or death to him, so you can expect trouble if he finds out about it before you're ready to go with what you've got. People everywhere —including in the biggest cities—move in cliques and thrive on juicy gossip. Don't impede your own efforts by loose talk.

No investigative story that meant anything was ever brought in entirely by telephone. You have to do the legwork. You have to get out of the office and observe for yourself. This is one of the hardest, and often most frustrating, aspects of the job. Investigative reporters have been known to put weeks into knocking on doors, keeping vigils in run-down neighborhoods, sitting in sleazy cafés and hotel lobbies, and the like, only to come back with an empty, or near-empty, basket. In reel three of the standard newspaper movie, the reporter either sees something so astounding that it makes the story, or some cornered ne'er-do-well sighs and says, "O.K. I'll talk. I'll tell ya what ya wanna know." In reality, few tell you what you really want to know, or even say anything at all. Some really don't know anything, but you can't know that until you ask them. Others, with faces that belong in nativity scenes, assure you that they haven't the slightest idea of what you're talking about when, in fact, they know exactly what you're talking about and have information you need. Often, though you never know when, face-to-face contact will tip the balance your way. People usually respond more honestly and completely when they are confronted by a questioner than they do over the phone for at least two reasons: (1) you can get your own personality into the conversation better when it's face-to-face, and (2) they lose a trump card—they can't hang up.

Don't do anything illegal, since it compromises you in two ways. First, any pretense at morality has to vanish when you do the same thing your target is supposed to be doing. Second, you leave your-self vulnerable to counterattack in court, in the media, or by word of mouth. Among other things, it is illegal to open other people's mail, enter private premises without permission, bribe public officials or employees, impersonate them, or harass, intimidate, or threaten anyone to the point where he suffers mental or physical anguish (which is highly subjective). In most places, it is also illegal to receive or copy stolen documents, but since the press does not use those things in ways that are competitive with a company or agency, it enjoys a certain amount of latitude under the First Amendment. The exception is anything construed as involving national security.

Impersonation—to do it or not to do it—depends on the circumstances. It is illegal to impersonate city, state, or federal officials and, depending on the locality, many others. In most cases, impersonation is unnecessary, since you can get much of what you need simply by using your wits and keeping quiet. When Richard Severo, then an investigative reporter for *The Washington Post,** worked on a story several years ago in which a sleazy realtor was trying to assemble parcels of property in Washington by intimidating homeowners into accepting relatively little for their land, he used an obvious, but effective, method for getting into the story. When he found that the realtor was going to speak to the neighborhood association, and that membership in the group cost $1, Severo simply joined. He then had a perfect right to sit in the audience, without identifying himself as a reporter, and listen to a harangue and threats that were later reported, verbatim, on the pages of *The Post*. The ploy, along with a thorough check at the municipal records office of who owned what land in the area, was simple, legal, and effective. It was so effective, in fact, that when Severo confronted the realtor after he had assembled the evidence, the man said, simply, "You've got me." Reporters are just that—reporters. They aren't spies, so there is rarely a need for subterfuge.

Don't pay for information. Nickel-and-dime stuff—buying a lunch or dinner, getting a ticket to a sporting event, or even passing along a bottle or two of rotgut on skid row—is done all the time. But exchanging money for information is dangerous to the profession because it inevitably breeds sources who come to the press for the wrong reasons or who concoct stories for sheer profit. In addition, it gives better-heeled news organizations an unfair advantage over their less affluent, but no less serious, competitors. The result is the bludgeoning of the opposition to oblivion, not with better reporting, but with a checkbook.

Keep your sources to yourself. As a rule, reporters don't even tell one source about another unless it is absolutely necessary and there is no risk to either. A source's confidence, as has been mentioned, must be respected at all costs. This is the principle on which the entire reporter-source relationship is built. Anything that erodes that principle damages the flow of information to the media and,

---

* He joined *The New York Times* in 1968.

perhaps worse, can hurt a person who is trying to help you. Since you wouldn't be doing an investigative story in the first place unless it was important, exposing your source almost automatically leaves him or her vulnerable to professional or physical trouble.

Evidence in support of any story, but especially sensitive investigative ones, has to be hard, particularly because of the possibility of court action. It is likely that a businessman or government official accused of embezzlement or graft, or an athlete accused of throwing a game, will come out of his corner swinging a lawyer in either hand. Your ultimate defense against libel, again, is the truth. And the truth is best shown with solid evidence. Ask to see, and hold onto: letters, memorandums, notes, tape recordings, movies, payroll records, rail, ship, and airline ticket duplicates or stubs, canceled checks, photographs, receipts, vouchers, invoices, and anything else that supports your story. Ask your sources whether they would be willing to testify for the record before a judge, jury, or commission, as to the truth of what they're telling you. But never rely exclusively on a source's promise to support your story later. There's usually a world of difference between how a source feels while confiding in you, and how he or she feels when confronted by the specter of repeating it to the whole world. Proof.

Telling the target of an investigative story early on that you're working on it is equivalent to a general telling his enemy counterpart that a major attack is in the works. It makes the whole exercise self-defeating. Try to avoid letting your subject know what you're working on until you've accumulated as much information as you need to go with the story—until you are in possession of everything necessary to produce a clean, effective, and tight story without "holes." Comes the day, however, when you have to tell your subject what you're up to. You must do that because, in this society, the accused has the right to speak in his own defense. Get down everything he cares to say, and when you put it in the story, don't bury it—that's a cheap shot. Say in the second, third, or fourth graf, or any other prominent spot, that he denies the charge (if he does), and follow with an explanation, at least in part in his own words, of his side of it:

> Elliot "the Virus" Coogan, the Nevada racketeer who is said
> by state authorities to own controlling interests in three gambling

casinos there, is extending his investments to Texas, records there show.

Coogan has in the last year bought two nightclubs in Dallas, and another in Houston, according to municipal records in both of those cities. In each case, the club's owner of record is not listed as Coogan, but is a close associate of his.

The establishments—the Gilded Bird and Samantha's in Dallas, and Oil's Well in Houston—have a combined value of $2.5 million, as shown by their tax assessments.

Coogan's associates, however, bought all three for him for less than $1 million.

Coogan, reached by telephone at his Reno home yesterday, emphatically denied that he had anything to do with the night-club purchases.

"This is the first I've heard of it," he said, "and I hope it's the last. I've got enough to occupy me here without looking for more problems someplace else."

Evidence accumulated in Dallas and in Houston suggests otherwise, however. . . .

If your subject does not want to comment about the allegation, you can occasionally get him to change his mind by telling him that you need his side of the story in order to produce as fair an account as possible of what happened. Your task is to balance the story, and you can usually do so with a little gentle prodding:

"There's no law that says I have to call you, Mr. Coogan, but I want to get your side of this before I write the story. Don't you think you owe it to yourself to get your position before the public?"

"No comment."

"Fine. Then, of course, I'll have to write what I've got, and that's what will appear in print. Your side won't appear, but remember that you had your chance and turned it down, okay?"

When you drop your investigative cards, do so one at a time, so the subject can respond as precisely as possible. You are, remember, taking notes and looking for statements that summarize his position or the position he wants to have publicized. Marching into Elliot Coogan's plush den, whipping out your trusty pad, and leading with, "I have proof that you recently bought three nightclubs in Texas. What do you have to say about it?" would probably get you thrown out and impaled on a very large cactus. Nor would Coogan, who has sensibilities like everyone else, be entirely wrong. No one has to tolerate cross-examination by an alligator. The usual result of that kind of pushing is to get pushed back—your subject turns belligerent and either tells you to take a long leap through a flaming hoop, or else refuses to say anything. But that's not why you're there.

So, while being firm, also try to be as pleasant as the circumstances allow. Time permitting, get into what you've got by telling Coogan that you hear that the Nevada authorities are after him for moving into casinos in Reno.

"Yeah, they are," he might answer. "But I haven't done anything illegal. It's all legal. Everything I do is absolutely legitimate, but they hound you, you know what I mean? They hound you all the time."

"Sure. I think I know exactly what you mean. You must be sick of Nevada. They say there are terrific investment opportunities in Texas.

"Like what?"

"Oh, like nightclubs . . ."

"Nightclubs?"

"Nightclubs. In fact, Mr. Coogan, that's what I'd like to talk with you about. I've just spent a couple of weeks in Dallas and in Houston, and . . ."

Most of the subjects of investigative stories don't have Elliot Coogan's underworld status. They are more often politicians and bureaucrats who received minor illegal payments or who mismanage programs, alleged criminals who have been wrongfully arrested and found guilty for having done things they didn't do, businessmen who are engaged in unfair practices or who are siphoning corporate funds, stock manipulators who are victimizing widows and orphans, unscrupulous merchants and landlords who are bleeding the poor, public utilities that are trying to compensate for inefficiency or other problems by raising their customers' rates, food producers who mislabel their cans, jars, bottles, or boxes, transit systems that don't keep their equipment in good repair, and so on. Important? Certainly. Glamorous? Rarely.

Nor does investigative reporting necessarily have to do with "bad guys." Say a company is releasing large amounts of toxins into a river, and the story has already been reported. The governor tells the company to stop doing it. The company responds by telling the governor that it is doing its best to clean up its emissions, but that the process will be long and costly (which is true). It also tells the governor that if it is forced to change its operations immediately, it will have to move out of the state. The governor is faced with two conflicting goals: to get the river cleaner, and to keep that company in his state for its economic advantages (jobs and tax revenues). At minimum, a good investigative piece presents the governor's problem to the public in clear, balanced form—it explains the nature of his quandary. Indeed, the whole area of environmental reporting abounds with stories about competing, but not necessarily evil, interests. Coming to the defense of creatures inhabiting a salt marsh that is going to be turned into a marina and amusement park is laudable, but so may be defending the residents of the area, who are desperate for jobs and enough revenue for a badly needed hospital. This is not to say that the marsh ought to be filled in and the environmentalists routed, but only that their opponents are probably not nature-haters, but well-meaning folk who have other priorities. Investigating this means getting both sides' views to the public so that, when the vote comes, the voters will have a balanced picture of what's at stake and why.

The sources for most investigative stories are all around you, not just in the E Ring of the Pentagon, or in the mayor's closet. The planet is loaded with frustrated, angry, competitive, and altruistic people who want to talk to someone—anyone—about their problems and those they see around them. City halls and municipal courts, sanitation departments and tax agencies, police precincts and real-estate divisions, public prosecutors' offices and welfare departments, fairly crawl with middle- and upper-echelon clerks, bookkeepers, and secretaries who every day witness mismanagement, corruption, and ineptitude. They constantly complain about it to their husbands and wives, friends and colleagues. Sit in a bus or subway car during rush-hour, or on a park bench at lunchtime, and listen to them. Tune in:

"Harriet should have been made department head, not Stanley."

"I know. She's been there fourteen years and knows the job backward, forward, and upside down."

"Well, you know he came right from the commissioner's office, and his father kicked in plenty during the last election."

"How do you know?"

"He *said* so, for heaven's sake. He told Myrna. I think he likes her. He took her out for a drink after work on Thursday."

"You're kidding!"

"I am not. He said he studied management in college, and that being head of the department is only the first step to bigger and better things."

"Like what?"

"Like the mayor's staff, *that's* what. I'm telling you, that's what he told Myrna."

"Poor Harriet . . ."

Corporations and government agencies, foundations and universities, election committees and military commands, school systems, churches, hospitals, and just about every other institution from New Orleans to New Delhi hold in their depths angry, frustrated, and unnoticed workers who see, or who think they see, wrongs. Those people are, for whatever reason, eager to see the wrongs righted. The best of them—the most honest—are the reporter's natural allies because they know that the best reporters—the most honest—are *their* natural allies.

A final word. Never hesitate to back off from a story in any stage of its development if you have serious reason to believe that it won't hold up. The amount of time, money, and energy that go into even the biggest story are nothing compared to the result of going with it and being wrong.

# chapter fourteen

# PUBLIC RELATIONS

Just about everything is packaged to look better than it really is. The Earth, itself, looks much better from space than it does from Main Street. The vast stretches of tan, green, and blue, set off in places by deep purple and covered elsewhere by swirling wisps of pure white, give no indication of the crime, crud, and corruption on the surface. You have to get up close and concentrate in order to see what's really going on. So it is with the news.

The public relations profession has grown with the news profession and is a parasite of it. Public relations specialists exist, in the main, because those who want or who are forced into media exposure—politicians, celebrities, government agencies, corporations, universities—have messages to get to the public and feel they need to look as good as possible while delivering them. Conversely, when something bad happens, they want to appear in the best possible light, given the circumstances. In truth, I think, so do you and I.

The public relations (PR) person's job is therefore not only to get news to news organizations but, very often, to package it as prettily as possible without making it obviously gaudy. The reporter's job is to take off the ribbon and wrapping and have a thor-

ough look at what's inside. Their relationship, consequently, tends
to be a subtle one of defense and attack.

It was no accident that former President Richard Nixon had as
his closest domestic advisers public relations and advertising specialists, not scholars. To Nixon, a man who had generally come off
badly at the hands of the press, his image—the package—wasn't
just important; it was crucial. Nixon felt (and with some justification) that since the liberal press would go out of its way to pounce on
him, he had to develop an extraordinarily effective public relations
team that would take the initiative in finding new and imaginative
ways to make him look good. The result was that appearance finally
came to dominate substance. When Ronald Ziegler, Nixon's press
secretary, told reporters that a statement he had previously made
was "inoperative," he was echoing Macbeth's tragic state of mind:

> . . . function
> Is smother'd in surmise, and nothing is
> But what is not.

While acknowledging that they are paid to promote "positive"
public attitudes, public relations men and women generally feel
that they are of genuine help to reporters in getting the news, and
that the causes they serve are just. They generally believe in their
employers and in their employers' products. Tell a PR person that
making a crooked politician look good is disgraceful, and he or she
will probably answer by saying that (1) it is no more disgraceful
than working for one of the nation's many irresponsible rags that
pass for newspapers, and (2) public relations people also work for
many environmental and consumer groups, charitable organizations, colleges, universities, hospitals, and . . . the press itself.
That is unchallengeable.

Yet reporters by and large think of the public relations man or
woman as being a kind of walking deodorant stick whose function is
to cover sweat and smell good, not to really clean anything. At
best, they feel, the "PR type" is a captive functionary who tries to
be cooperative within severely imposed limits. At worst, he or she
is taken to be an obstructionist or a liar. Nomenclature is indicative
of how public relations people see themselves and their products,
and how reporters see them. In their own trade press, PR people

call themselves "practitioners" who send "news releases" to the news media. Reporters and editors call them "flaks" (probably after the antiaircraft fire put up around enemy targets) and somewhat contemptuously refer to the releases as "handouts."

In 1974–75, 48 journalists on the staff of the Austin (Texas) *American Statesman* and 25 public relations representatives were polled to find out how all viewed the practitioners and what they do. The result, as published in the August 1975 *Public Relations Journal,* was in part as follows:

Practitioners help reporters obtain accurate, complete and timely news:

|               | Agree | Disagree | No Opinion |
|---------------|-------|----------|------------|
| Journalists   | 48%   | 44%      | 8%         |
| Practitioners | 91%   | 7%       | 2%         |

Practitioners often act as obstructionists, keeping reporters from the people they really should be seeing:

|               | Agree | Disagree | No Opinion |
|---------------|-------|----------|------------|
| Journalists   | 82%   | 12%      | 6%         |
| Practitioners | 38%   | 56%      | 6%         |

Practitioners too often try to deceive the press by attaching too much importance to a trivial uneventful happening:

|               | Agree | Disagree | No Opinion |
|---------------|-------|----------|------------|
| Journalists   | 89%   | 4%       | 7%         |
| Practitioners | 33%   | 56%      | 11%        |

Public Relations is a profession equal in status to journalism:

|               | Agree | Disagree | No Opinion |
|---------------|-------|----------|------------|
| Journalists   | 10%   | 79%      | 11%        |
| Practitioners | 76%   | 16%      | 8%         |

(Courtesy of *Public Relations Journal*)

For better or worse, virtually every phase of modern reporting brings the journalist and the public relations person together. A call to the president of almost any major company or to any city office, branch of state government, college or professional sports team, federal agency, large police department, or movie studio is routinely routed through someone in public relations. The overwhelming proportion of information (which is not necessarily synonymous with news) coming out of those places, as well as many others, comes from a public relations, public information, or community relations officer, a press agent, or some other kind of spokesman who is paid to get that information to the press in its most positive light. The public relations people are usually also responsible for generating good publicity and, if at all possible, for "playing down" the other kind.

Political PR does not consist simply of writing and distributing handouts. It involves "consultants" who are paid quite adequately to mastermind campaigns, manipulate the results of polls, and do everything else, from inventing slogans for bumper stickers (BURNSIDE'S AT YOUR SIDE . . . BURNSIDE'S HOT ON CRIME . . . BURNSIDE AGAINST THE TIDE . . .), to buying radio and television time, placing ads in newspapers, writing speeches, staging media "events" (baby-kissing, tree-planting, hot-dog–tasting, and the rest), to telling reporters that the mayor is unavailable for comment when comment is very much in order.

Governmental PR is, in many ways, even more pervasive. Every branch of state and federal government, as well as large municipal departments, has its own public information office. The Department of the Air Force is typical. SAFOI, another of those acronyms cherished by the military, and meaning Secretary of the Air Force, Office of Information, is headquartered in the Pentagon. It also has offices in the larger cities that exist to service the local press and maintain community relations. If a reporter wants to do a story about the Hurricane Hunters, he or she contacts the local SAFOI office for permission, even though the Hurricane Hunters fly out of bases in southern Florida and Puerto Rico. In addition, every Air Force base has its own public information officer, usually a captain or a major, who is responsible for maintaining "liaison" (keeping contact) with the media and the community as a whole. It's his and his staff's job to publicize the base's annual picnic and challenge softball game with the fire department, get a picture of the base's Airman of the Year into the local paper, and arrange for evening-long talks explaining "The Air Force Mission" (accompanied by color slides or a film produced by SAFOI) to the garden club or the Loyal and Secret Order of Honorable Octogenarians. It's also his job to assure the town that the nine airmen who got drunk on Saturday night, and who smashed windows and molested three girls, will receive appropriate punishment, or to listen sympathetically while an angry farmer complains that the fighters coming into final approach over his barn are turning his cows' milk to sour cream before it leaves their udders. He tells the farmer that the matter will be investigated. It might, too, but the fighters generally win.

The very fact that what used to be called the War Department is now called the Defense Department illustrates the importance of public relations. "War" implies aggression. "Defense" connotes a turning of the other cheek. The primary goals of governmental public relations are to show taxpayers that their trust is well placed and their dollars well spent.

Good publicity and favorable publicity are not necessarily the same thing. It is axiomatic among many in show business that *any* mention of a star's name is better than no mention at all. Gossip columnists thrive on petty scandals fed to them by press agents. Celebrity love affairs, arguments, and brawls would seldom make the newspapers were they not planted by press agents, and neither would the theft of Va Va Voom's jewels. Muhammad Ali, the fighter, got a good press ride early in his career by reciting poetry calculated to taunt his opponents and by making nasty, pompous remarks in order to anger the public. He knew perfectly well that he was making people so angry that they would pay outlandish prices for tickets in order to see him flattened. Besides turning out to be a pretty nice guy, Ali also turned out to be a genius where his own publicity was concerned—two facts generally missed by the press during those first years of covering him.

The best public relations people, like the best reporters or the best anybody else, are credible. They are believable. When getting news stories to the press, they maximize what is truly important and play down or ignore what is superfluous or incorrect. Since most of them started as reporters, they can and do anticipate what reporters need—plenty of solid, accurate information. When asked follow-up questions, they answer as completely and as honestly as possible. When they don't know an answer (which is usually the case because of our society's enormous technical specialization), they go to the right person in the organization, or to their client, get the answer, and get it back to the reporter as quickly as they can. The very best PR man or woman will admit that the axles on a particular model car have been collapsing because of faulty workmanship. But the practitioner probably hasn't been born who will take it upon himself or herself to explain for the record why the company employs incompetent workers, why quality control failed to spot the problem, or how many axle-related accidents have been reported. He or she is not, after all, being paid to destroy the company. But it is up to the reporter to get answers to such questions. The worst in public relations peddle lies camouflaged as obvious fact, leave out even rudimentary material that could balance the story, and otherwise make themselves and those they serve unreliable or disreputable.

### Trick or treat.

There is an enormous amount of money in this world. A surprisingly large percentage of it is earmarked for press relations. If you accept presents of any kind you must be prepared to admit that you are on the take. If you're on the take, well-balanced reporting becomes difficult or impossible, since it's against human nature to be impartial toward those whose gifts are accepted. Obviously, this means reporters take no cash, liquor, silver pen-and-pencil sets, or expense-paid trips. They also do not accept free tickets to shows, concerts, operas, sporting events or the like, unless it's for coverage (even then, the practice of accepting press passes has come under increasingly heavy attack by news organizations themselves). Weekends out of town and vacations are paid for by you, which hurts your bank account, but does wonders for your self-respect. If you're invited on a junket—a press trip—and you think that going along is necessary, ask your editor if your company will pay for it. If he says no, don't go; if he says yes, find out what your share comes to (including transportation, accommodations, and meals) and pay it in advance, if possible, and by check. Press parties are all right, provided (1) they're not in your honor, and (2) you're able to stay awake through them.

**Lunch.**

Lunch is an American institution as sacred and as deep-rooted as, say, the tax deduction and the padded expense account—not lunch-the-meal, but lunch-the-game. As played by a good public relations person and a good reporter, lunch is a combination of the exquisite subtleties of good bridge and the probing and feinting of chess. The food doesn't matter.

"Hello, Scoop," says the spokesman for Granite Consolidated over the telephone. "How about lunch at The Salty Sailor? Hank Warner says they've got a new chef and that the lobster thermidor'll knock you out."

Over his first drink, the reporter learns that Reuben Junior is racking up straight A's in plane geometry, earth science, and Spanish, and has lettered in bowling; little Daphne's orthodontia bill has passed the $1,500-mark and is still climbing; the Braves will win the Pennant. With the second drink comes news that Hank Warner has been promoted and is going to the Washington office, leaving the department a man down (or two men down, counting Merwin Ackerman, who is recovering from a heart attack). The clams are fat and juicy and so, apparently, is Granite Consolidated, which in a few days ("You got it first!") will announce a breakthrough in the development of prefabricated stone houses. "The ad campaign's thrust," confides Reuben Senior as he jabs at a piece of lobster, will be: "It's cheaper and safer to get stoned."

You should know that the expense account lunch is a frill that goes with the public relations job. It is paid for by Granite Consolidated, not by your immediate host, and Granite Consolidated is not in business to subsidize journalists without getting something in return. Second, the chances are good that when Reuben returns to his office, he will write a "contact report" listing the name of the journalist, his organization, and the topics of substance that were discussed. This is not to say that Reuben Senior doesn't enjoy the reporter's company but only that, at bottom, it's business. In theory, reporters pay for their own meals. In practice, fumbling and arguing over bills is embarrassing and splitting them is awkward. You should therefore keep the books balanced by agreeing the first time out that you and your contact will alternate picking up checks. Keep a record.

**Handouts.**

Handouts are supposed to give reporters important information. The catch, of course, is that what's important to one person or group may be insignificant to another. Yet all are pushing, shoving, and elbowing for limited space or air time. Every day, in every newspaper, magazine, and radio and television station in the country, forlorn clerks or editorial assistants sit at desks sorting out blizzards of handouts: Mayor Burnside's daughter will be married on November 19th; Interstate Rt. 81 is to be widened by two lanes between West Clarksburg and Tulipville; Our Lady of Perpetual Hope church is abandoning bingo; Melvin D. Bateman is to be named Scout of the Year; the United States Government is going to send 10,000 orange and lemon trees to Siberia as a goodwill gesture; the Department of Defense says that the French Navy has a submarine that can go as fast backward as forward while under water; Wisconsin cheese production increased by 3 percent last year; a jetport is to be named in honor of a famous quarterback who has "gone to the air more times than Pan Am and TWA combined," and so on.

There are two basic kinds of handouts. The first is the purely factual variety containing nothing but hard, unbiased information: the verbatim transcript of a speech or key elements from one; a fact sheet detailing the background, component, or history of something in the news; a biographical sketch of someone important. Handouts describing how a new electric locomotive works, listing the wildlife in the Grand Canyon, or the history of the Winter Olympics, are valuable, time-saving aids to reporters who must include background material on such things in their stories. Transcripts of speeches are useful when long quotes are needed. Instead of writing like mad, or playing back a tape, the reporter with an advance text of a speech simply reads along as he or she hears it given (to make certain it is being delivered as prepared), then pulls appropriate quotes from the transcript.

The second kind of handout, and by far the more common, is the one that describes the event itself, and that can therefore be hard or soft, tightly written or wandering, valuable or unimportant, depending on the nature of its contents and the way in which the public relations person chooses to put it together. This type must be approached critically, not only for what it says, but for what it doesn't say. Here, admittedly in parody form, is an example.

**ABYSMAL PRODUCTIONS, INC.**
120A Sunset Boulevard
Hollywood, California 90010

Contact: Buzz Gaddis                    FOR IMMEDIATE RELEASE
(213) 545-6969

    Arthur B. Ratznest, President of Abysmal Productions, Inc., has announced that Lance Pointe and Cherry Bomb will star in the forthcoming film, "The Goddog," scheduled to go into production in late September.
    The picture, based on Mario Macaroni's best-selling novel of the same name, concerns the life-and-death struggle between rival packs of dogs out to control Palermo, Sicily. Fang, the Wonder Dog, will play Stiletto, the top dog and title role.
    "The Goddog," which will be filmed on location and cost an estimated $3.5 million, will bring Mr. Pointe and Miss Bomb together for the first time since "The Honduras Connection," another Abysmal production. "The Goddog" is scheduled for release a year from now.
    Mr. Pointe will play the role of the director of the Palermo equivalent of the ASPCA. Miss Bomb will play Angelina, a psycho-clepto-schizo-killer and the only human Stiletto trusts. Barry the Poodle will play the Boss of All Bosses. Guy Pan, the brilliant Japanese who won an Oscar in 1975 for "I Was a Motorcycle Kamikaze -- III," will direct.
    "This is a truly exciting -- I will say stupendous -- undertaking," Mr. Ratznest said, "and one which will bring to bear the full array of talent and resources of Abysmal Productions. I've just finished reading the shooting script and I can guarantee that the scene in which the Goddog makes the promiscuous cats on Via Francesco Crispi an offer they can't refuse will leave audiences absolutely numb. This picture will be far more than a work of art; it will be a penetrating social statement. We have another sure winner here."

- 30 -

This handout closely approximates the spirit, if not the appearance, of the real thing. Its job is to get news space or time. Ratznest, of course, didn't actually announce anything. He pays Gaddis to fashion good quotes that can be attributed to him. Notice that the handout mentions Gaddis, not Ratznest, as the contact for questions. The reporter who wants to find out why Abysmal is making yet another Mafia exploitation film, why Cherry Bomb got a part in it even though she isn't good enough to do voice-overs for cartoons, or exactly why Ratznest thinks the picture is a stupendous undertaking, will have to go through Gaddis to get the answers. Ratznest has three very protective secretaries and an unlisted phone number. When Gaddis has the reporter's questions, he will either formulate the appropriate answers himself, or he will on rare occasion go to one of Ratznest's immediate subordinates for a conference before supplying the answer to a particularly tricky question. It is getting information through the middle man that most frustrates reporters because they feel, and often with good reason, that what they end up with has been carefully filtered and has all impurities removed.

There is a good deal of hard information in the Abysmal handout—the cost of the film and its approximate release date, its story line and stars, and the fact that it will be directed by an Oscar winner. But there is also a lot of self-serving, unnecessary fluff. Reference to *The Honduras Connection,* for example, is simply a way of plugging another of the studio's films. More obviously, nothing allegedly said by Ratznest contributes to the story, so all of it can be discarded, including the fact that he made the announcement in the first place. The handout can therefore be boiled down to something like this:

> Abysmal Productions will begin filming "The Goddog" in Palermo, Sicily in late September. It is due to be released in about a year at a cost of $3.5 million.
>
> Lance Pointe, Cherry Bomb, Fang, the Wonder Dog, and Barry the Poodle will play leading roles. Guy Pan, the Japanese Oscar-winner, will direct.
>
> The film is based on Mario Macaroni's novel of the same name, and concerns rival packs of dogs fighting to control Palermo. Fang will have the title role.

When working from handouts:

1. Check all facts, starting with a call to the source of the handout, to make sure it is legitimate. This is particularly important with

political handouts during campaigns. As former President Nixon's dirty tricks group demonstrated, the day of the hoax is far from over. For less than $100, anyone can go to a printer and have run off blank press releases which bear the imprint of the White House or the Committee to Reelect Blowharde. Then it's just a matter of typing in the desired message, photocopying a batch, and mailing them. Go to the clips to find out whether the news release is really news at all, or whether its really a rehash of an old story. Even if it is new, the clips will likely raise questions that should be answered.

2. Separate the news from the embroidery and be tight about it. Be alert for self-serving nonsense and unsubstantiated claims. If the mayor announces a new drug rehabilitation center, for example, and is quoted as saying that he has a deep and long-standing concern for the plight of addicts, look for proof of that assertion.

3. Push hard for relevant information not covered in the handout and look for holes or discrepancies. If you were writing a release about yourself for the world to read, would you concentrate on your good points, or on the bad ones? So do the pros. Glopco's handout will say where and when the new plant will be built, when it will start production, how many persons it will employ, and how much mustard and relish it will turn out every year. It will probably not say how the building will affect the aesthetics of the area, how much pollution it will contribute, whether the plant will be unionized, how many workers will be hired locally versus the number that will be moved in, how the influx will affect the school district, and so on. It is not the release-writer's job to volunteer the fact that the plant will not have adequate waste disposal facilities, or that it will overload the local elementary school. It is the reporter's job to ask about such things. If the spokesperson says that he or she doesn't know the answers to the questions, say so in the story because, (1) the record should show that the company didn't know, and (2) attentive readers will know that their newspaper bothered to ask.

4. Anticipate and answer obvious questions and translate slang or jargon. Acronyms, as has been said, must be explained. Technical terms such as linear accelerator, circuit breaker, fusion, psychosis, or binary fission, have to be defined. If NSA, the *National*

*Security Agency,* says that it has launched a SPOOF with a perigee of 450 miles, you must explain that: (1) SPOOF stands for Satellite Peering Over Others' Frontiers; (2) the perigee is the satellite's lowest point in orbit; (3) its apogee (whatever the distance) is its highest point in orbit. Many writers of releases either forget that the general public doesn't know such things, or assume that those processing the releases will explain them in sufficient detail.

5. Follow release dates and times. FOR IMMEDIATE RELEASE means what it says—that the story can run as soon as it is received by the news organization. Sometimes, though, you will see FOR RELEASE AT 4 P.M. JANUARY 13, or simply, PMS JANUARY 13. This is called an "embargo," and it is usually done so that the release is made public in conjunction with the news event it describes or supports. If you "break" the embargo—get the story out ahead of time—you are not only betraying those who sent you the release and who expect you to honor its embargo, but you're sabotaging your news competitors. Keen competition and sabotage are very different. Instances in which embargoes have been broken are rare and are usually remembered. Don't do it.

If the text of a speech, or parts of it, must go to press before the speech is actually given, refer to it as "prepared for delivery" until you have heard the words as they appear in the handout. Say the first edition closes at 7:30 p.m. and is to include a speech whose text you have, but which isn't due to be given until 9. You refer to that speech in the first edition as having been prepared for delivery, and only after you or someone else in the organization has heard it given as prepared, does "said last night" (or "today") get substituted:

> A coast-to-coast subway offers the only hope for ending air pollution, Sen. S. Erasmus Blowharde said in a speech prepared for delivery here last night.

becomes:

> A coast-to-coast subway offers the only hope for ending air pollution, Sen. S. Erasmus Blowharde said here last night.

The history of journalism is strewn with the bones of reporters who wrote "said here last night," only to learn that the speaker either dealt with another subject, deviated significantly from his prepared remarks, or never said anything because he was snowed in at an airport 600 miles away.

Above all, never forget that you are in the business of disseminating news, not advertising. That means you must use your critical faculties to turn public relations material—even the best of it—into the hardest, most concise, best-balanced stories possible.

# part three

# SPECIALTY

# Introduction to Beats

Beats—specialized areas of reporting—were until recently thought of as being similar to the watertight compartments on a ship. Each was handled by a specialist who stayed securely behind his or her own door and who rarely, if ever, ventured into someone else's area. Each reported directly to the section officer (desk editor), and each section officer reported to the captain (managing editor) on the bridge. Well, the lower ranks still report to section officers, and section officers still report to the captain, but something has changed: there's a lot more movement below decks.

The complications and interdependence of modern society have forced news organizations to take fresh approaches to the coverage of traditional beats. Just as scholars have recently learned the virtues of interdisciplinary study, so newsmen and -women have learned that the events they cover usually overlap with those they don't cover—that the people they report about don't go through their lives on clearly defined tracks like sprinters in a 100-yard dash. Instead, they weave, often getting in each other's lanes.

Until the late 1960s, for example, public utilities were in the exclusive domain of the financial reporter who could understand and translate profit-and-loss statements and pass along all references to kilowatt hours, whether he knew what they were not. Then, seem-

163

ingly overnight, he found himself listening to confrontations between utility executives and environmentalists who kept referring to
strange things like the ecosphere, hydrocarbons, emissions, temperature inversions, fish kills, alpha particle half-life, heavy water, and
meltdowns. He scratched his head and ambled over to the science
department for help from the eggheads. While he was gone, the
sportswriter showed up, also groping for help. Clyde Hammerhead,
whose mighty bat had led the Des Moines Daggers to three World
Series titles in four years, was selling turkey sandwich (with a secret
ingredient) franchises coast to coast and wanted to get on the Big
Board. Until that morning, the sportswriter mumbled darkly, he
had thought that the Big Board registered scores by innings or
quarters, that tender offers happened in French movies, and that
SEC stood for ticket Sales Exceeding Capacity. It was no better on
the police beat. The garden-variety lunatic, bank robber, and
bomb thrower had been replaced by Josef-Cinco, a lieutenant in the
Popular Front for the Liberation of the Nicobar Islands (PFLNI),
and a man whose tapes showed him to be a Guevara-style Maoist
with paranoid schizophrenic and Oedipal tendencies and an insati-
able appetite for white heiresses and smoked mushrooms, both of
which he learned to enjoy while completing a graduate degree at the
Sorbonne. It had gotten very complicated—very complicated,
indeed.

This is the beat reporter's new world. It is a three-dimensional,
kaleidoscopic one in which almost every answer raises two more
questions and practically nothing stands unaffected by something
else. The best beat reporters therefore accept the fact that everything they report, however seemingly unimportant or isolated, is
somehow related to the larger fabric of society. Furthermore, the
solid general assignment reporter—the one who can be thrown on
short notice into an interview with a prima ballerina or a rocket
engineer and bring back an incisive story—is prized like a precious
gem. Not long ago, the reporter who was "promoted" to education,
religion, or science started thinking about updating his résumé
within minutes of being told about his new assignment. That is less
often the case now, and rightly so, because the better reporters
understand that there's no such thing as a bum beat—only bum
reporters. Good and important stories are literally everywhere.

Beats are made or broken on initiative. Beat reporters are expected to know their specialties thoroughly, stay on events as they unfold, and dig to generate stories. Here are some general rules about beats:

1. Get thoroughly briefed by the reporter you are replacing. Don't depend on him or her to volunteer everything you ought to know. Ask. Find out about immediate and long-term problems and about stories that could be developed, but that are not yet ripe. Put them in a notebook or on your calendar and follow up.

2. Brief yourself on the nature of the beat by doing as much reading as possible—quickly. On some beats, that means only going over relevant clips; on others, it means hitting source books, trade journals, and old but good handouts.

3. Get the names of reliable and chronically unreliable sources. Keep an index file or directory with the names of the good ones, plus their addresses and home and office telephone numbers, on your desk. Carry with you a "little black book" containing the same information.

4. See as many of the good sources as possible as quickly as possible. Ask them to tell you about what they do, what their problems are, what stories they think are important, and where you can find other good sources. Give them your home phone number and tell them not to hesitate to use it, provided they really think a call at home is warranted. In addition to making yourself available for important breaking news after hours, you will also be showing them that you take a real interest in your work (and therefore in what *they* do).

5. Sources have to be carefully trained to come to you with good information. That can be done through a reward system. Reward your best sources by giving them exposure in print provided it's warranted and they have no objection (which is usually the case). Treat them to informal, little-or-no-shop-talk lunches or dinners, sports or cultural events, or weekends on your oceangoing yacht. Husbands, wives, and boy- and girl friends should be invited, since the accent is on socializing, not on digging up dirt. If your sources

are well trained, they'll bring you the dirt on Monday morning. Be careful, however, about accepting such favors in return. You will be able to socialize occasionally with probably no more than two or three of your best sources, and discrimination is critical. Back off if you have any reason to think that you're being used as a patsy.

6. If the beat requires daily or weekly phone checks, make them on a regular schedule, and sound interested every time. The minutes of city council meetings may represent drudgery to you, but to the keeper of the minutes, they represent his or her finest professional effort and are the product of a full day's work: don't demean them and their keeper by sounding as though you'd rather be doing number painting than making the call.

7. When Fenster tells you that Bromley is out to end civilization, remember that you are going to have to check with Bromley to find out his side, rather than run with a one-sided story. If Fenster's allegations not only turn out to be wrong, but to have been deliberately invented, tell him politely, but firmly, that you are not in the business of doing his hatchet jobs for him, that the wasted time has given you heartburn, and that you don't care to go through anything like it again—ever. If that doesn't penetrate, Fenster goes on the least reliable sources list.

When covering meetings or groups (which can be difficult because of the number of people and the resulting confusion):

1. Pull the clips beforehand to familiarize yourself with the issues and the participants.

2. Get there early enough so that you can ask key participants for comment on what they're going to say or do. The chances are they'll tell you to hang around and find out with everybody else, but try anyway—it shows them you care.

3. Collect all handouts as soon as you arrive and quickly look them over. If you see something important, you'll be ready to concentrate on it when the meeting begins. In a prepared speech—

again—read along, line by line, and pencil in or cross out when there are deviations.

4. Get a good seat. Plant yourself in front of a large room without audio equipment or in the back if you can hear all right and have to run for a telephone. Always sit on an aisle for mobility. The tigers of the trade, by the way, have been known to hang "Out of Order" signs on public telephones in highly competitive situations when seconds count. It's a bit much.

5. Pursue participants with relevant follow-up questions after the meeting. As in all interviewing, don't ever assume that you have the story just because you have the formal statements. Use remarks by one speaker to stimulate rebuttal from another. The result is usually revealing and sometimes explosive:

"What did you think when Councilman Babbitt said that there's widespread corruption in the Highway Department?"

"It takes one to know one. Ask Babbitt how his brother-in-law passed the bar examination. . . ."

You can sometimes unearth a fair amount of crud by hanging around after the meeting—even after you've phoned in the story— and talking.

6. Official crowd estimates, particularly at parades or at outdoor meetings, are rarely reliable, especially when they come from the police. That's not because policemen are stupid or can't count, but because they have to justify the number of men they use (often on time-and-a-half) according to the size of the turnout. Numbers therefore have a way of being multiplied by a factor of two or three. If marchers pass, count the number in the first row that goes by and then try to tick off succeeding rows. Do the same thing in auditoriums by counting the number of seats in a section and multiplying by the number of sections. If all seats aren't filled, try to block out clusters of 10, 50, or 100 persons, or whatever is most convenient and accurate. If an auditorium has a seating capacity of, say, 1,000, and every seat seems taken, the estimate is easy. You can rarely rely on numbers given by participants because perceptions vary widely,

or by public relations representatives on the spot, since their success or failure is often judged by the turnout.  Do it yourself.

Beats are arranged here by chapter, but remember that much of the information in one is applicable to some or all of the others.  A new lead or a second-day story, for example, applies to almost all of them.  So does codebreaking.  If religious reporting has to do with fundamental social issues more than it has to do with ecclesiastical technicalities, so do sports, financial, and science reporting, among others.  Think of them, again, as that ship with its doors wide open.

# chapter fifteen
# OBITUARIES

My Aunt Lillie, when she was able, read the obituary page of the New York *Daily News* every day of her adult life. Although she spent most of that life in the borough of Brooklyn, which at that time had a population of something like two million, she used the obit page to keep track of those of her friends and distant relatives who were surviving and those who were not.

"Look at who died," she would announce dramatically over her morning coffee. She would say his name. Then she might say, as she did on at least one occasion, "He wanted to marry me."

Aunt Lillie used the obit page as her most dependable source for the most important news. What could be more important, she reasoned, than the deaths of friends and relatives? Not only did her former suitor's obit tell her that she had outlived him, but it also filled her in on what he had managed to accomplish in the 30-or-so years since she had last seen him, how old he was when he died, what he died from, where he lived, the names of his wife and children and where the children lived, and where he was going to be buried. Maybe there would even be a nice picture she could study for comparison's sake.

Such obits were more important to Aunt Lillie than were the

blockbusters about Lindbergh flying the Atlantic or Roosevelt's third election to the presidency, and for very good reason: she had never met either Lindbergh or Roosevelt, much less been privileged to receive marriage proposals from them. The obits were more important. They were about "real" people.

Most reporters react to a stint on obit work pretty much the way they would react to being used for common-cold experiments. That's because most obits are relatively short and are written by formula, allowing little, if any, creativity. The exceptions, though, can make them a formidable challenge. There have been great and celebrated obits that, in every case, captured the essence of their subjects' personalities and accomplishments with real flair.

Obits are not the same as death notices. The latter are usually small boxes or single grafs, arranged alphabetically on the obit page, which contain a short message or prayer and funeral and burial details. They are paid for by the family. Obits are news stories whose length and position on the page are dictated by how important the editor thinks the subject was. They are never paid for.

Obits are important to any reader who is curious about someone who has died, but they are especially important to those who knew him or her personally, or who were otherwise involved, however remotely. First, the obit tells the world that so-and-so has died, and it is therefore a good way of getting the word to interested parties (those who want to pay last respects, who want to know for business reasons, or who want to make a grab for the estate). Second, since the obit is a news story in a public forum, it represents what is probably the dead person's last crack at immortality—a final summary of what he or she did. For the survivors, it is the way in which their friend or loved one will be remembered by the world at large, and that's extremely important to them. Even the parents of the most blatant stinker therefore usually want their boy to be portrayed in the best possible light.

There are two basic kinds of obit leads: supplementary and self-sustaining. A supplementary lead obit accompanies another story— an immediate news story—describing the details of the person's death and other relevant information. The obit therefore only recounts his or her life. Supplementary obits are used mostly for important politicians and bureaucrats who die suddenly while in office, for retired statesmen on the order of Winston Churchill and Charles de Gaulle, and for ordinary folk whose manner of dying is in itself newsworthy (spectacular suicides, murders, auto accidents, and so on). Self-sustaining leads, on the other hand, stand by themselves and must therefore contain all of the news elements, including details of how the person died.

Let's kill our old friend, Lieut. Gen. Rockingham Smedley, two ways and see how both obits would begin. If Smedley were to be assassinated by an enraged ecologist in the Environmental Protection Agency's cafeteria, the resulting immediate news story (not the obit) would likely go on page one and begin like this:

> Lieut. Gen. Rockingham Smedley, Administrator of the Environmental Protection Agency, was shot and killed yesterday by a self-proclaimed ecologist as he was eating his lunch in the agency's cafeteria.
> The 63-year-old official had just started on his pork chop when the gunman . . .

Since that story would go on to explain in considerable detail how Smedley died, recounting the circumstances of his murder again in the obit would obviously be unnecessary, so the supplementary version would lead something like this:

> Lieut. Gen. Rockingham Smedley, the Environmental Protection Administrator who was shot to death yesterday, often told friends that "cleaning up enemy positions was easier than cleaning up the environment."
> Smedley, who was affectionately called "Rock" by his friends and colleagues, was appointed to his post in 1976 after a six-year hitch in the Army Corps of Engineers.
> Rockingham Smedley was born in Topeka, Kansas on . . .

If Smedley were to die from compound pneumonia, however, the event would probably not warrant a page one story, since his illness would have been referred to in at least one previous story. Again, though, remember that such would be the case because he was only the head of one of many federal agencies. If the President of the United States died after a similar illness, it definitely would make the front page. Smedley's self-sustaining obit would carry the whole story and start like this:

Lieut. Gen. Rockingham Smedley, Administrator of the Environmental Protection Agency, died of pneumonia here yesterday at Veteran's Hospital. He was 63 years old.

There is no single formula for obits, self-sustaining or otherwise,
because subjects and circumstances vary widely, and so do the
editorial policies and audiences of newspapers and magazines. It
says below, for example, that grandparents are not listed in obits.
Your grandparents and mine are not listed: the King or Queen of
England's grandparents *are* listed, however, because royal bloodlines
are considered important enough to trace. Grandparents are also
often listed in newspapers serving relatively small communities, and
particularly those having long traditions and "old" families, whereas
they're skipped in the big cities unless the subject was prominent in
society. The following, then, is applicable to self-sustaining obits,
but its body, in particular, is in no sense rigid. There is room, in
other words, for creativity.

The lead gives the subject's name, age, position or claim to fame,
and the cause and location of death:

Pamela Wilcox Turner, the first woman to cross the United
States on a motorcycle, died of a heart attack yesterday at her
home in Nashville, Tenn. She was 71 years old.

The body should give the subject's career highlights and survivors
and, if relevant, his or her education, professional affiliations (the
American Chemical Society), and honors (Phi Beta Kappa). The
subject's date and place of birth go in if space permits (meaning, if
he or she was sufficiently important), though getting the age in the
lead is usually enough.

Survivors are listed near the end and generally go in this order:
(1) widow or widower; (2) children, including those by a previous
marriage (but not the previous spouse); (3) the number, but not
the names or ages, of grandchildren. Siblings can go either after the
widow or widower or after the children or grandchildren and are
generally listed with their home towns. Leave parents out unless
you're writing about a child or someone in the social register. Ages
are given for surviving youngsters (Glenn, 8, and Phoebe, 6) and
domiciles are given for adult offspring (Mrs. Robert Harrison of

Cleveland and Jerome Smedley of Fairfax, Va.). Leave out aunts, uncles, cousins, brothers- and sisters-in-law, godparents, and the rest unless reference to them is germane.

The last graf or two gives the time and place of the funeral service and burial. If the family requests that contributions be made to charity rather than to a florist, say so in the last sentence.

Here is Rockingham Smedley's self-sustaining obit. Since he died in Washington, newspapers there would not use a dateline, but those elsewhere would:

WASHINGTON, July 28—Environmental Protection Administrator Lieut. Gen. Rockingham Smedley died of pneumonia here today at Veteran's Hospital. He was 63 years old.

Smedley was born in Topeka, Kansas, on July 24, 1914. According to friends there, he wanted to be a soldier from early childhood.

He graduated from West Point in 1935 with a varsity letter in wrestling and earned an M.S. in mechanical engineering from the University of Kansas in 1938.

When war broke out, then-Capt. Smedley was sent to England, then to North Africa, and finally to France just after the Normandy invasion. He served in the infantry and left the war as a colonel with two Silver Stars for heroism under fire.

The second Silver Star was awarded for leading a successful charge into heavy machine-gun fire and capturing an important enemy fortification.

"There were only two ways to go," Smedley later recalled, "and the wrong way would have meant getting shot in the back. I didn't want that, so I had to move forward, and fast."

Smedley also served as an infantry commander in Korea during the war there, and as commanding general of the 44th Infantry Brigade in South Vietnam. He was severely wounded in the legs when his helicopter was hit by Vietcong fire and crashed near Danang.

The wounds caused him more mental suffering than physical, friends said, since they forced him to give up wrestling, which he had continued to do since his academy days.

"Rock," as he was called by those who were close to him, had stayed trim and muscular through wrestling and other hard exercise. After the crash, however, he went into a physical decline.

Smedley was assigned to the Army Corps of Engineers after Vietnam and spent six years as its chief. He was appointed to head the Environmental Protection Agency last June.

Smedley's appointment drew sharp criticism from environmentalists who charged that his years in the Army engineers made him "incompatible" with the EPA job. He vigorously denied it.

"Cleaning up enemy positions was easier than cleaning up the environment," Smedley remarked after only two months at the EPA. "But our environment is more important. If we lose it, no foreign enemy will matter."

The general was rushed to Veteran's Hospital last Friday after he collapsed at home. Doctors who diagnosed his advanced pneumonia said they probably could have cured it had it been caught sooner. One doctor said that Smedley must have been walking around in great discomfort for weeks.

He is survived by his widow, the former Constance Berryman; a daughter, Mrs. Robert Harrison of Cleveland; a son, Jerome, of Fairfax, Va., and three grandchildren.

A funeral service will be held at 10 a.m. Thursday at the Cleveland Park Congregational Church, followed by burial at Arlington National Cemetery. The family requests that in lieu of flowers donations be made to the Environmental Defense Fund.

The best obits are those that capture the personalities of their subjects—the distinguishing traits that made them unique individuals, worthy of a final story. We've had some fun with "Rock" Smedley, but now that he's dead, we can learn a few things about him by studying his obit.

Although the obit in no way gives undue praise, it does provide a portrait of a man who was anything but a buffoon. Irrespective of whether we admire Smedley's choice of career, we are left with a picture of a man who always seemed to have done the job required, even when the demands were difficult or emotionally contradictory. That quality does not warrant snickering. Smedley obviously let his dedication to his new job be so well known to his family that his wife asked for contributions to environmental preservation rather than the purchase of wreaths. It can also be inferred that he put off going to a doctor because of the workload that was wearing him out. That isn't ludicrous, either.

We learn from the obit that Rockingham Smedley was a brave and industrious man who pursued higher education, loved to be physically vigorous, and who flew low over combat areas when he probably didn't have to. We learn that the wounds from the crash badly damaged his spirit, but not so much so that he didn't defend himself against his critics or try to do the best job he could. Smedley's own words (pulled from clips) and interviews with family and friends, portray a fairly thoughtful, conscientious, and brave individual—an individual who *lived*.

Now a question arises. If the obit is the last lunge at immortality, the final imprint on an enduring record, what happens when a blatant stinkard dies? The answer is that he gets treated with taste and fairness, but not as though he was a cross between Winnie the Pooh and Geppetto. As is always the case, let the truth tell itself. Let's temporarily liquidate Elliot "the Virus" Coogan, too, and see how we might write him off:

RENO, NEV., Sept. 3—Elliot "the Virus" Coogan, the millionaire mobster who controlled several gaming establishments in this city, died here today after a long illness. He was 78 years old.

The one-time bootlegger and suspected hit man was born Elliot Ronald Coogan on New York's Lower East Side on January 18, 1899. He was the youngest of four sons and a daughter born to an immigrant tailor and his wife.

Coogan first achieved wide notoriety for the defiance he showed at a trial in 1928 in which he was being prosecuted by federal authorities for bootlegging.

"There isn't a jury in this country I can't buy," Coogan was quoted as having boasted. He was found guilty and served four years in prison, proving, apparently, that there was at least one jury he could not buy.

After repeal, in 1933, Coogan became a partner of Ira Sadisky, the gambler who was later convicted of operating brothels and fixing horse races in California and of extorting money from casino operators in Reno and Las Vegas.

Sadisky electrified a Senate crime committee hearing in 1953 when he named Coogan as his partner in an effort to take over most of the gambling in Reno. The two men apparently had had a falling out before the hearing.

"They call him 'the Virus' because he's unhealthy to be around," Sadisky told the Senators before television cameras.

"Let him say that to my face," Coogan answered from his guarded estate outside this city, "and he'll regret the day he was born. I've been viciously and maliciously slandered by a plain creep."

It was brought out at a tax evasion trial in 1962 that Coogan started his career as a gunman in Chicago during World War I. He never denied the charge and, in fact, implied that it was true.

"I had to eat, like everybody else, and I knew that nobody was going to send me to Harvard. This is the greatest country in the world, but you have to help yourself because no one else is going to," he said at the trial. He was not convicted.

Although the stocky, graying man suffered from chronic asthma and arthritis in his later years, he continued to direct far-flung business operations from his estate.

It was reported last year that Coogan bought control of three nightclubs in Texas through associates and, in each case, paid far less than their market value. This, too, he denied.

He is believed to have become terminally ill early this year and was treated almost entirely in his large, two-story home, one of several buildings that sit on a 38-acre oasis 10 miles north of here.

Coogan is not believed to have ever been married.

The funeral service and burial will take place at the estate on Wednesday morning and will be private.

*The New York Times* obit on Otto Skorzeny, the Nazi commando leader who achieved fame by a daring rescue of Mussolini in 1943, was a classic "mean man" obit. In it, Lawrence Van Gelder described the unrepentant former SS officer as a "hulking, scar-faced Nazi Elite Guard colonel" before going on to recount Skorzeny's record of World War II activities and neo-Nazi affiliations in Spain after the war. By noting that Skorzeny was acquitted of charges of murder, robbery, and arson in Czechoslovakia, Van Gelder fashioned an honest, but unsavory image of his subject. The obit's last graf amounted to a perfect snapper. After describing how Skorzeny's body lay in the back of a Madrid funeral home, wrapped in a white shroud strewn with carnations, and that his widow was going to take the ashes back to Vienna for burial, the writer finished his portrait with this deceptively simple, but very telling quote:

" 'Nobody has come to see him except the photographers,' an attendant said."

## RULES

### Avoid sentimental slop.

People ought to either "die" or be "killed." Use "died" if the cause of death was nonviolent, and "killed" if it was violent or deliberately caused (except for suicides). If you want to be more specific, which is usually a good idea, specify whether the victim was shot, stabbed, or strangled. Stay far away from all of the following and their ilk: passed away, succumbed, ascended upward (or downward), met his end or his Maker, drifted into the great beyond, went to life everlasting, entered permanent slumber or repose or the house of the Lord, was taken, dwells in eternity or with his ancestors, left this earth, or was separated from his spirit or soul. If you use "departed," be prepared to give a track number. . . .

Avoid non sequiturs. A non sequitur is an inference that doesn't follow from a premise. In other words, it's two disjointed thoughts that are incompatible when taken as a whole. For some reason, possibly because they think they can get the most information into the smallest space, beginners on obits find non sequiturs irresistible:

Born in Kentucky in 1958, she went to medical school.
A veteran of the Navy, he loved to eat Chinese food.
Convicted of voluntary manslaughter, she liked to sew.
Fond of Morgan horses, he skied throughout Canada.

You can unsnarl non sequiturs in your head before they go on paper by thinking of that good old straight declarative sentence, by beginning it with a personal pronoun, and by joining clauses with "and."

She was born in Kentucky in 1958 and went to medical school.
He was a veteran of the Navy and loved to eat Chinese food.
She was convicted of manslaughter and liked to sew.
He was fond of Morgan horses and skied throughout Canada.

## Never treat death humorously.

Some people think it's amusing to have a heart attack on Halloween, drown in a puddle, be trampled by a horse or bitten by a venomous snake in the heart of the city, be electrocuted while shaving or putting up a television antenna, or be accidentally buried alive. It's far from funny to the victim and to the victim's friends and loved ones. Death can be ironic but, by definition, it cannot be funny. To treat someone's death as a joke is to betray immaturity, insensitivity, callousness, or all three, and that's not what good reporters are all about.

## Give the specific cause of death when possible.

Avoid "died of natural causes" because that hackneyed expression covers everything and explains nothing. When a bullet shatters a heart it is quite natural for the heart to stop functioning. Carried to its logical extreme, then, all deaths can be said to be natural. Avoid using "old age," too. No one dies of old age. Old people die because one or more of their parts break down or become diseased. Name the part, if possible, and explain what happened to it. "After a long illness" generally means that the victim died of cancer. The fudging is used because there are still many people who are embarrassed by having it known that a relative had cancer. You should respect their wishes. As a service to the American Cancer Society and to cancer research in general, most newspapers and magazines use the word "cancer" whenever they can, since recurrent mention of it helps to keep potential contributors aware of the disease. But if the family says no, it's no. If they say yes, be specific, but not technical: brain cancer, lung cancer, leukemia, Hodgkin's disease.

### Interviewing survivors.

Be empathetic when interviewing survivors. The death may be just another obit to you, but it's probably the source of deep pain to those you interview. Begin by giving condolences and keep an even level of respect and politeness throughout the interview. You can often change the minds of those who are reluctant to give information by pointing out that an obituary (*not* an "obit") is public acknowledgment of accomplishment and that many friends and relatives want and expect it as a kind of memorial. Further, it will notify those who don't know of the death that it has happened, and many of them will want to pay respects. If this doesn't work, politely back off with a thank you and a second condolence. If you do get the interview, concentrate on material that will reveal the personality and uniqueness of the subject, rather than going after stuff that can be pulled from clips. The obit is a kind of profile and should be approached accordingly.

### Double-check.

There exist in almost every community some souls who think that having their friends read their own obits in the newspaper is hilarious. So one of them occasionally phones in such "news." Most real obits, or at least the rudiments of them, are phoned in by the funeral home that has the body (*not* where the body is "reposing," "resting," or "waiting," but where it *is* . . . ), so call back for routine confirmation if you don't know precisely who you're talking to the first time. Use the number that's in the telephone directory or on the office master list, not the one given to you by the caller. You won't embarrass yourself by calling back, since funeral directors don't like such practical jokes, either.

# chapter sixteen
# PUBLIC SAFETY

## POLICE

Although many enlightened city administrations are making serious efforts to improve police-press relations, a fair amount of mutual mistrust, and in some cases, antagonism, remains. When a policeman doesn't like reporters, it's usually for any or all of the following reasons:

1. He thinks reporters are procriminal. Most investigative stories, in the crusading tradition, have helped or tried to help accused criminals, not those who have locked them up. Even more annoying, many notable news stories have drawn attention to police corruption and inefficiency.

2. He has a natural bureaucratic revulsion for anyone on the outside knowing his business (perhaps even better than he does). He therefore considers reporters smart alecks, meddlers, know-it-alls, or plain troublemakers.

3. He knows that the police beat on most newspapers is where beginners try their wings and where tired old hacks are put to pasture. He is therefore offended, however subconsciously, because "police science" is subject to coverage by "kids" and "has-beens."

For their part, many reporters assume that all policemen are at bottom frustrated Wyatt Earps who delight in locking up people, bashing in their brains, or shooting them. The police reporter muses about the fact that policemen are the only members of the community who openly carry revolvers and who are legally entitled to shoot anyone they think deserves to be shot. "They're all carrying weapons, and they can make mistakes," he reflects early into the job. "They can make mistakes." They can, and have. But, as we well know, so can reporters. There is a brave and honest cop for every careful and conscientious reporter and there is a surly, incompetent redneck for every lazy, numbskulled hack. For every policeman who has erroneously or deliberately shot the wrong person, there are probably three or four who have been murdered in the line of duty. Police work is a dangerous, high-tension profession, precisely because it involves lethal weapons.

"Kids" do, indeed, often start their careers on the police beat, and with good reason. Police reporting is an excellent primary training ground because most of it is neatly contained and is therefore manageable for beginners. On its most basic level—say, a grocery store robbery or a traffic accident—there is no theory or supposition required. You collect the facts accurately—who got robbed, who did it, how much was taken, when it happened, and so forth—and you arrange them in a tidy little story of perhaps three or four grafs. There is no speculation about real motives, long-term effects on the economy or the political system, or other heavy stuff. Most police reporting therefore easily lends itself to the collection of plain facts for use in tight stories. This is excellent for easing beginners into the profession and for easing those who are old and tired out of it.

Now for the catch. If the late 1960s taught the American press nothing else, they taught it that the "big" stories had shifted from the Kremlin, East Africa, and even from Indochina, right back to our own communities. We learned, somewhat unpreparedly, that an apparently routine arrest of the sort most experienced police reporters would have yawned at in the early part of the decade could ignite a riot in Watts, Detroit, or Newark. We discovered that student protests at a political convention could fill hospitals and that one on a campus could leave four youngsters dead. We came to find out, as the years of increasing anguish and cynicism continued, that a car driven off a bridge in the middle of the night could profoundly affect a Senator's career. Most astonishingly, we found that a "third-rate burglary" in reality amounted to a first-rate knife thrust at the heart of our entire political system. That seemingly routine bit of breaking and entering—a police story—sent convulsions through the nation and destroyed a President.

As we turned inward, we stopped politely scorning those of our colleagues who covered the PTA, fires, budget hearings, zoning board meetings, and the police beat. We came to realize, terribly late, that a seemingly dull zoning or school board meeting could in reality be a vicious battleground for entrenched and volatile racial or financial interests and could easily send angry citizens onto the streets looking for blood. The catch, then, is that even the most innocuous-looking story can have very serious repercussions. This certainly applies to police reporting.

On the police beat:

1. Get to know the workings of the department as quickly as possible. Know who is responsible for what, where key offices are, who is in charge of the department and its divisions, and who the press spokesman is. Cultivate sources in each division: traffic, homicide (*not* homocide . . . ), vice, burglary, larceny-theft, motor vehicle theft, robbery, and the others. Let your source or sources in each division know that you want to be contacted immediately on important stories—that you're interested in police work and want to do it justice.

2. Establish a reputation for fairness immediately and hold onto it. A few reporters begin antagonizing policemen from day one. Some others, however, get to like the vicarious police role so much that they go to the other extreme. They start thinking that they're one of the boys. Riding around the worst section of town in the company of armed policemen, with the two-way radio on, or being allowed at murder scenes and serious accidents, can touch off the

Charlie Chan-Number One Son syndrome ("Gee, Pop, the gardener had the best motive . . . "). If you find you're addicted to it, don't live with frustration—trade in your press card for a badge. Otherwise, remember that you're not one of the boys. The "boys" have their work to do and you have yours. Reporters who take to wearing regulation police cardigans, slapping police stickers on their cars, and running coffee into the captain's office are put down for what they are—patsies—and are treated accordingly.

3. If you share a press room in the police station with reporters from other news organizations, you will from time to time have to double-cover and share information. One will perhaps watch the police teletype while the other makes the rounds of the divisions. That's all right when there is a lot happening. But you're expected to beat the opposition, not supply it with news, so remember that an exclusive is just that. When you dig up something out of the ordinary, as is expected, keep it to yourself.

4. If you're responsible for checking the booking sheet, which is used to record the names, addresses, and charges made against most (*but not all*) of those who are arrested, do so at regular intervals. Pay close attention to the names on the sheet, since you could come up with somebody important. If permitted, check arrest forms, too. They usually go into considerable detail about the crime and contain the names and addresses of the suspects and the names of the arresting officers. Some police departments allow reporters to look at arrest forms as a matter of routine. Others technically don't allow it, but in practice, it comes down to the reporter's relationship with the desk sergeant.

5. When a suspect is charged with a crime he or she has been formally accused of having committed it and the police are prepared to say so in court. Being arrested and being charged are not the same. A person is arrested when he is physically brought into the police station. In theory, he might sit in a corner for hours, or even be put in a cell, without anyone accusing him of anything. A charge, however, is a written accusation of his having committed a crime. Further, a person can be charged, but not arrested (as is the case when a grand jury hands up an indictment, a judge issues a warrant,

or a public prosecutor submits information). When writing about someone who has been brought in and booked, you should therefore say that he was arrested and charged with . . . No one gets his name in the news unless he has been charged. Then, report the charges exactly as they are worded by the police. If you make a murderer out of someone who has been charged with involuntary manslaughter you have maligned him and brought yourself a lot of trouble. (There is a list of crime classifications at the end of this section.)

6. Criminal or victim identification should come only from the police, other law enforcement officials, or from hospital officials— never from bystanders, witnesses, friends, or relatives. Even if you pull a wallet from the victim's pocket, his identity must be confirmed by the police. That victim could be a thief who stole the wallet an hour earlier. Don't kill the person he stole it from. Try to check all victim identifications in the telephone book and, when possible, call their homes for confirmation.

7. Since the accused is taken to be innocent until he is found guilty by a court of law, those who have merely been arrested and charged are generally referred to as "suspects" who have "allegedly" committed crimes:

> Cherry Bomb, the movie actress, was arrested and charged here last night with possessing five pounds of cocaine brought from Sicily.
> Miss Bomb returned from the Mediterranean island last Thursday after completing *The Goddog,* a film shot on location there.
> The suspect was released on her own recognizance, police said, and has been ordered to appear at a preliminary hearing in District Court on Friday.
> Miss Bomb declined to comment on the charge.

Some beginners believe that sprinkling arrest stories with "suspected" and "alleged" wards off libel suits the way crosses are supposed to ward off vampires. They are wrong. As has been mentioned, news organizations are legally responsible for everything they print or air, and no amount of equivocation alters that. It may be more tempting for someone to sue in the absence of such phraseology, but if he thinks he has a good enough case, he'll probably sue even if he's depicted as a "reputed alleged perpetrator" (to carry it to the point of the absurd). In *World Without End, Amen,* Jimmy Breslin described with great humor, but also with more than a touch of truth, a New York policeman who referred to someone who had been murdered as "the alleged victim." That, of course, is preposterous. But protecting the rights of citizens who have only been accused of crimes isn't preposterous at all—it's crucial. Think about how you would feel if you were arrested and charged with a crime you didn't commit, and then saw reference to your having done it splashed in the newspaper.

8. The race, religion, or nationality of criminals, suspected or otherwise, are not put into news stories unless such information is germane. Most often, such descriptions are printed only about those who have committed particularly nasty or sensational crimes, and who are still at large. This is done as a public service, usually to help law enforcement authorities find murderers or kidnappers, or when such information is relevant to the crime, itself: a nationalist group blowing up a bank or staging a political assassination are obvious examples. Youths—generally those under 18 years old—are not named as alleged or actual criminals. Write that "his [or her] name was withheld because of age," and remember to give the age. Rape victims' names are also left out unless the victim agrees otherwise.

9. Suicides must be ruled as such by the coroner or medical examiner. Don't take it upon yourself to label any death a suicide, even if there is a note saying as much. The police usually say "apparent suicide" until they get the result of the coroner's autopsy, and so should you:

> Morley Bascomb, a 41-year-old College Hills tavern owner, was found dead by his wife last night in their home on Cedar Avenue. He was listed as an apparent suicide.
> Mrs. Bascomb, who told police that she discovered her husband's body in their bedroom shortly after midnight, said

that he had been brooding about business problems for several weeks and that he was in serious debt.

A half-empty bottle of sleeping pills was found in the bathroom, according to police, who are ruling the death a tentative suicide until they get a report from the county coroner.

"Jumped or was pushed," or simply "fell," usually takes care of those who go off bridges, out of windows, or onto train tracks.

10. Robbing and stealing, which constitute most police stories, are not synonymous. Robbery, in its legal sense, is done openly against persons or property and with the threat or use of violence. A bank robbery or a store holdup are obvious examples. "Mugging" is a form of robbery, but it is a lay term and is so imprecise that it ought to be further explained: "He took her purse and wrist watch, pushed her into the bushes, and ran toward the subway." A bit of trivia: since hands are considered weapons (you can strangle or beat someone to death with them), "armed robbery" is redundant. All robberies are really armed robberies, even if the robber isn't carrying hardware. Through common usage, though, "armed robbery" is universally accepted. Stealing and theft, on the other hand, are done with stealth by sneaks—when the victim is not aware of it—so violence or the threat of it are not factors. Persons who steal pens from a store (shoplifting) or securities from their own firms (embezzling) are obvious examples. Burglary involves entering a building and staying there with the intent of committing a crime against property. Since many burglars walk past unlocked doors or climb through open windows, they aren't necessarily "breaking and entering," so watch out for that hackneyed term. Burglars operate with stealth—when you're asleep or aren't home. If you walk in and surprise a burglar, and he pulls a pistol and continues to clean out your home while keeping you covered, he turns into a robber (or a bandit, or a gunman).

11. Pistols, revolvers, and guns are not synonymous. A revolver is a hand weapon with a revolving chamber that holds cartridges. An automatic pistol holds cartridges in a magazine, usually in its handle. Either can be called a pistol, but it's better to be specific:

.38-cal. revolver; .45-cal. automatic. Neither of these, nor any other hand weapon, is a gun. Guns are larger weapons, starting with rifles and shotguns, going through heavy machine guns, and ending with cannons. A cartridge is a case that contains an explosive charge and either a bullet or pellets. The bullet or pellets are fired from the weapon and hit people. What remains behind is the cartridge or shell. Don't substitute "slugs" or "lead" for bullets unless you're writing a detective potboiler.

### Attribution.

Go on the assumption that for routine or favorable stories, every policeman you know wants to see his name in the paper, since that is one of the ways they (and many others) help to get themselves promoted. This is far from being the reporter's major working tool, but it isn't exactly inconsiderable, either. Reporters routinely reward their most reliable police sources with "exposure." It's the lubrication that keeps Lieut. Gallagher's jaw working. He tells the reporter that the department has an excellent lead in the Butterfield multiple murder, and either gets his name in the newspaper in connection with that story, or, if he'd rather remain a "reliable police source," he gets a credit for one cookie later. This is generally accepted, but when doing it, remember not to cheapen your cookies by handing them out indiscriminately.

In routine, but serious stories, name the policemen you quote for the usual, very good reason—it keeps them responsible for what they tell you. It isn't necessary to use names in routine, nonserious stories, or in those for which attribution doesn't contribute much. Candy store robberies, muggings, or highway accidents, to take three of many possible examples, don't usually contain anything so sensitive that they require pinning quotes on a policeman. Neither does a homicide in which there is only a description of what happened. You don't need to write that Lieut. Lionel Gallagher said that the victim was shot three times in the head. You can write it if you want to give Gallagher his cookie, but you don't have to: "according to police," or "police said" is generally enough.

### The Mafia.

Great exploits require great adversaries. There is no glory in
arresting Luigi Fettucini, the small-time bookmaker and vest pocket
crook. But arresting Luigi Fettucini, the soldier in Carlo "Il
Disonesto" Brutto's crime "family," carries with it heroic overtones
of Wagnerian proportion. An astounding number of alleged criminals whose last names end in vowels are therefore put in the Mafia
throughout the United States every year by policemen, district attorneys, and other law enforcement officials who feel they need to
justify the funds they use, and who want the best possible media exposure. And since reporters are as attracted by the dramatic as are
their sources, we keep reading and rereading that Frank "Five
Fingers" Cassata, "a reputed captain in the Gino Gelati crime
family," was arrested for, well, for income tax evasion . . . or in
connection with the killing last August of . . . . Italian-Americans,
the vast majority of whom wouldn't know a criminal if they tripped
over one, are becoming increasingly annoyed at being equated with
the criminal class.

There may or may not be a Mafia in the United States. It depends
on definition. If the term means a group of blood relatives who control one or more rackets in a given area, or a fairly tight-knit association of lower- and middle-echelon neighborhood gangsters, it's
probably fair to say that there is a Mafia, in the sense that there are
also tong societies among the Chinese and a variety of closed syndi-
cates among other ethnic groups. But if it means that there is a pervasive criminal conspiracy by some "Boss of All Bosses" who has his
fingers in everything from heroin and prostitution to shaking down
third-graders for milk money, then such an operation surpasses
reason. In any case, if everyone who was named a mafioso by the
police, FBI, and the Justice Department actually belonged to such
a shadowy band, it would very likely have more, better armed, and
tougher members than the Second Marine Division.

When you are told that so-and-so is in the Mafia, or is a member
of someone's crime family, ask your source to prove it. There may
be proof that the culprit is a sadistic killer, but that's not the same
thing as being part of some ethnocentric criminal conspiracy. If you
don't get proof, let the Mafia (including the Black Mafia and the
Jewish Mafia) remain in the hands of those who fashion fast fiction.

### Listen to the radio.

Press rooms in most police stations, nearly all city rooms, and the company cars used by police reporters, almost always have police radios that are used to monitor communications between headquarters and squad cars around the city. The radios are left on all the time. When headquarters orders a police car to get to the scene of a robbery, murder, accident, or anything else requiring a response, the editor or reporter hears it at the same instant as the policemen who are being directed to the scene. This can save reporters enormous amounts of time. To someone not paying close attention, chatter on the police radio sounds a little like hyperactive pygmies debating in an echo chamber. Experienced editors take it all in with one ear even while they're working on something else. In New York City, an editor who picks out "10-13" on the radio automatically begins listening more closely, and if he hears "10-34" immediately after, he notifies the police reporter or starts looking around for someone else to send out.

In New York, 10-13 is a code signal that means a policeman is calling for assistance, and 10-34 means that an assault is in progress. These numbers are part of the so-called Signal-10 system, which, while varying from one municipality to another, is used throughout the country as a quick and accurate code for exchanging information between headquarters and the officers on the street. You should familiarize yourself with the more common signals in your area, since they vary (10-30 is a robbery in progress in New York; signal 40I means the same thing in Fairfax County, Virginia). Police communications are more common in plain English than they are in code, but remember that code is just that—a way of transmitting information that is not generally understood by outsiders. If you know that the N.Y.P.D. uses 10-46 as a rapid mobilization signal for eight sergeants, 40 patrolmen, and possibly a lieutenant, and you hear it, together with a location, you go there fast. If you understand this, acknowledge with a "10-4."

As a rule—not only in police stories, but in all related stories—death and serious injury, followed by money, are the most important factors. That is not to say that in reality there aren't many things more important than money, but only that, when a bank is robbed, readers have a natural desire to want to know how much was taken. This applies to all robbery and theft stories, since money is the reason the event happens in the first place. Similarly, readers and listeners want to know about the monetary loss from property damage as a result of fires and natural disasters. But loss of life always takes precedence:

> The manager of the Topps Burger Bar at 19th and Spruce was killed in a robbery last night in which two gunmen made off with about $400.
>
> Robert H. Fletcher, 32, was putting the day's receipts in a safe just before the usual midnight closing, according to three employees, when the gunmen entered and demanded the money.
>
> Fletcher did not resist, one employee told police, but apparently he did not move fast enough. He was shot twice in the chest by one of the bandits and was dead on arrival at the Downtown Medical Center. No one else was injured.

Notice that Fletcher is not named in the lead. Except in very small communities, where his death might be more newsworthy because he was known by all, the fact of the robbery, his death, and the amount taken are better because they get readers into the story faster. This is also true of highway fatality stories:

> A Bethesda dentist and his wife were killed last night when their car crashed into a bridge abutment on Rt. 70, three miles west of Rockville.
>
> The occupants, identified as Dr. Lester Sykes, 29, and his wife, Francine, 26, were traveling over the speed limit, according to state police, when he apparently lost control. They were alone in the car and no one else was injured.
>
> The Sykeses had been to a party in Gaithersburg, friends said, and were rushing home because they promised their baby-sitter that they would get back by midnight. The accident happened at about 11:30.
>
> There are two Sykes children, ages 4 and 7.

Note: (1) Before giving the victims' names and ages, the reporter writes that they were "identified," which is always taken to mean that they were identified by officials; (2) the state police are quoted as having said that Sykes was driving faster than the speed limit; (3) it is made clear that no one else was hurt or involved in the accident; (4) the car crashed, it did not collide: only two objects in motion can collide, so since the abutment wasn't moving, there could be no collision; (5) having written that the couple was rushing home to relieve the baby-sitter, and therefore raising a likely question, the reporter answers the question by including the fact that there are two children (giving their names, under the circumstances, would be a little tasteless).

Let's try the same basic structure on a domestic quarrel resulting in homicide:

A Culpepper Heights man was allegedly stabbed to death by his brother last night over a card game, according to police.

The victim, Rupert McCoy, 45, was pronounced dead in his apartment at 103 Beecher Ave. at 11:40. He was stabbed twice in the left chest with an eight-inch kitchen knife found at the scene.

Rupert's brother, Calvin, 48, was taken to the Third Precinct and charged with second-degree murder.

The fight took place in the victim's apartment after Rupert accused his brother of cheating at poker, according to two other men who were playing. After a heated argument, they told police, Calvin went into the kitchen, got the knife, and stabbed his brother.

"Cal was drinking beer since the afternoon and right through supper," said Rupert's widow, Elsie, who was also present. "He has a bad temper when he's sober, but gets real mean with alcohol."

Police found several empty quart beer bottles in the room and $1.75 in nickels and dimes on the card table.

This is the kind of story that happens virtually every Friday and Saturday night in July and August in every city in the country. Hot weather, small apartments, and alcohol lead to husbands shooting wives, women stabbing lovers, fathers throwing children out of windows, youngsters dueling on roofs or in dark alleys, and a great deal more.

The technical elements of the story should be self-evident, and so should its structure, except for one thing. Instead of merely run-

ning through the material and getting rid of the story, the writer
ended it with a snapper based on a nice bit of observation. By counting the change on the table, the reporter was able to bring a final
touch of irony to the story of the death of Rupert McCoy. He was
murdered for nickels and dimes.

## TYPES OF CRIMES

Here is a list of the most common crimes, with short definitions
for them. Remember, though, that each state has its own criminal
statutes. Although most definitions are basically similar, there are
differences, so approach working terminology accordingly.

Crimes are divided into two broad categories: misdemeanors
and felonies. A *misdemeanor*—literally, misbehavior or poor de-
meanor—is the less serious. Shoplifting, trampling someone's
tulips, playing the trumpet at 4 a.m., taking a bus or train ride without paying the fare, being improperly dressed, being drunk and disorderly, or anything similar that results in a complaint, is a misdemeanor. So, usually, is the theft of $100 or less. A *felony* is a
serious crime: murder, rape, robbery, burglary, kidnapping, arson,
and others that jeopardize life, health, property, morality, or public
safety. Misdemeanors are, by definition, not terribly newsworthy
unless they happen in towns with populations of less than 40 or are
committed by very well-known persons (even then the news value is
dubious).

### Crimes Against the Person

| | |
|---|---|
| Assault | Threatening to injure someone in a way that makes him afraid, and having the clear ability to carry out that threat. |
| Assault (aggravated) | Attacking someone with a dangerous or deadly weapon with the intention of causing serious harm or death. |
| Battery | Illegally striking someone, throwing |

|  | something at him, or even spitting at him. |
| Homicide | The killing of one person by another, generally when the victim dies within a year and a day. |
| Homicide (justifiable) | Killing in self-defense (as when a person is attacked with intent to kill), or in the line of duty (by a policeman or other law enforcement official). |
| Homicide (felonious) | Manslaughter or murder. |
| Manslaughter (voluntary) | A killing committed intentionally, but without malice, as can happen in fits of passion (arguments in bars or between members of a family). |
| Manslaughter (involuntary) | An unintentional killing done through negligence, as happens when a drunken driver runs over someone. |
| Murder (first degree) | The malicious and premeditated killing of one person by another, as is the case with all assassinations and gangland executions. |
| Murder (second degree) | Maliciously killing someone, but without premeditation, as can happen during street fights or robberies. |
| Rape (forcible) | Forcing someone to have sexual intercourse, almost always with the use or threat of violence. |
| Rape (statutory) | Having sexual intercourse with a female who is under legal age, even though she consents. |
| Robbery | Taking someone's property through fear or the use of force. It can also be a crime against property, as happens when a safe is robbed. |

## Crimes Against Property

| | |
|---|---|
| Embezzlement | Illegally taking money or property entrusted by others, as happens when a corporate official dips into the firm's bank account, perhaps to bet on horses or repay personal debts. |
| Extortion | Taking someone's money or property with his consent, but through the use of fear: blackmail is an obvious example. |
| Forgery | Illegally altering or creating a piece of writing (usually a check) for profit. |
| Larceny (grand) | Major theft of money or other possessions. The minimum amount varies among states. |
| Larceny (petty) | Minor theft, which, again, varies in amount from one state to another. |
| Malicious mischief | The deliberate destruction or defacing of property (usually personal) or the killing of animals. |
| Receiving stolen goods | Taking possession of goods obtained illegally, either for sale or concealment. This is what the renowned "fence" does. |

## Crimes Against Habitation

| | |
|---|---|
| Arson | The malicious burning of a building or other structure, including one's own, which is usually done in order to collect fire insurance. |
| Burglary | Illegally entering a building in order to commit a felony. |

## Crimes Against Morality and Decency

| | |
|---|---|
| Adultery | Sexual relations by a married person with someone he or she is not married to. |

| | |
|---|---|
| Bigamy | Marrying a second time (or several times) with the knowledge that the first marriage is still in effect. |
| Contributing to the delinquency of a minor | Causing, inducing, or helping someone under legal age to break the law. |
| Fornication | Sexual relations between persons who are not married. |
| Incest | Sexual relations between persons who are so closely related that they are legally forbidden to marry, as for example, between a father and his daughter or between a brother and his sister. |
| Indecency | Any act, generally committed in public, which is taken to be disgusting or morally offensive. Being underdressed (or undressed) in public is an example. |
| Miscegenation | Illegal marriage between persons of different races. |
| Obscenity | Anything taken to corrupt public morals because it is indecent or lewd. The publication of photographs showing persons having sex is an example. |
| Prostitution | Sexual relations by a man or a woman for profit. |
| Seduction | Getting someone (almost always a woman) to have sex through persuasion or deception, but without the use of force. |
| Sodomy | Sexual relations done in "unnatural" ways between two or more persons or between a person and an animal (a horse, for example). |

## Crimes Against the Public Peace

| | |
|---|---|
| Affray | A public fight between two or more persons that terrifies everyone not participating. |

| | |
|---|---|
| Disorderly conduct | Any behavior forbidden by law. This can mean almost anything—talking too loudly in a public place or drinking beer in a park, for example—and is therefore a favorite catchall for making street arrests. |
| Disturbing the peace | Interrupting or adversely affecting the good order of the community, usually by making too much noise. |
| Gambling | Betting on the result of games or events (usually in sports) in which the bettors have little or no control. |
| Riot | An unlawful assembly of persons who are acting tumultuously or violently and who may be endangering life or property. |

## Crimes Against Justice and Authority

| | |
|---|---|
| Bribery | Illegally paying with money, goods, or services anyone involved in the administration of justice, government officials, witnesses, or voters to act contrary to duty or dishonestly. |
| Compounding a felony | The victim of a felonious crime agrees not to prosecute the person who committed the crime on condition that reparations are made. |
| Conspiracy | Agreement between two or more persons to commit a crime—to conspire against the law. |
| Contempt of court | Deliberately disregarding a court order, making a disturbance in the courtroom, or doing anything that can erode the authority of a court. |
| Counterfeiting | Making an imitation of something—almost always paper currency or securities —with the intent to defraud. |
| Obstruction of justice | Impeding the law in any way. Here's another catchall, occasionally used to |

harass. Resisting arrest is in this category, but so is refusal to aid an arresting officer, or even talking back to one in a way he interprets as being insulting or demeaning. Treat this charge warily.

Perjury     Deliberately giving false testimony under oath.

Subornation of perjury  Getting someone to commit perjury.

## Crimes Against Safety, Health, and Comfort

These include the whole range of public nuisance laws, traffic regulations, health regulations (landlords not keeping their buildings clean), food and drug laws (inaccurate labeling), safety regulations for the use of explosives, public and private transportation vehicles, marked exits in theaters, availability of fire extinguishers, properly checked elevators, and so on.

## FIRE

For reasons that are not really understood, very many people are fascinated by fire, and the bigger the better. Perhaps this relates to man's other self-destructive impulses as a kind of cleansing and purging tool. Whatever the reason, though, big fires attract big audiences both at the scene and in the news. They can be very important because they often combine heavy property damage with injury or loss of life.

Generally, those three elements—death toll, injuries, and property damage—start the story, along with the name and description of what burned. They don't all have to go into the lead, but all should be way up there, and are followed (in whatever order is most appropriate) by: likely causes acts of escape or heroism, number of firemen and pieces of equipment, a chronological account of the fire (when it started, when its climax came, and when it was declared to be out), the owner of the property, and any human interest angle. Again, the order in which the facts are given varies as much as the circumstances, so you don't have to wed yourself to any pat formula. Let's burn down Stanley's department store ("Significant Savings for Sensible Shoppers") and start the story from a few different angles.

Each of the following openings represents a different approach based on a different news element. Since death, injury, and the destruction of the store are judged to belong in the first graf, an immediate dual lead is selected, with human and property destruction put in separate grafs for clarity. And having noted at the end of the lead that the $3 million store was destroyed, the writer opens the second graf by returning to the victims, which is more compelling. He then keeps the parallel structure intact by closing the second graf with more detail about the store—that is, where and how the fire started.

An immediate single lead, reporting that Stanley's burned down and giving the probable cause of the fire, is used in the second version because there was no loss of life and injuries were slight (both factors are noted high in the story to satisfy reader curiosity). Since the second version is pegged on property loss, not death and injury, reference to the loss of merchandise is put in higher than it would have been in the first version.

In the third version, a fireman has died, and that one fatality, again, is more important than the loss of the store. Death again opens an immediate dual lead and destruction closes it. The fireman is not named in the lead because of space limitations, but he *is* named in the beginning of the second graf, and is referred to again in the fourth. This version would, of course, go on to give information about him and his family and would probably run with a supplementary obit in the same edition.

> Sixteen customers were killed and at least 60 were injured yesterday when fire spread through Stanley's. The department store, valued at about $3 million, was destroyed.
>
> All of the dead and most of the injured were trapped in the basement, which is where the blaze started, according to fire officials at the scene. They said that a cigarette discarded among the piles of fabric, linens, or clothing was the probable cause.
>
> The fire began at about 10:15 a.m. and quickly spread upward to the main floor, where hundreds of other customers began fleeing in what witnesses described as panic.
>
> The first fire unit arrived at 10:29, but it was too late to

help many of those caught in the basement, despite repeated efforts by firemen to penetrate the smoke and bring out customers.

or

Stanley's department store burned to the ground yesterday, apparently because of a carelessly tossed cigarette in the basement.

There was no loss of life, but 14 customers and three firemen were treated for smoke inhalation at St. Luke's Hospital and released.

The building was valued at $3 million and contained an estimated $2 million more in merchandise, according to Stanley Robinson, the president.

The fire, which began in the basement at about 10:15 a.m., quickly spread to the main floor. There was no panic as customers hurriedly left the building.

Fire officials said that there was evidence that a cigarette ignited fabric, linens, or clothing piled in the basement and that . . . .

or

An Osmonton fireman was killed by falling debris yesterday as he tried to rescue customers trapped in a fire in Stanley's basement. The blaze destroyed the building.

Matthew Goodrich, 24, was one of about 50 area firemen who responded to the fire, which began in the store's basement at about 10:15 a.m. He was the only fatality. Hundreds of customers left by climbing up fire stairs and through the building's 12 exits.

The building was estimated to be worth about $3 million and to have had another $2 million in merchandise. The fire is thought to have been caused by a carelessly tossed cigarette.

Goodrich, who had been a fireman for only a year, was among the first to reach the scene at 10:29. He . . . .

The store's location was not given only because it is assumed to be so well known that providing that information is unnecessary, which is usually the case in relatively small communities. Otherwise, always put in the location, as well as any damage to neighboring buildings. Notice, too, that an official gave the apparent cause of the fire (he would later have been named). Don't take it upon yourself to determine why a fire starts. Most fire departments have inspectors or other specialists whose job it is to sift through the rubble in order to get that information. They always think about arson, which, in turn, usually leads to a very large insurance policy.

You can collect plenty of factual material from fire officials (chiefs, inspectors, or battalion commanders), from policemen, and from hospital officials. You can also usually get good color material from survivors and witnesses but, as is the case with others kinds of public safety stories, don't misuse your sources. A survivor is excellent for providing descriptive detail on what it was like inside the department store after the fire was discovered, but he or she is probably not reliable for information on the cause of the fire, and is definitely unreliable for fire-fighting information and the events of the fire as a whole.

Where arson is suspected, fire officials usually say that they are looking into such a possibility, and that they will not know for certain for a couple of days or more. Since an arson investigation is no less a detective job than trying to solve a robbery, they are telling the truth. All you can do then, of course, is to report the fact that arson is one of the possibilities being investigated. Having been told that your source suspects arson, or that it is a possibility, you then want to find out: (1) who, if any, the suspects are (which is usually answered with, "It could have been anybody."), and (2) when the fire department expects to know, one way or another. If you're told that they ought to know by Wednesday, call them on Tuesday— follow up. For major fires in which lives are lost, and especially those taking place in public buildings (theaters, department stores, stadiums, office buildings) or in apartment houses, routinely question firemen about the adequacy of safety precautions: fire escapes, exits, sprinklers, frequency of fire drills, availability of extinguishers, and locations of call boxes.

### Gutted.

It means that the contents have been removed or destroyed. It is also far and away the most overworked word in fire stories. A six-story building is not gutted because three or four of its floors have had a fire. It is gutted only if there is nothing left standing but the walls. And if that happens, why not say that there was nothing left standing but the walls?

# chapter seventeen

# MAJOR ACCIDENTS

There is no qualifying level of injury, suffering, death, or destruction with which to determine what is, and what is not, a major accident. A thumb smashed by a hammer amounts to a major accident when it is *your* thumb. This ought to be kept in mind when interviewing accident victims and their loved ones. They feel the suffering infinitely more than you and I can. Trying to empathize with them—to plumb the depths of their anguish, not just for the story, but for the emotional and intellectual growth it affords—provides one of the better possibilities for the development of the sensitive reporter-writer.

Major accidents (as opposed to weather calamities and other natural disasters) always involve machines or things made by machines. That's because machines and their products are everywhere in our society, because people have become increasingly dependent on them, and because the machines are being used by increasingly large numbers of people at the same time. Most machine accidents, in turn, have to do with transportation—movement—at high speed. Transportation machines that crash at high speed force metal against muscle with great violence. The metal, however twisted or burned, always wins.

A bad highway accident or, less frequently, an airplane crash, usually gives the beginning reporter his or her first experience with gore. And because of the suddenness of accidents there is no preparation, no mental conditioning, possible. It almost always happens in about the same way. You're sitting in the newsroom, chatting with a colleague or thinking about how to get into a story on bugles, when the city editor looks up at you and says: "There's a bad crash on Rt. 41 near the Magnolia Mall. They're calling for three ambulances." It's just like that.

Ten minutes later, you're pulled off to the side of Rt. 41 near the Magnolia Mall. What you see is a car turned over, wheels up, another on its side many yards away, and a third with its front smashed in. There are police cars, ambulances, and a rescue unit. Traffic in the opposite direction is crawling; there are intent faces in every car. There is a lot of broken glass on the road, and oil, and you smell gasoline. You also see the victims. A woman, laid out on the grass, is being treated by a medic while a state trooper looks on. She stares at the sky and says nothing because she is in shock. Her husband is in the car with the smashed front, another state trooper tells you, and they're trying to get him out. The trooper says that a medic told him that the man is cut in half. So you look over there. Your curiosity makes you look, but your sensibility keeps you from looking too closely, so you're content to see rescue workers trying to pry open the door. A stretcher goes by with a body that is completely covered by a sheet spattered red. Now you notice that they're pulling another one out of the car that's turned upside down. Your first thought is to walk over for a closer look. But you don't. You tell yourself that a closer look isn't really necessary. In fact, you're afraid to go over there. While you stare at his broken face, with its dark bruises and smears of blood, you begin to steel yourself. You tell yourself, as they lay his limp body on another stretcher, that you're tough. You try to pretend that you've seen it all before, that it's strictly routine. But it isn't routine at all. No matter what anyone says, it will never get to be routine so long as you maintain the sensitivity necessary for your work.

Theories abound on how to cope with the sight of victims at serious accidents. Some say that it's best to pretend that they were always that way; that if they had never lived, they couldn't have died, so there is no tragedy. Others try to work up an anger at whoever was responsible for the accident—a kind of "serves you right" approach. Still others get philosophical. They keep telling themselves that life and death are inseparable and that what they see is simply the way of the cosmos. I used another method. I'd tell myself how immensely relieved I was that it had not happened to me. That is not to say that I wasn't sorry it had happened, but only that, given the fact that it *had* happened, I had not been the victim. I was still alive, and with others around who were not alive, that fact became cause for a certain deep relief—in fact, for celebration. But nothing really works. If you feel sick at the scene of a bad accident, you at least have one great consolation—you're human. That is a strength in reporting, not a weakness.

## HIGHWAYS

Here is a checklist for road accident stories:

1. Exact location. This means the street or intersection in the city and a meaningful spot on the highway (Rt. 95, a mile south of exit 38W; Lee Highway, opposite the Europa Arcade at Staunton).

2. Time. This generally comes from the police. It ought to be accurate to within 10 minutes of the accident, and remember that the official "approximately 5:45" becomes "about 5:45."

3. Cause. This, too, comes from the police. Major accident stories are often helped by eyewitness accounts, but that's exactly what they are—descriptions of how it looked to bystanders. Only the police are trained and equipped to determine how the accident really happened. Theirs is the version you give readers when you write the lead; witnesses' accounts, provided they are credible, support the official account.

4. Vehicles. You want to know how many are involved, what kind they are, and what happened to them. Cars are usually identified by make and type, but the year is unnecessary unless it's an antique, and so is the color: Oldsmobile sedan; Triumph sports car. If a car is demolished (which is rare), say it, but leave out "totally"

because that's redundant. Buses and trucks also take description: a Hermitage High School bus; a Trailways bus; a tractor-trailer; a Yum-Yum Bakery delivery van.

    5. Persons directly involved.
        A. How many and in which vehicles.
        B. Who was driving.
        C. Their names, ages, addresses, and conditions.
        D. Where they have been taken for treatment.
        E. Anything special about them.

    The police will give you some of the information, but the rest requires a hospital check, either in person or by telephone. Both the the dead and the injured are almost always taken to the Emergency Room (ER), where there is a supervisory nurse on duty around the clock. She has what you want: confirmation of the names, ages, and addresses you got from the police, and the victims' conditions. DOA means Dead On Arrival; as with other code, spell it out. Generally, patients are assigned one of five rather imprecise conditions: good, fair, satisfactory, serious, or critical. "Stable," which you will sometimes hear, means a great deal to the doctors who are treating the patient, but it means nothing to those who don't know the condition in which stabilization takes place. You can stabilize with a broken toe or at the brink of death. Don't use it without a description of the patient's injuries. Except in stories about well-known persons, it is not necessary to detail injuries, but a general condition has to go with each patient. Readers want to know what's happening to the survivors of the accident. Tell them, but don't make the diagnosis yourself: "Lefcourt was listed in serious condition." That "listed" is taken to mean that he was listed in serious condition by the hospital, not by you.

    Special, or so-called human interest, angles usually concern the victim's profession, circumstances of the accident, or particular irony: they were returning from a picnic; she was celebrating a promotion; he is the father of eight. Incidentally, since it's unlikely that he is the father of eight baboons or alligators, reference to "children" is unnecessary: "the father of eight" suffices. If the eight are adults, reference to his being a father is superfluous.

6. The effect, if any, on traffic. Many readers or listeners who were caught in the jam that resulted from the accident want to know what happened, and so do those who were home or in the office waiting for them.

7. Ask the police whether charges are going to be placed against anyone involved. If they are, follow through by checking the book or the arrest form. If the police say they plan to charge someone who has been taken to the hospital for treatment, write it that way, being sure to list the charge or charges exactly as given to you *and* the full name and rank of the officer who told you.

Here is a typical major highway accident story:

> Five persons were killed and six others were injured late last night when two cars loaded with vacationers collided in fog on the Chesapeake Freeway two miles east of Dover.
>
> One of the cars, a Chrysler with Ohio plates, somehow got into the southbound lane, according to police at the scene, and collided with a Maryland-registered Cadillac. Two persons in the Chrysler and three in the Cadillac died instantly, police said.
>
> The accident happened at about 11:20, just after both cars sped into one of the patches of fog that often appear suddenly along the highway at night.
>
> The accident scene, bathed in milky yellow light from a nearby lamppost, showed clearly that the Ohio car had been going in the wrong direction and that both vehicles had been moving fast when they collided.
>
> Bodies, luggage, and pieces of metal and glass were scattered across the north and southbound lanes and on the grass in the median.
>
> The injured, three of them from Maryland and three from Ohio, were taken to Bay Memorial Hospital at Sea Beach. All were listed in serious or critical condition.
>
> "Judging by the disposition of the vehicles and the fragment area, I'd say that they were traveling in excess of 75 miles an hour," said Sgt. Jason Collins, a state trooper, as he looked around.
>
> "That's a combined impact speed of about 150 miles an hour," he added, shaking his head slowly. "You don't stand a chance of walking away from anything like that."

The dead, who were also taken to Bay Memorial, were listed as:

Francine Jefferson, 25, of Cumberland, Henry S. Powell, also 25 and from Cumberland, Doris Ames, 20, of Silver Spring, Nelson Tubbmann, 52, and his wife, Stella, 49, both of Columbus, Ohio.

Those in critical condition were listed as:

Melvin Tolliver, 28, and his wife, Elizabeth, 27, of Cumberland, Janice Hopkins, 24, of Baltimore, and Stephen Tubbmann, 22, a son of Mr. and Mrs. Tubbmann.

Two other Tubbmann children, Phoebe, 17, and Harold, 16, were listed in serious condition.

The Tubbmanns were apparently on their way to New York City from Florida. The six Marylanders were on their way to Florida, according to members of their families who were reached last night.

Note how the description of the scene—the yellow light, scattered luggage, and so forth—and the quotes from trooper Collins make the story more immediate than it could have been without them. Incidentally, tempting adjectives like "eerie yellow light" or "grotesque scene" weren't necessary. Straight narrative did the job. When the reporter learned that one of the cars was going to Florida, and that the other was coming from there—fun-filled Florida—he found it ironic enough to use as a snapper. Note, too, that Maryland locations are not identified with their state, while Columbus takes Ohio. You can tell from this that the story was written for publication in Maryland, where readers would be expected to know that Cumberland, Silver Spring, Dover, Sea Beach, and Baltimore are in their state. They would not be expected to know that Columbus is in Ohio, however, so it was explained for them. (No, Marylanders are not ignorant: there are also Columbuses in Georgia, Indiana, Kansas, Mississippi, Nebraska, New Mexico, North Dakota, Texas, and Wisconsin.)

## AVIATION

Here, too, there are official accounts and those of witnesses, but with a significant difference. Since airliners are very technical and complicated contraptions, you are more dependent on official accounts of what happened before a crash than you are when reporting highway accidents. Aviation people and their equipment inhabit a world of thrust-to-weight ratios, sink rates, Instrument Flight Rules, separations, alternate runways, patterns, climbouts, flap angles, crabbing, and a great deal more. If Harold Beemis, ordinary citizen, had been standing on the median near where our two-car collision happened, he would have been perfectly capable of telling you that "One of them was going in the wrong direction and they were both going too fast." But there's no way that Harold is going to be able to tell you why an airliner crashes while trying to land, even if he's standing on the side of the runway and sees an engine on fire. Of course the engine was on fire, but (1) *Why* was it on fire? and (2) Was that burning engine really responsible for the crash? Don't ask Harold; he doesn't know.

The responsible officials won't know on that first day, either, but they can make better guesses than Harold can. When an airliner crashes on takeoff or while attempting to land (both situations account for a relatively large number of accidents—there's almost no problem flying high and straight), the best people to question, in order, are: (1) the control tower operators who visually and verbally monitor all air traffic around the airport; (2) the airport administrators who are supposed to keep track of what's going on at and around the place; (3) the Federal Aviation Administration, which is responsible for aviation safety in the United States; (4) any pilots who were in the air at the time of the crash and who therefore might have heard communication between the pilot who crashed and the tower. Airline officials that first day rarely know more than their passengers, not because they don't care, but because following the minute-by-minute progress of their companies' planes is not their job. You should ask every official you can find about the probable cause because your readers ought to be told, but don't get your hopes up, since the answer will most likely be six months or more in coming.

The answer will come from the National Transportation Safety Board, a Washington-headquartered federal body with regional offices, which is empowered by law to investigate all air crashes. NTSB investigators are usually at the scene of a crash, looking for clues, while the wreckage is still smoldering. The best clues are almost always found in the plane's flight recorder, which keeps track of all maneuvers, and its voice recorder, which contains the crew's cockpit conversation. If the recorders don't provide the answer, every piece of debris—every nut, bolt, cable, and turbine blade—can be put back together like a giant puzzle in order to try to find out what went wrong. Examination of the recorders, collecting other evidence and taking testimony, or reassembling the whole plane, takes months, which is why there will not be an immediate ruling on the cause of the accident. Meanwhile, as usual, you go with what you have.

Here is the core of information you will need:

1. Time and exact location of the crash.

2. Name of the airline, type of plane, its flight number, where it was coming from, when it was due to land, and its final destination.

3. Number of passengers and crew, and how many were:
  A. Killed.
  B. Injured.
  C. Unharmed.

4. Where the dead and injured were taken and details of the rescue.

5. Obvious circumstances of the crash (collision with another plane, foul weather, failure to make it off the runway, or whatever).

6. Whether the airport was closed because of the crash and, if so, where other planes were diverted to.

You will also want a passenger list and eyewitness accounts, including those of passengers. The passenger list will probably not be immediately available, since airlines need time in which to get that information together, so it will likely go into the second-day story (see below). Meanwhile, get as many passenger names as you can, along with their professions, from airline officials at the scene. If someone who is noteworthy was on the plane, you will want to get that high in the story.

Eyewitness accounts are important, not only for use in establishing what *apparently* happened, but for getting the human dimension into the story. Within the bounds of taste and reason, survivors can be quoted for the apparent cause of the accident, but remember that those inside a plane are aware of less than those on the ground who are watching it. Both of the following would be acceptable:

"I could see the airport lights as the plane banked to come in, and I saw a radio tower as high as we were, too. I think we hit the tower."

"I was looking out of the window when, suddenly, the outside engine burst into flames and we just dropped like a rock."

The following is not acceptable:

"The pilot, copilot, and stewardesses are absolute screwballs. I could tell that as soon as I got on at St. Louis."

## THE NEW LEAD AND SECOND-DAY STORY

Because a major air crash amounts to a story that is continuously changing as new information comes in and, in fact, may continue for a couple of days or more, it is updated as often as is necessary. Stories are updated on any given day by writing new leads to replace the old ones. This can happen four, five, or more times in a single day. What follows uses an air crash for a model, but understand that new leads and second-day stories are used whenever necessary for *any* kind of story: bank robbers holding hostages, a kidnapping, a flood or other natural disaster. It is therefore important that you thoroughly grasp the workings of the new lead and second-day story.

If we were to write a story about a major air crash, we would probably slug it AIRCRASH, and it might start something like this (we're reporting in Washington, D.C.):

An American Airlines Boeing 727 carrying at least 90 passengers and a crew of 10 crashed while landing at National

Airport here this afternoon, killing at least 50 persons on board and injuring many others.

The three-engine jet, which left Chicago at noon as Flight 66, was seen to approach the runway at a very steep angle. It hit hard, exploded in flames, and broke apart, according to witnesses.

Weather conditions at the time of the crash, 1:10 p.m., were excellent and control tower operators at National said that visibility was virtually unlimited.

Takeoffs from National were immediately suspended and incoming flights were diverted to Dulles International Airport in Virginia and to Friendship International outside Baltimore.

The Federal Aviation Administration, which operates National Airport and sets aviation industry safety standards, was at a loss to explain the reason for the crash.

Many persons around the airport had a good view of the jetliner as it approached, however, and they seemed to agree that it came in very steeply and hit the runway hard.

"For some reason, I looked up at that one, and saw immediately that it wasn't landing smoothly like the others," said Michael Torrens, who was fishing from his small boat in the nearby Potomac. "It came down like a rock and blew up as soon as it hit the runway."

Now, we've sent that and a couple more takes that further describe the scene, rescue efforts, and where the victims were taken, to the editor for processing. Then we call American Airlines (again) to find out whether the passenger list is available, since we will want to run it as a separate box accompanying the main story and sidebars (which other reporters are putting together). Our source at American Airlines tells us that the full list is not yet ready, but that there have been a few developments that we might find interesting: (1) there were 98 passengers, 76 of whom were killed, along with all 10 crew members, making a total of 86, not "at least 50" as first reported; (2) one of the dead passengers has been identified as Julius Burnside, the Mayor of Chicago, and (3) this was the worst air crash in National Airport's history. "Interesting" isn't the word for it. We say thank you.

Then we make a long-distance call to Burnside's office and are told that he was, indeed, on Flight 66. Why was he coming to Washington? we ask. We are told. Next, we call the Federal Aviation

Administration office at National and ask a source there whether this crash was the worst in the airport's history. It was. There is no point in calling anyone for verification of the number of fatalities because we know that the airline is in the best position to know that and, if anything, its spokesman would want to minimize the number of victims, not maximize it.

The new information is sufficiently important to justify starting the story all over again—to write a new lead which might go a take or more. We tell the editor what we've got and that a new lead is on the way, slugged NEW LEAD AIRCRASH:

> An American Airlines jet carrying 98 passengers, one of whom was Mayor Julius Burnside of Chicago, crashed while landing at National Airport here this afternoon, killing 86 persons, including Burnside and the plane's crew.
>
> It was the worst air crash in the history of National Airport, according to the Federal Aviation Administration, which operates the facility.
>
> END NEW LEAD AIRCRASH AND PICKUP
> GRAF 2 AIRCRASH BEG: The big three-engine . . . .

The reference to the plane's being a Boeing 727 was taken out because Burnside went in—there wasn't space enough for both. The plane will be correctly identified at some likely place deeper in the story.

Notice that the editing and typesetting instructions at the end of the new lead are explicit: they are typed upper case to be easily seen, say that the new lead ends right there, and tell those working on the story that the original lead picks up with the second graf, beginning. . . . The original lead will be killed; it has been replaced. We don't have to replace the old copy, graf for graf, either. We could have written, say, a five-graf new lead to replace the first two of the original lead. We in fact could have written a *five-take* new lead had there been enough new material to warrant it, with successive takes appropriately numbered: NEW LEAD AIRCRASH, NEW LEAD AIRCRASH—2, and so on. The next new lead is: 2ND NEW LEAD AIRCRASH.

But we're not finished. We can't possibly report that the Mayor of Chicago died in a plane crash at Washington National Airport without explaining what he was doing there. This calls for an insert that is one or more grafs long, *typed* on a separate piece of copy paper, and clearly labeled: INSERT A AIRCRASH (not NEW LEAD AIRCRASH because it is going to be inserted in the body of the original story):

AFTER GRAF 5 AIRCRASH ENDING: . . . reason for the crash.
INSERT:

Mayor Burnside was coming to Washington to ask for federal funds to supplement public transportation costs in Chicago. He said last week that the recent transportation strike settlement there was financially "untenable."

He was to meet tomorrow with congressmen and Department of Transportation officials to explore some form of aid, according to Donald S. Black, an assistant to Burnside who was reached in Chicago by telephone.

END INSERT A AIRCRASH AND PICK UP
GRAF 6 BEG.: Many persons around the . . .

In reality, not only would the graf numbers be put in, but for clarity's sake, so would the take numbers (TAKE 2, GRAF 5). It wasn't done here to avoid confusion, since you're reading this in a book, not as separate sheets of paper. Inserts are given consecutive letters, not numbers, so they don't get confused with takes.

Things are moving. While we are making more calls for additional information about the actual crash, other reporters have been given sidebars to do: the rescue operation (RESCUE); the scene at the hospital where the dead and injured were taken (HOSPITAL); a description of the overall scene at the crash site (MOOD), and interviews with air traffic controllers and other officials for possible causes of the accident (FAA). A careful look at the clips has also shown that other 727s have crashed while approaching Dulles International, New York's JFK, and airports at Chicago, Cincinnati, Salt Lake City, and Tokyo. A reporter is therefore working on a story slugged BOEING, and is calling company and other industry sources to find out whether there is a thread—mechanical or human—common to all the crashes. Finally, someone has called Chicago and pulled all of the clips on Julius Burnside and is writing his supplementary obit:

Mayor Julius Peabody Burnside, who was killed in the air crash at National Airport today, may not have been Chicago's most loved mayor, but he was by all odds one of its toughest. He was 68 years old.

On hearing of his death, city administrators and many of his close Democratic cronies said that his likes would probably never again be seen in a major American city. It is truly, one said, the "Last Hurrah."

It is now the second day. The air crash story is still being pursued, but from different angles. We have a full passenger and crew list, which will go into the newspaper in alphabetical order and with a city or town beside each name. We also have an update on the fatalities, since four more died in the hospital during the night, bringing the total to 90. We have an interview with Chief Petty Officer Robert Crowder, who was aboard Flight 66 when it crashed. Crowder was returning to his assignment at the Pentagon after visiting his mother in Chicago. He was thrown clear on impact, sailed at least 75 yards onto the grass beside runway 18–36, and walked away with a broken left thumb and "a Sunday morning headache." (It happens.)

The main piece, which will wrap up the hardest remaining news elements, will also go on page one as a second-day story. This type of story is a continuation, though fresher, of the previous one. The trick in writing it is to introduce the new information while getting in enough of the background so that the new stuff makes sense. On the one hand, then, it has to be sufficiently self-contained so that it can stand alone, but on the other, it can't repeat too much of the first story, because that's no longer news. We therefore have to sneak in the background material in such a way that it helps the story, not detracts from it:

The number of deaths resulting from yesterday's jetliner crash at National Airport climbed to 90 last night as federal investigators sought a reason for the worst accident in the facility's history.

The four additional deaths, all of them at St. Elizabeth's Hospital, were attributed to severe burns inflicted when the American Airlines 727 slammed onto runway 18–36 and exploded in flames. The plane had taken off from Chicago about an hour earlier with 98 passengers and a crew of 10.

A team of investigators from the National Transportation Safety Board (NTSB) worked through the night to find any clue that might explain the cause of the accident. The NTSB, which is headquartered here, is responsible for trying to determine the cause of all air crashes in the United States.

Working under gasoline-generated floodlights, 14 investigators carefully picked their way through the charred debris searching for the plane's flight and voice recorders, which record maneuvers and conversation in the cockpit.

"There's no way of telling exactly what happened," said Dexter Foss, one of the NTSB's on-sight team. "It could have been engine failure, or structural failure, or pilot error, or a sudden gust of wind, or anything. You don't know until you put all the pieces together.

"If it was engine failure, then you want to know why that engine or engines failed," Foss added as the eastern sky began to lighten. "Maybe birds were ingested. There are a lot of birds around here."

Flights in and out of National were resumed at 11:33 last night, with some of the planes taking off 100 feet or so above the investigators, the floodlights, and the wreckage.

One of the departing pilots, Capt. Arven Adams of United Airlines, said that the runway's closeness to the Potomac might have been a factor, since pilots are sometimes forced to approach the runway from the south at relatively high altitude, rather than risk hitting the jetty.

A third-day story, and a fourth or fifth, would follow this general structure. Again, the idea is to get in the necessary background as unobtrusively as possible. That's why the four burn deaths (whose names would have appeared further into the story) were used to get in the fact that the plane exploded and burst into flames.

As with any accident, don't take it upon yourself to establish the cause. That crash would cause millions of dollars' worth of insurance claims and possibly lawsuits. The situation would therefore be very sensitive, not only for those who wanted to collect insurance or sue, but for the airline, the plane and engine manufacturers, the airport, the pilots' union, the traffic controllers, the FAA, and everyone else who was involved. Get what you need from those who are in a position to know and you'll seldom, if ever, go wrong.

Most other serious transportation accidents can be handled in ways roughly the same as what we've been doing here. There's no great secret to covering a major subway accident or a ship's sinking, since you always need the same basic information: cause, casualties, location, effects, and so on. In every case, the speed with which you get the information, and the quality of that information, are the factors that determine whether you've done your job effectively. This just as surely applies to water- and gas-main explosions, mine cave-ins, reservoir breaks, nuclear-reactor meltdowns, collapsed buildings and bridges, and other kinds of catastrophes. Although circumstances vary, all follow the same essential form. In each case, you need answers to the same basic questions, so think about applying the accident reportage in this chapter to the possibilities mentioned above. If you were to report that a gas main exploded, for example, one of the things you would want to know would be the length of time the neighborhood was to be without gas. This is precisely what we were doing when we found out that flights into and out of National were suspended for 10 hours and 23 minutes following the crash. The circumstances may vary, then, but the basic approach does not.

In all situations, the most effective reporters are the ones who can get the information they need as quickly and accurately as possible, particularly when there's a sudden, major accident. The great "trick" in this kind of reporting, as in every other kind, is almost ridiculously simple: *Know what you need and know precisely where you can get it quickly.*

# chapter eighteen

# WEATHER AND ITS EFFECTS

Most experienced reporters don't like to do weather stories because they think that every conceivable kind of weather story has been reported and written. They're absolutely right.

It's been raining and snowing on and off for millions of years now, and except for the time of the Ark or when tribes were chased south by advancing ice, it's always been pretty much the same old story:

Thousands of commuters were stranded downtown and widespread flooding occurred throughout the area yesterday afternoon when a sudden thunderstorm dropped six inches of rain in two hours.

There were no reported deaths or injuries, but early estimates put property damage at more than $4 million in the wake of the worst rainstorm in this city's history.

Hundreds of homes and businesses in and around the city were flooded, sewers backed up, and roads were awash by 5 p.m., less than 30 minutes after the start of the downpour. And then it really began to rain.

Gertrude Parsons, a taxi driver, said that she had to abandon
her cab at . . .

Give or take a technical detail or two, change Gertrude's name
and sex and put her in a chariot, and the same story could have been
written in Rome at the time of Caligula. There is nothing really new
or different about high winds, hailstorms, lightning, freezing temperatures, heat waves, or drought. Not only have they been around
forever, but they are likely to continue to be around forever, which
means that they're not unique. Which means that coverage of them
follows a fairly predictable pattern. Which means that they can be
boring to report. Which means that when the city editor stands and
looks around the office during exceptionally bad weather, reporters
begin running to the lunchroom, disappearing behind their desks
to fidget with their shoelaces, or making hurried telephone calls for
stories they abandoned weeks before.

The economists have this old saw: When your neighbor is unemployed, it's a recession; when you're unemployed, it's a depression. The meteorological counterpart might be: When your neighbor gets rained on, it's shower; when you get rained on, it's a storm.
The point is that weather, and especially bad weather, is more important to those it directly affects than to those it doesn't. It has been
said many times on these pages but, here, it has to be said again:
Reporters do not exist in bell jars or closets—they are people who
are affected by the same basic things as are other people. When
they wash the ink off their fingers and go on a camping trip that is
ruined by rain, or have their flight to Europe delayed because of
snow, they, too, want and need to know what has happened. They,
like sports fans, travelers, commuters, farmers and fishermen, and
everyone else, are dependent on the weather. The very fact that
weather is there all the time is the reason it's usually taken for
granted, but that's also the reason it's so important, and particularly
so as people get older and less able to cope with its extremes. Old
people talk about the weather every day, not only because there is
often little else for them to talk about, but because they understand
that an inch of snow can keep them indoors and a rise in humidity
can cripple them with arthritis. It is important to them, and it
should therefore be important to you.

Sooner or later you will get a weather story, almost undoubtedly because of a storm or a blizzard that is happening while you're in the office. Normally, you will be fed wire copy, and will be expected to call the weather service. You will sit there and, every 15 minutes or so, a copy boy or girl will drop the latest AP or UPI story on your desk. You will be expected to spread them all out, sort them by location, integrate them with the latest forecast, and turn the whole thing into a story. This is usually done as a rewrite job. But covering a weather story that way is like covering a battle from a hotel room—it has to come out sterilized.

Go outside and look around. Get wet or scorched with everyone else. It will do wonders for the quality of your writing. Watch the umbrellas being blown inside-out and people leaning into the wind, or wading through snowdrifts, or huddling in doorways, or stripping to their underwear, or pouring water into steaming automobile radiators. If there's flooding, and someone goes by rowing a boat, you will have the human dimension to the story. You will also have it if you're in the city during a snowstorm and see people on skis or snow shoes, or tunneling into or out of their stores. In blistering weather, look for people dangling their feet in fountains, children swimming in rivers or reservoirs, fire hydrants spraying tenement dwellers who can't afford to leave the city, animals that are panting and dizzy from the heat.

Talk to the sufferers. Some years ago a resident of Portland, Maine, was asked what he thought of the five-or-so feet of snow which covered the city for as far as he could see, and which had practically brought all movement to a standstill. He looked around, rubbed his chin, and said in the classic tradition of Maine humor: "Ain't no musquitas. . . ." Push for the quotes that best summarize what has happened and reflect the feelings of those who are caught in the weather.

A story about normal weather is routine and not very interesting. Put in the latest forecast, the mean and hourly temperatures when relevant, the humidity, barometric pressure, wind strength and direction, comparison with record highs and lows for that date and season, and, in hot weather, the THI—the Temperature-Humidity Index. The THI is found by adding wet- and dry-bulb thermometer readings, multiplying that number by 0.4, and adding 15 to the product. When the THI hits 75, the theory goes, half of the population is uncomfortable; when it hits 80, everyone is uncomfortable.

Stories about abnormal weather are, of course, more interesting. They usually take some or all of the elements in the normal story, but those elements have to give way to more pressing news, and they are therefore written lower. The most pressing news in an abnormal weather story concerns: death, injuries, property damage, accidents, transportation problems, and physical description of how the area was generally affected. There also has to be information in the lead about precisely what the weather did, and that information ought to be supported by statistics, particularly when a record has been broken. The statistic—say, 17.5 inches of snow in 24 hours—doesn't have to go in the lead, but it has to be fairly high in the story, since that is basically what the story is about.

Official weather information and prediction come from the National Weather Service of the National Oceanic and Atmospheric Administration (NOAA), which, in turn, is part of the Department of Commerce. In addition to studying and monitoring the environment, making land, sea, and air surveys, preparing nautical and aeronautical charts, and doing other things related to the environment, NOAA, through the National Weather Service, provides a constant barrage of weather information through offices all over the country. NOAA is second to none where keeping statistics is concerned, and the terms it uses for the weather are precise (even if its predictions are often far from so). A storm, for example, is taken to have winds of between 55 and 63 miles an hour, no more, no less. A blizzard must have winds of 35 miles an hour or higher, a temperature of 20°F or lower, and be carrying enough snow so that visibility is reduced to less than a quarter of a mile. There is a list of wind speeds and their definitions at the end of this chapter. Suffice it to say, don't toss the terms around with abandon, because they are used carefully by those in the weather business.

National Weather Service reports—monthly and yearly statistical data, weather just past, its current state, predictions, and advisories —can be gotten either off the press wires or by telephoning the nearest NWS office. But remember that the information should be used as core meteorological data (properly attributed), and not as a complete story in itself. It is, after all, about physical occurrences, not about the people affected by those occurrences.

The general rule: Inform people about elements of the story

which they wouldn't be able to get for themselves simply by looking out of their windows.

> Rochester is mostly underwater today following two days of heavy rain.

That lead is all right, as far as it goes, but, aside from being written in a somewhat pedestrian way, it doesn't tell the inhabitants of Rochester a single thing they can't see for themselves. Its news value is therefore very light.

> Almost 15 inches of rain in two days has caused flooding in Rochester that has left two persons dead and at least $8 million in damage.

There is no way an inhabitant of Rochester who was just looking out of his window could know that: (1) there were almost 15 inches of rain; (2) two persons were killed because of it; and (3) there was at least $8 million in damage. He has therefore been informed.

As you know by now, there is nothing funny about death, injury, or destruction. There is usually nothing funny about inconvenience, either. But that doesn't mean that all weather stories have to read as though they were penned by Edgar Allan Poe and dictated by his celebrated Raven. Look for the lighter elements of the story in the absence of heavy ones.

> Thousands of Peninsula Railroad commuters were subjected to a novel kind of snow-job yesterday when a storm unexpectedly swerved down from Three Rivers, catching them and their beleaguered line unprepared.
> All trains—believe it or not—were late.

Then comes the amount of snow that fell, where it fell, when it started and stopped, how many passengers were inconvenienced, which trains were latest in arriving, and the pandemonium it all caused at Union Station. In there, somewhere appropriate (perhaps after a graf describing the way Union Station looked filled with frustrated commuters), you could allow one or two persons to speak on behalf of all the others:

"I can't say I'm surprised," said Jules Bernstein, an advertising executive who sat on his attaché case and poked angrily at the olive in his martini.

"We have $1 billion worth of weather satellites up in the sky, another $1 billion in computers, and thousands of weathermen. But Mr. Rauch, the president of this alleged railroad, relies on his corns, and this morning his corns evidently told him that it was going to be fair and warmer."

George Rauch, the president of Peninsula, was not available for comment. His secretary said that the railroad uses the same weather data as is used by everyone else—that supplied by the National Weather Service.

Because weather stories are very often ongoing, they are prime candidates for new leads and second- or third-day follow-ups. Here are the beginnings of BLIZZARD, NEW LEAD BLIZZARD, and 2ND NEW LEAD BLIZZARD, written perhaps an hour-and-a-half apart:

Heavy snow driven by winds of up to 55 miles an hour hit the Hartford area late yesterday, bringing traffic to a standstill and closing schools today.

An estimated 11 inches of snow came down between 3:30 and 6:30, according to the National Weather Service, but biting winds pushed most of it into drifts as high as six feet.

Most businesses, heeding heavy-snow warnings that had been in effect since Monday, let employees leave early. There were no reported deaths or injuries.

We then learn that two elderly women have been killed because the roof of their house collapsed under the weight of the snow:

Heavy snow driven by winds of up to 55 miles an hour hit the Hartford area late yesterday, causing at least two deaths and bringing traffic to a standstill.

All schools in the area, public and private, have been ordered closed today.

An estimated 14 inches of snow came down between 3:30 and 8 last night, according to the National Weather Service. Drifts were reported to be as high as eight feet in some areas.

Both of the blizzard's victims were elderly women who lived together near Goodwin Park. They were crushed to death when the roof of their two-story house collapsed under the weight of the snow, police said.

The women were identified as Sandra Keene, 68, and Doris Schwartz, 71, of 106 Fairfield Ave. Both were widows.

Most businesses . . .

Later:

The Hartford area was battered yesterday by a blizzard that took at least five lives and brought traffic to a standstill.

An estimated 16 inches of snow, driven by winds of up to 55 miles an hour, hit the area between 3:30 p.m. and 10:30 p.m. according to the National Weather Service. Drifts were reported to be as high as nine feet in some areas.

Two of the blizzard's victims, both elderly widows who lived together at 106 Fairfield Ave., died when the roof of their house collapsed under the snow. The other three apparently drowned in Wethersfield Cove when their 36-foot cruiser capsized shortly before 10 p.m., police reported.

The widows were identified as Sandra Keene, 68, and Doris Schwartz, 71. They lived alone. The three occupants of the boat had not been identified by late last night, nor was it known whether anyone else had been aboard.

All schools in the Hartford area, public and private, were ordered closed today.

Highway crews worked into the night to . . .

Note that: (1) since it is likely under such circumstances that there will be other deaths, "at least" was used with the number of victims; (2) weather conditions were updated in each version and the verb "battered" was used when it became clear that that was exactly what was happening to Hartford; (3) references to schools being closed and to businesses letting out early (which would have followed) were dropped successively lower because they had to give way to more important news. Here is the beginning of the second-day story:

Hartford area residents spent yesterday digging out from the second-worst blizzard in the city's history, and one which took at least six lives.

Twenty-one inches of snow, driven by winds that reached 55

miles an hour, hit the city between 3:30 p.m. Tuesday and 2 a.m. yesterday, according to the National Weather Service.

Two of the victims died when their roof collapsed under the weight of the snow. Four others, one of whom was discovered yesterday, drowned after their cruiser capsized in Wethersfield Cove.

All schools and many businesses were closed yesterday and many services, including mail delivery, were seriously curtailed.

The city's worst blizzard struck on February 4, 1936. It left 30.4 inches of snow in 16 hours and claimed three lives.

More snow is expected early tomorrow, the National Weather Service predicted late last night.

Heavy drifts effectively closed most streets in Hartford yesterday and limited movement on the Wilbur Cross Highway, Main Street, and Rts. 84 and 91.

"This is the worst pounding this city has taken in my memory," Mayor Gerasi said yesterday morning before he requested emergency aid from the state.

Notice, again, that the most important developments of the first-day story were recapitulated and blended with later developments. Also, having said that the blizzard was the second worst in the city's history, we had to satisfy reader curiosity by telling them about the worst blizzard, though such information ought to be tight enough so that it doesn't get in the way of the news. Those who lived through our blizzard would be understandably curious as to whether conditions were going to improve, or whether the city was going to get hit again, so they have been told. There would be a detailed summary of the National Weather Service forecast further into the story, as well as information on what the city and state were going to do to cope with more snow.

Second-day stories usually lend themselves to lighter, more novel approaches, since the death and destruction is generally taken care of in the first-day story.

The name Dolores comes from the Spanish word for sorrow, and the hurricane of the same name lived up to it here Thursday.

or

It rained for two days and two nights. Then all of the Highway

Department's trucks, and all of its men, tried to put things together again. They could not, though.

For the sake of those of your readers with sensibilities, avoid: water, water, everywhere; any reference to an ark or to a storm that strikes "like lightning" or thunder; all hail (lots of it) to Decatur; when it rains, it pours; it came down dachshunds and angoras (and left poodles on the streets); fog that could be cut with a knife; sidewalks that could be used for frying eggs; God's icebox, and other tripe of that sort.

The almanac has a reasonably good list of meteorological terms and definitions, temperature and precipitation charts for selected cities, weather records, a wind chill table, and such fascinating bits of trivia as the fact that one inch of rainfall on one acre of ground leaves 27,154 gallons of water. Most good-sized newspapers also carry explanatory information about isobars, fronts, high and low pressure systems, and wind direction symbols near the daily weather map and detailed forecast. Below is the list of wind speeds and their definitions.

Wind Force
(In miles an hour)

| | |
|---|---|
| Less than 1 | Calm |
| 1 to 3 | Light air |
| 4 to 7 | Light breeze |
| 8 to 12 | Gentle breeze |
| 13 to 18 | Moderate breeze |
| 19 to 24 | Fresh breeze |
| 25 to 31 | Strong breeze |
| 32 to 38 | Near gale |
| 39 to 46 | Gale |
| 47 to 54 | Strong gale |
| 55 to 63 | Storm |
| 64 to 73 | Violent storm |
| 74 and up | Hurricane |

# chapter nineteen

# SCIENCE AND TECHNOLOGY

The average American high school or college student reacts to practically anything having to do with science pretty much the way he or she would react to being forced to swallow a whole walnut, including the shell. The thought process in either case comes to about the same thing: "If I do this, I'm going to choke and die." That's because he or she equates science with equations:

$$f(x) = (5y_1 + 6y_2)^2 - (3y_1 + 10y_2)^2$$
$$= 16y_1^2 - 64y_2^2$$

Looking at that makes me a little queasy, too. But those letters and numbers are not scientific, they are mathematical, and mathematics is simply a scientific tool. Further, you don't have to be able to understand mathematics in order to appreciate and enjoy science. For starters, then, forget about numbers.

Science is incredibly important, especially to journalists, for at least two reasons. First, as the world continues to technologize, scientists and what they do become increasingly necessary. They are

225

already the new priests. And since what they do is unintelligible to most of us—or so we assume—they are mysterious priests. St. Thomas Aquinas's *pange lingua* has given way to the table of atomic weights. The new icons have names like linear accelerator, electron microscope, light water reactor, and space shuttle. The new churches are called the National Science Foundation, the Jet Propulsion Laboratory, the Center for Advanced Studies, and so on.

Second, the results of the new priests' best efforts are proving to be a mixed blessing. Hydrogen bombs, ICBMs, and other military hardware are obvious examples of dangerous scientific products, but at least we (and those who designed them) knew what they could do from day one. There is a growing list of supposedly benign and helpful items, however, which are turning out to be quite the opposite. DDT, intended to kill agricultural pests, turns out to kill animals and harm humans; estrogen, which was developed to ease menopause problems is thought to induce certain kinds of cancer; birth control pills, designed to help prevent unwanted births, increase the risk of premature death for women over 40 who take them. Every item on the lengthening enemies list was invented by a chemist or other scientist, or is a by-product of something invented by them, in every case to serve mankind: thalidomide, saccharin, monosodium glutamate, sodium cyclamate, Red Dye #2, aldrin-dieldrin, endrin, toxaphene, polychlorinated biphenyls (PCBs), vinyl chloride, fluorocarbons, diethylstilbestrol, and others.

We were informed a while back that we should eat more fish because the cholesterol in meat and eggs is dangerous for our hearts. After our third mouthful of swordfish or sturgeon, we were told that some of those fish contained enough mercury and PCBs, respectively, to be lethal. Mercury and the PCBs are waste from factories that produce things designed or invented by scientists. The answer, they advised, was to drink water and eat more fruits and vegetables. Only some of us began to notice small things waving at us from inside the water glass. We also began to notice that some scientists were saying that fruit and vegetables can be excellent carriers of poisonous pesticides and nitrogen fertilizer. I am waiting for them to tell us that we should eat more meat and eggs.

All this has given some people a severe case of *malaise scientifique*. This is not because scientists are individually untrustworthy, but because there are now so many of them, producing so much, that mistakes are bound to happen, if only because of inadequate testing and failure to explore far-reaching side effects. The people who developed DDT did so with the single-minded (and laudable) purpose of controlling pests and therefore increasing our food supply. The chemical's effect on the ecosphere, if it was considered at all, took second place to solving an immediate problem. Scientists are always hammering away at immediate problems, and they can't be blamed for that, either. Otherwise, little or nothing would be done. But who is looking at the larger picture? Who is going to hold them accountable for *all* of the effects of what they spawn? The press certainly ought to.

In addition to being a legitimate and necessary press function, science reporting can be of great benefit to those who do it, too. First, it forces them to understand how something works, which is good for their reservoir of knowledge. Second, it forces them to reduce the complicated to the simple, which is one of the most difficult, but most important, elements of all serious reporting and writing.

Science reporting, more than any other speciality, concerns codes. But fear not. Every code that has ever been invented can be broken. Further, those who use code are human beings, just like you. They know the code, not through osmosis—*effortless filtration through something*—but because they have put in thousands of hours in medical school, a physics lab, chemistry class, or someplace else, memorizing it. Given the same amount of time, degree of interest, and basic ability, you could, too. Very few scientists are geniuses; the nature of research, in fact, requires that they be intelligent, careful pluggers, not Merlins. And best of all, though you may not believe it, every Latin name, every physical property, every element under the sun and stars, is reducible to plain ole English. Given the fact that none of them were born speaking Latin, or knowing what biochemistry—*the chemistry of living things, as opposed to minerals and other lifeless matter*—is, how could they have learned it, except in their mother tongue? They started, that first day, in English, and it was on English that their codes were built. And it follows from that that their codes can be turned back into English if they really want to do it.

You can get them to break their own codes into simple English by asking them to do so. The best doctors, engineers, and scientists

—those with the most wide-ranging intellects and humanistic instincts—are able to clearly explain what they do in such a way that
an average 12-year-old can understand it:

"The Earth appears to be getting slightly colder."

"Why?"

"Because the circumpolar vortex is expanding more and contracting less."

"What's the circumpolar vortex?"

"It's a very large mass of cold air that covers the top of the planet.
It whirls, like a ballerina's skirt, expanding in winter and contracting
in summer."

That climatologist (one who studies long-range weather patterns
and their effects) has not only answered the question, but has drawn
an analogy that makes the answer easier to understand. What could
be clearer than the picture of a spinning ballerina whose skirt is
whirling and moving up and down?

The analogy is the single most useful tool in science writing aside
from the short, clear, descriptive phrase. Good science writers are
invariably good analogists, which is to say they have excellent imaginations and are capable of reducing the complex to the simple. As I
said, this is a quality all reporters and writers ought to have, but it's
particularly important when dealing with such code as capillary
action. According to my science dictionary, capillary action is "A
general term for phenomena observed in liquids due to unbalanced
inter-molecular attraction at the liquid boundary; e.g., the rise or
depression of liquids in narrow tubes, the formation of films, drops,
bubbles, etc." Hmmm. That seems to mean that when you have two
different substances, and one of them is liquid, the liquid can be
attracted to the other one and move toward it or through it. That,
in fact, is the way trees and other plants feed—nutrients carried by
water go into the roots and move up the trunk or stem. It is also
the way *raw wood soaks up stain.*

Or consider the rocket engine, a formidable piece of very complicated machinery that can weigh a couple of tons and have thousands
of intricately arranged parts. But what, in essence, does a rocket
engine do? It burns fuel, which turns into hot gases, which try to
expand in all directions. But, with the exception of one place, the
gases don't get very far because they run right into the metal walls of
the combustion chamber and bounce back under great pressure.

There is a way out, though, and they take it. They rush through the small hole at the rear of the engine. Before they have found their way through that hole, though, they have managed to exert enough pressure—enough "push"—in the other direction to make the engine, and whatever the engine is in, move forward. As those gases fight to get through that small hole, then, they push the engine in the opposite direction. And that, in essence, is exactly what happens when you drop *a lighted firecracker into a tin can* or release *a toy balloon filled with air*—gases rushing out under pressure make them move in the opposite direction.

The key to thinking in analogies is to loosen up and let your mind wander in likely directions. When possible, and without being flip, draw analogies that will be most familiar to the general reader. Saying that a synchrotron is a kind of circular linear accelerator doesn't really help much, does it? What is a shark? It is a scavenging fish. It is a scavenging fish that can be dangerous. It is, then, a kind of nautical vacuum cleaner with teeth. How good is that new spy satellite, which can get excellent, high-resolution pictures of a Soviet SS-9 missile's warhead? It's obviously very good. It's so good, in fact, that *if rooftop sunbathers could see it coming, they'd probably run for their towels.* That mental picture, of being clearly photographed in the nude from 500 miles up, is much more vivid than can be any reference to an SS-9's warhead or to mobile missile launchers.

Avoid clichés—and particularly any reference to something's being two or three times as long as that cursed football field. . . . The concept of something 200 or 300 yards long is not so difficult to grasp that readers have to have it measured off for them by a football field turning end-over-end two or three times.

Don't write down to readers. Even those who have never had a science course, or who never completed high school, know a little more today about basic science than they did before. In many cases, their knowledge has come while they switched channels to avoid commercials, but it nonetheless is there. It will therefore not come as news to most people that the Earth revolves around the sun, that cancer involves cells and is deadly, that helicopters can fly vertically as well as horizontally (straight up and down as well as forward), snakes are reptiles, microscopes magnify, and that ocean water is salty. Explain the complicated, but leave out the blatantly obvious.

Science and technology are not the same thing, but they are often treated as such, even by scientists. That is because the distinction between basic research and applied research gets blurred. Science in its purest form, has to do with basic, or "pure" research—research for its own sake. Doctors who do basic research in immunology (the body's resistance to disease and infection) simply want to learn what attacks the body and what the body can do to defend itself. Applied research in immunology uses that information to produce specific kinds of chemicals, or other immunological weapons, with which to turn back or destroy specific kinds of attackers. Applied research gets into technology, which is pragmatic and which has to do with the development of "defensive weapons," not with the theory of why they're needed. On an even more basic level: science produces the concept of the sail; technology makes it and puts it on a boat for propulsion.

In either case, but especially where applied science is concerned, the heart of the matter lies in its significance. What is it supposed to accomplish? This question raises the hackles of many pure scientists, who are prone to shoot back: "The *significance* of science is to contribute to knowledge, and even basic research that has no immediate application is valuable because it adds another dimension to mankind." Too true. But the pure scientist's job and the reporter's are not the same. Reporters, including those on science beats, deal with what is newsworthy. They need to find out how a given idea is supposed to affect *people*. That is what the intelligent reader wants to know, and what all readers are entitled to have made available to them. You want to know, then, about its applications and intended effect.

You also want to know—and here's the hardest part—about its likely or possible side effects. What could go wrong, how long will it take to find out, and what will the effect be? Getting the answers to these questions, which is a rarity, is the heart of the science writer's mission because few scientists seem to have the inclination to seriously pursue such matters, and federal regulatory agencies have a record of being very late. The problem exists, I think, because relatively few scientists in or out of government take an interdisciplinary approach—a long look in all directions—at the development and use of new techniques, chemicals, and hardware. Nuclear waste disposal is only one example. Who among the scientists working to develop and improve power reactors during the quarter century immediately after 1945 tried to grapple seriously with the problem of waste disposal? Their attitude, an understandable one, was: My job is to invent better reactors, not worry about the radioactive crud that comes out of them. Not until the mid-1960s did environmentalists begin to challenge nuclear waste–dumping policies, and then to little avail.

Such myopia is understandable. If every scientist took time to consider every conceivable side effect of what he or she was working on, research and development would probably grind to a halt. But someone has to raise such questions. It ought to be the science writer, not simply passing along developments, but pondering their significance and likely consequences.

For interviews:

1. Be prepared. Go not only to the clips, but to the trade or technical journals for a briefing on the basics of the area and an idea of where previous research ended. Make a list of questions, going from the simple to the complicated, and ending with ones about significance and wide consequences.

2. Be as patient with your scientist as you would like him or her to be with you. Some, and they are usually the biggest "names," have a kind of press presence. They know what reporters want and they give it with gusto: good quotes, vivid analogies, dramatic implications. They are outgoing, occasionally funny, and sometimes even solicitous. Others, however, are quite the opposite. They have very low-key personalities, are shy around those who don't understand what they do, and have problems communicating with outsiders. This, of course, has nothing to do with the quality of their work. Adjust the character and pace of the interview accordingly, remembering that the information is there, but that you have to be gentler and a bit more persistent at digging for it.

3. If you don't understand something, say so—six times, if necessary. People, and particularly those with highly technical skills, have more compassion for ignorance than is generally imagined.

The best reporters have been known to lead off with, "This may seem like a dumb question, but . . . " It won't be dumb at all.

4. Raise the analogies right then and there. Not only will inventing them on the spot help you to understand the subject as you go along, but you'll be getting confirmation that they're right to use in the story. If they're good but not excellent analogies (which is almost always the case), say so in the story: It is roughly similar to. . . It works about the same as. . . It is something like. . .

5. Quote accurately. You know by this point that accurate quotation is important in all reporting. But it is especially important in the scientific and technical area, since one wrong word can change the entire meaning of the story. No matter what the discipline of the person you interview, his or her common denominator is, by definition, a degree of precision unmatched anywhere else. Don't compromise it.

6. Get the names of others who might be engaged in the same work and find out, if you haven't already, what agency, body, group, or individual is responsible for monitoring and passing on the work. Anything controversial or doubtful will need to be pursued. In addition, you don't want to credit one person or institution with something that others have also worked on. It is entirely fair to write a story around, say, one scientist's work and also get in the fact that "Similar experiments are being done at . . ."

7. Keep single ideas sufficiently isolated so they don't get mixed up, and put them in the story that way, too—strung out, in logical order, one at a time.

Here is a science story put together for illustrative purposes. Note the use of analogy, selection of quotes, simple style, adequate backgrounding, and perspective.

> That "death ray" pistol used by Buck Rogers in comics and movie serials is here.
> Scientists at the U.S. Army's Weapons Development Center at Fort Bragg, North Carolina, have produced a hand-held weapon

that can fire a laser beam with greater range and accuracy than ordinary pistols.

The weapon, called SPLASH, for Special Laser (Hand-held), can fire a laser beam up to 500 yards with absolute accuracy. Bullet-firing pistols are generally not effective beyond 100 yards.

"Buck's Baby," as the gun has been unofficially named, looks like a round, black liquor bottle and is about the same size. It weighs 3.2 pounds, is connected by a wire in the handle to a back pack, and shoots out of the "spout."

Laser is an acronym for Light Amplification by Simulated Emission of Radiation. A laser device makes coherent radiation, or radiation of a given frequency with all wavefronts in phase, and in very short wave bands. The coherent beam does not diffuse like normal light radiation and therefore can be directed in a highly concentrated form. The beams are made of light particles called photons.

Lasers are widely used in science and industry. They are also being studied for use as larger weapons. Experiments have already shown that they could be used to damage or destroy planes, ships, missiles, or satellites, and can direct bombs with great accuracy.

SPLASH is said by its developers to be the smallest laser weapon in existence, and to have these advantages over ordinary pistols:

• It has more than five times the effective range and shoots in a straight line, as opposed to bullets, which are pulled down by gravity as they move toward the target.

• It has eight times the destructive capability and, at 300 yards, can knock the treads off a tank.

• It makes no sound and gives off no smoke when it is fired, so its user's position is less easily found by the enemy.

• It carries 48 precisely measured "shots," or about seven times as many as a standard automatic pistol.

There are two main disadvantages, though: the back pack weighs 19 pounds—a hefty load to carry into combat—and has to be charged from a special field generator, thereby limiting its mobility. Dr. Anthony Driscoll, SPLASH's project director, is not worried.

"This isn't a weapon that everyone is going to carry, and it will not replace the standard .45 automatic," he said. "It's meant for specialized requirements, such as sniping or bringing down low-flying enemy aircraft.

"There's no reason to kill a fly with a cannon," Dr. Driscoll added. "Standard weapons are going to be around for a long time."

Since laser equipment has been reduced to pistol size, it is probably fair to say that it would easily work for such larger weapons as the guns on fighters and ships. Dr. Driscoll declined to comment on that.

A SPLASH demonstration is eerily similar to what happened in those old Buck Rogers movies. The weapon is pointed at a 55-gallon sand-filled drum that stands 400 yards away. There is no indication that "Buck's Baby" has been fired until the drum explodes in a shower of sand and metal. Close inspection shows that it is nearly cut in half.

What would happen, Dr. Driscoll was asked, if laser pistols got into the hands of criminals?

"That's most unlikely. In the first place, they will be very secure. In the second, you just don't charge them by plugging them into a wall socket. It's complicated," he said.

But what if it happens, regardless of the security, and criminals either get one of the Army's generators (which weigh about 400 pounds and are on wheels) or find some kind of equivalent?

"Then," said Dr. Driscoll, "I would have to say that you would have a potentially serious problem on your hands."

# chapter twenty

# SPORTS

The best and the worst writing in a newspaper, according to honored legend, can be found on the sports pages—often side by side.

For reasons that may never really be understood, sportswriting has attracted a determined cadre of deadbeats, dullards, and hacks, most of whom use multiple adjectives and clichés the way soldiers in the trenches use hand grenades. But it has also yielded Jimmy Cannon, Heywood Broun, and Red Smith, and sent the likes of Ring Lardner, Damon Runyon, Paul Gallico, and James Reston off to fertilize other fields.

In Spain, those who review the performances of matadors are not only paid by the newspapers for which they work, but often by the matadors, too. In America, such blatant bribery is a thing of the past, in no small part because it's unnecessary. There's no reason to pay for something you can get for nothing.

Sportswriting the world over has traditionally drawn those who are compelled to act out their own fantasies, however vicariously, through the athletes they cover. They share that trait, I think, with their brethren who cover show business and write reviews. Although there are signs that a new generation of thinking and questioning sportswriters is beginning to make itself heard, some in the

235

old guard still have the sensibilities of marine lance corporals and the journalistic instincts of pilot fish. They continue to call baseball teams "clubs," which sounds chummy and fun, rather than "companies," which smacks of business and profit. Since many of these reporters want to be the stars they write about, it follows that they tend to see them in heroic dimensions and portray them accordingly. This is certainly true in the United States, and it is only fitting, since the United States is an intensely physical country with muscular roots. The nation was "won" with brawn, reflex, and courage, all tied together with competitive instinct. Or so we have been led to believe. Survival of the fittest. The harrowing epics of wagon trains pushing through Indian country have been written about endlessly. Who, though, has bothered to write about the people who made the wheels for those wagons?

Sports are cherished by Americans for a number of reasons, most of which have been instilled, and all of which have been puffed up, by the most myopic of those who have written about them. They have created an enduring sports mythology.

Sports are inherently democratic: they are the great equalizer for minorities, for the poor, and for the less endowed of all stripes. Relatively few people have the combination of brains and money (both bestowed by God) necessary to go to a good college and become a Nobel physicist. But anyone with enough determination, we have been told, can simply practice running until he can do a mile in 3:53, or knock the "apple" out of the park almost every time. Jackie Robinson and Joe Louis, they say, are obvious examples. That is true. But it also conveniently ignores the pain, humiliation, and eventual exploitation suffered by both of those men, as well as by all their brothers and sisters, as they climb tortuously closer to the top of the white male sanctum. The mythology pays tribute to their all-American guts, but conveniently ignores the equally all-American gauntlet that made such guts necessary.

The corollary of this is that, unlike organic chemistry, Miltonian poetry, and thermodynamics, anyone who bothers to learn the rules can enjoy watching a sport and can understand it. Enjoy it? Certainly. You can enjoy a total eclipse without understanding why it happens. In the same way, you can enjoy a football game if you know why a fourth-and-goal situation is exciting. But you can't completely understand the game unless you also understand that you're watching humans, like yourself, who are under enormous physical, emotional, and mental stress. You can't understand them unless you are able to relate to them in human, not just athletic, terms, for the very simple reason that they are humans first and athletes second.

Finally, most fans, if they think about it at all, assume that athletic competition takes place within a comfortingly finite time frame. A sports event begins and ends like a train trip, by the clock; it doesn't drag on, inconclusively, like relations with Pakistan. If the Yankees have four runs and the Twins have five runs at the end of nine "full" (as opposed to "partial") innings of play, the Twins are the winners. They have shown the universe that they were one run better than their opponents. There is little or nothing to argue about or to question. There is nothing that requires contemplation the next morning. Or so we have been conditioned to think. In fact, no athletic event is ever finite. Each must be prepared for, each has an aftermath that can be physical, psychological, social, emotional, or any combination of them, and each in some way affects the evolving state of the sport. But that's pretty heavy stuff and is better ignored in favor of the old play-by-play, or so some of our sportswriters still seem to think.

Like every other form of human interrelationship, athletic competition is essentially psychological and social, not statistical. It is too often forgotten or ignored by many sportswriters and sportscasters that athletics involves human beings who are held together by exactly the same muscle, sinew and bone that hold you and me together. The greatest athletes have brains the size of ours, emotions and sensibilities like ours, and even blow their noses just like we do. They get hot, cold, angry, stubborn, mean, sick, hungry, and they die, just like you and I. That should be noted. It should provide the framework for sports coverage, I think, because it might help draw the race of man together, not further stratify and divide it. A hockey player who takes an unusual delight in trying to knock out his opponent's teeth not only ought to have that fact put in a story about him, but some serious effort ought to be made to learn why he does it (*really*), why his team encourages it, why officials ignore it until there is blood on the ice and stitches in some young man's head, and why the crowds thrill to it. By probing in such directions the sports reporter may well be able to tell us something about ourselves—all of us—and our addiction to violence and danger. But this hardly ever happens.

Instead, we get questions like these:

"Do you really want to win here today?"

*"No, Mel, I don't. I think losing builds character. . . ."*

"How did it feel to lose this one?"

*"It felt real good. . . ."*

"Do you think you'll improve by next season?"

*"I'd have to say, Mel, that the chances are I'll get worse. . . ."*

"How does it feel to be sidelined with that broken leg?"

*"It feels wonderful: The pain helps keep me awake and I love the daisy my daughter painted on the cast. . . ."*

"What will you do if the Bombers don't make the playoffs?"

*"I'll swallow red-hot razor blades and leave my right arm to the Smithsonian. . . ."*

"What advice would you give to youngsters who want to do what you've done here today?"

*"Chew uppers and wash them down with straight vodka, Mel, that's what they ought to do. . . ."*

"Would you say you're better than McGirk at this point in the season?"

*"McGirk's a slob. . . ."*

"Do you really mean that?"

*"No, I don't, Mel. I just kind of said it. Everybody who knows me knows I never mean what I say. I lie like a rug. . . ."*

"Would you say that this is an important game."

*"Certainly not. . . ."*

"How does it feel to be the best?"

*"Awful. All the magazine stories and TV appearances, the money and fame, have made me an impossible egomaniac. I felt much better when I was a poor, starving nobody. . . ."*

There's more to learn along these lines:

"Why, exactly, do you smash at other players with your stick?"

*"You have to."*

"Then why don't most of the other players do that? Why is it that you and a few others do it all the time and collect most of the penalties? Do you like to hurt opponents?"

*"No, I don't really like to, but it's part of the game. I usually get hit first."'*

"That's not what the game films show, and it's not what the officials see. You seem to start most of the trouble. Why?"

*"The fans like to see it. They come to see a little blood now and then. You know. . . ."*

"And if they didn't get to see some blood, you think they'd stop coming to hockey games?"

*"Sure. They love it."*

"If there was no nasty fighting, and ticket sales dropped, how do you suppose the owners would feel?"

*"They'd feel very unhappy."*

"Do the owners encourage you to draw blood?"

*"Put it this way: They want to win games and pack the house, and anything that accomplishes that is all right with them."*

"What about the opposing players you hurt? How do they feel?"

*"They understand. Some of them do the same thing. I have stitches, too, because they have to do what I do. Like I say, you have to. The first thing you learn in this business is that all the rules aren't in the rule book. . . ."*

Most athletes, I suspect, are smarter than most of those who report about them. The suspicion is not unique. In his book, *Sports-World*, Robert Lipsyte, a former *New York Times* sports reporter and columnist, explains the contempt many athletes feel for the "jocksniffers" who buzz around them like gnats, asking inane questions, slapping backs, and trying to bask in glory they are incapable of earning for themselves. "Many athletes are very sensitive to this," Lipsyte says, "and while they will tolerate—in fact, try to cultivate and exploit—jocksniffers among the press, owners, and well-connected businessmen, they have a very special hatred for people who dehumanize them by making them fantasy objects." Lipsyte was anything but a sports nut as a youngster, so after briefly reporting the way the herd did, he was able to change course and come to see professional sports for what they are—businesses run by people who exploit other people (fans as well as players) for profit, and which have profound, though far from obvious, effects on the national mentality.

"Winning isn't everything, it's the only thing," was the motto of

Richard Nixon's ill-fated reelection committee. And the Nixonians were far from alone. Dwight Eisenhower had his celebrated golf games. John Kennedy played touch football for votes as well as for exercise. Gerald Ford's days as a center on the Michigan football team were carefully resurrected right after he became President. American politicians, businessmen, bureaucrats, and everyone in the military use sportstalk the way Eskimos on dogsleds use "Mush!" —to urge those in harness to pull harder: Don't let the team down. . . . Play the game. . . . Nice guys finish last. . . . Get on the ball. . . . Don't miss your turn at bat. . . . Shape up. . . . Cover all bases. . . . Second-best doesn't count. . . . Don't be a foul ball. . . . Don't be a bonus player. . . . Don't go down swinging. . . . . Don't strike out. . . . Don't be an eight-ball. . . . Pull your weight. . . . Give it the extra effort. . . . Bounce back. . . . Winner takes all. . . .

Sports, like everything else, do not exist in a vacuum. They are inseparably—organically—a part of the human current in which they exist. They at the same time affect the society in which they exist, and are affected by it, in a continuing interchange. If you bear this in mind, and follow a few modest suggestions, you should be able to cover sports in a way that will not only make you proud of the undertaking, but which will produce stories that inform, as well as merely entertain.

### Avoid clichés.

Although colorful phraseology lends itself to colorful activities like sports, and can even enhance coverage, clichés do the opposite where the discerning reader is concerned—after a while, it's like getting a shot of Novocaine in the brain. Train yourself to wince when you think of or hear a cliché or one of those exhausted expressions that are the hallmark of the dedicated dullard.

The Possums crushed the Water Moccasins 48–6 here today before a delirious homecoming crowd of loyal partisans.

The victors were smarting from last week's drubbing by the Alligators and were not to be denied. They needed a big win,

and a convincing one, to stay alive as the race for the championship comes down to the wire and nears its end.

First blood was drawn early in the opening seconds of the
first quarter by Elmo Ryzyski, the blazing bulletback who has
been warming the bench most of the season because of a multiple
concussion he sustained in combat against the Cobra secondary
on Oct. 10. The Possums went on to pound the Cobras with a
decisive 21–12 drubbing.

Ryzyski scooped up the opening kickoff, a long, high, end-over-
end boot, on his own 10-yard stripe and then sailed the distance
for the day's first tally. It came 31 seconds into the first period.
The Moccasin defensive unit knew at that point that they were
in a football game.

With Frank Grogan and Steve Cutler blocking like two slabs
of pure granite, Casper Morris, the standout from Eternal High,
split the uprights for a one-point conversion. It was 7–0 for
Ole Poss.

It was also the beginning of the end for the Water Moccasins
and their junior field general, Bert Higgenbottom, who went into
the one-sided contest hoping to land a berth on the All-State
Eleven.

The Possum safeties, Hank Schramm and Cosmo Nimbus,
dumped Higgenbottom no fewer than 18 times. The Moccasin
Menace was repeatedly upended and forced to eat the pigskin
by the dynamic duo dogging him relentlessly all afternoon.
Schramm and Nimbus came here today to play football. They
had done their homework, too.

The second Possum score came only a minute and a half later
after a costly Moccasin turnover in which Higgenbottom was
nailed on his own 19 by Schramm, who hit him from the blind
side like a battering ram, forcing the sphere loose. It was recovered by Boyce Potter, the Deep Purple's aggressive defensive
end, who emerged from the pileup flaunting his trophy.

It was a costly Moccasin miscarriage, and a serious setback
from which they were not to recover.

Ryzyski, who is usually anything but an aerial artist, called
for a down-and-out to Tyrol Tannenbaum.

With 30,000 frenzied alumni chanting "P-L-A-Y, Possum,"
the intrepid quarterback, his feet planted, looked to the sky.
He shot a flat screen to Tannenbaum, who picked it off in the
coffin corner and plunged onto pay dirt—right on the money.

Onlookers of both persuasions began to sense a rout. So far
as the Water Moccasins were concerned, it was the Little Big
Horn all over again. . . .

This compendium of clichés might strike you as amusing, but if
it does, it's probably because you don't have to read its like four
times every Sunday all fall long, which would be numbing. There
are literally hundreds of clichés in the major sports. Baseball ("the
national pastime,") is infested with them: strafed a line-drive,
knocked out in the fourth, fanned nine batters, picked off or tagged
at the bag, fast-ball artist, emptied or cleaned or cleared or swept the
bases, and others. Like the camp followers who once granted their
favors to soldiers, hack sportswriters ply their trade around hurlers,
keglers, hoopsters, grapplers, matmen, pucksters, anglers, mermaids,
netmen and harriers who fire horsehides, blast pucks, connect for
doubles, boot through the uprights, sink baskets, go to the air, grind
out yardage, or serve with blinding speed.

It doesn't have to be so. The best of the new sports reporters,
such as Paul Zimmerman, Pete Axthelm, Sandy Padwe, and
Larry Merchant, have a command of the mother tongue, are
original, and can be as acerbic as the situation requires. They get
the color into their stories by closely observing those they write
about, and by portraying them cleanly but powerfully. They don't
need to use clichés to mask incompetence.

### Avoid inane or gratuitous questions.

Sports lend themselves to shallow or pointless questions when
they are approached on their simplest or most obvious levels. The
mindless banter that goes on during televised football games and
tennis matches typifies this kind of verbal pollution:

MEL: You've certainly come a long way since Wimbledon,
haven't you?

SALLY: I think I have.

MEL: Are you ready for Forest Hills?

SALLY: Well, the competition this year is going to be real
tough, but I've been working real hard.

| MEL: | On what? |
|------|----------|
| SALLY: | On my serve. |
| MEL: | Very important. Your serve let you down at Wimbledon, didn't it? |
| SALLY: | Yes, it sure did. It let me down. |
| MEL: | How? In what way? |
| SALLY: | Well, that first serve wasn't going in the way it should. You want to get that first serve in there. |
| MEL: | Right. It's very important to get that first serve in there. |
| SALLY: | It wasn't going in there the way it should. |
| MEL: | Why was that? |
| SALLY: | Concentration. I wasn't concentrating enough on the ball. |
| MEL: | Concentration is important in tennis. |
| SALLY: | Right. |
| MEL: | Why weren't you concentrating? |
| SALLY: | Oh . . . |
| MEL: | What was the problem? |
| SALLY: | I was concentrating too much on getting up to the net fast. |
| MEL: | Putting the cart before the horse, huh? |
| SALLY: | Right. That's what is was—putting the cart before the horse. |
| MEL: | Now a word from Glopco, makers of . . . |

Sportscasters, and particularly those on radio, have a special problem. They don't want so-called "dead air," so they have to keep talking even when there isn't much, if anything, to say. A long silence is anathema to a medium that depends on voice communication. Any running commentary or exchange, however banal, is therefore better than nothing. Print reporters are free of that problem, though, so their questions ought to be incisive.

Since it's usually easier to explain what went wrong than it is to explain what went right, don't ignore losers. Again, losers have more to tell us about ourselves than do winners. Push to find out what really happened. Sally's concentration might have been off, for example, because she was exhausted by the time she got to Wimbledon. That, in turn, could be because of the international tennis circuit's killing pace—a pace set by promoters, not players, in order to maximize profits. It's also possible, to go farther out, that Sally did a lot of drinking the night before her match at Wimbledon. Athletes, again, are humans first. But if over-drinking was the real problem, we would want to know about the nature of the pressures that caused her to do it, especially given the likely consequences that she would have been able to anticipate. If Sally is using liquor to fend off otherwise unbearable pressure, she is speaking for more of us than is the player who eats Wheaties out of her trophy cup and flashes sparkling teeth at photographers.

You can find out what Sally's schedule has been during the last six months or so by going to the clips before you interview her, or asking her at the appropriate time during the interview. You should also observe her closely, as you would if you were working on a profile, and raise the matter of personal or professional problems if there is any reason to think they exist.

### Don't make athletes bigger than life.

You are in the business of reporting the news fairly and accurately, not of helping to mold enduring heroes with which owners and promoters can finance large automobiles and estates with swimming pools.

On its most basic level, the bigger-than-life syndrome has to do with adjectives. The best basketball player in the league doesn't need to be called a dazzler, a wizard, an immortal, or Mr. Magic, since everyone who cares knows that he's the best, anyway. The worst player in the league obviously doesn't deserve accolades. Those in between will establish their levels of competence, too, so you needn't help them with hyped-up and unnecessary verbiage.

The more complex level has to do with tone but it, too, is marked by careless adjectives:

> Simpson, on the ropes, took two hard jabs in the stomach and one on the face before he broke away, caught his breath, and began a fearless counterattack.

Everyone who fights for a living, or who plays body contact sports like football, rugby, or hockey, knows fear in its many shades. Some overcome it better than others, but all have known its presence. A fearless boxer—one who absolutely knows no fear—would have to be a human wind-up toy, an automaton devoid of brains.

Beyond simple adjectives, tone has to do with the entire approach you take to athletes and to the games they play. Here is where the bad sportswriters have committed their foulest deeds, not only by going along with "club" owners, league officials, and promoters in their quest for glory and grandeur (money), but often by going them one better. There is nothing whatever about the "World Series," for instance, that makes it competitive on a worldwide scale. Lipsyte thinks that the "North American Professional Baseball Championships for Men" would not only be more accurate, but less arrogant. Yet in American sports, and particularly in the professional ones, overblown splendor—the religion of being the biggest—prevails at the expense of lifelike proportion to the point at which real-life and phony-life become inseparable. This is the case with the U.S. Open Tennis Tournament held each summer at Forest Hills, which has been promoted from a rather sedate and serious affair to a major spectacle reminiscent of what Ebbets Field was like when the Brooklyn Dodgers were there. This is also the case with the Super Bowl, which started only as a gaudy professional football playoff, but which, thanks to the promoters and their allies in the press box, has evolved into a grotesque Roman circus brought to perhaps 80 million viewers annually by sportscasters hawking the latest in chariots. It might be noted here that, among journalists, sportscasters are virtually alone in the business of selling cars, deodorants, airline tickets, beer, trucks, and clothing. That, unfortunately, is how many of them see themselves—as pretty faces with compelling voices. They see themselves for what they choose to be: salesmen.

Kept in honest perspective, the world of sport abounds with good stories, not only about games, but about what goes into the games and why. Good sports reporting, like every other variety, is multidimensional, serious, and searching. The public ought to know what athletes really do when they aren't competing or practicing; what relations are really like between the races on one team when it isn't in the locker room or on the field; how the media, themselves, affect sports; what role business really plays in sports (including the selling of increasingly sophisticated and expensive equipment to a society that has been taught to equate quality hardware with quality performance); how new ballparks and franchises affect their cities, both beneficially and adversely; how college athletic scholarships and the sports programs they feed can corrupt academics in a dozen or more ways and victimize ten youngsters for every one they help. There is a better story in the college football player who says, "When I make a tackle, I know it's his scholarship or mine," than there is in yet another piece of pap about the National Football League's outstanding flanker, or safety, or quarterback, or . . . The selection process for amateur and professional awards and trophies ought to be looked at closely, as should the careers of the winners and the also-rans. We need stories about the officials in all sports, about how many times they make bad calls and decisions, and we need to find out why that happens. There are countless others.

Finally, and I think most important, sports fans ought to be told about *themselves*. Their motivations should be picked at and probed, and what they want from sports—especially speed, violence, physical damage, and the flirtation with death, itself—should be questioned. They ought to know who they really are. Away from the Sunday Stadium, the fan is also a family member, a job holder, and a voter. The national frenzy after the attack on Pearl Harbor and the great anger whipped up after the Tonkin Gulf incident have their parallel in the real hatred felt by the ordinary football fan who sees a player on "his" team (whatever that means) get hit late or be thumbed in the eye. What, in fact, makes that fan loyal to a team whose players he does not know personally and whose receipts he does not share? What manner of allegiance is it, why does he seem to need it, and how does it manifest itself elsewhere? Finding out, or even just trying to, is an honorable undertaking. It is not work for jocksniffers.

## COVERAGE

Sports reporting is basically no different from any other kind, and in at least one regard, it's among the easiest of the reporting areas.

Unlike a homicide, which is covered after it happens, an athletic competition is a staged event at which the reporter is present. As is the case when covering a political speech or an opera performance, the reporter is able to see and hear what happens as it is happening, so nothing has to be reconstructed or pried out of the authorities.

Further, and this is particularly true in most college sports and all of the professional ones, there are virtual armies of public relations persons around whose sole function is to provide the press with statistics, biographical and physical information about players and coaches, and other basic material about the event. Many college, and all professional, teams issue handy press pamphlets that are loaded with averages, total won-lost records, details of championship games, lists of players and their positions and identification numbers, seating capacity of the stadium, and more. Believe it or not, it is therefore easier to cover the Super Bowl than it is to cover a high school game, at which such press material is either unavailable or, if it is available in mimeographed form, is quite likely wrong.

Understand the nature of the game you're covering. Reporting a football game without knowing the difference between a lineman and someone in the backfield is like covering an opera without knowing the difference between a soprano and a tenor. It's impossible to do a good job. There are scores of books on every major sport that explain rules, procedure, and technique. If you're unfamiliar with what you're going out to cover, then, do your homework.

Watch out for the "friends" you make on the team. Having said that many sportswriters are not objective about what they cover, it now ought to be noted that living with a team at home and on the road often makes objectivity—or at least objective reporting—very difficult. Five or six reporters who drink with, eat with, travel with, and party with a baseball or football team often find it impossible to separate business from pleasure. There is no easy way out of this dilemma. Some newspapers have their baseball writers switch teams in mid-season to reduce the kind of thorny personal ties that would encumber fair reporting as the summer wears on. There probably is no good solution to the problem. But know it exists.

**Sources.**

The players themselves are generally the best news sources. Obviously, they are well aware of their performance, what is expected of them, and how the team is working as a whole. Today's more educated, more vocal athlete is also less bewildered by or accepting of front office policies than was his predecessor. Support personnel—water or bat boys, trainers, assistant coaches, and team doctors—are also usually reliable. Cultivate as many of them as possible and use one to verify what another says when it is questionable or controversial. They can be found in the locker room before and after the game. (After is better, since the action is over and there is therefore more to discuss.)

Head coaches, as a rule, are second only to public relations representatives for being poor sources about anything controversial. The head coach's role is not only to teach the members of the team and get them to play together, but to inspire them. That's why many head coaches make a show of arguing with officials during games— not because they think the officials are clearly wrong, but because they want to show their players that they're actively participating in the game, too. Given this understandable situation, no coach is likely to denigrate his team or any player on it by telling an unhappy truth that would hurt morale. Imagine the effect on the team, for example, if the players read this in the newspaper right before the season started:

> Coach Grady Armbuster predicted yesterday that the Water Moccasins will not win a game this season.
> "Here is a classic instance of the whole being even worse than the sum of its parts," said the exasperated coach.
> "Most of them aren't very good individually, but when you put them together, it's chaos. Higgenbottom has trouble tying his shoelaces, so how can I expect him to understand the play book?"
> Having looked over the schedule and his players, Armbuster added, he could come to only one conclusion: "We're gonna get killed."

Coaches know that such a story would be tantamount to guaranteeing a losing season. And since coaches, too, have families to support and therefore like steady employment, they are prone to fall back on equivocation or distortion in the face of a very unpromising game or season. "If" is the word to watch out for:

> Coach Grady Armbuster predicted yesterday that the Water Moccasins will have a winning season if Bert Higgenbottom stays healthy and the defensive unit continues to improve.

As he said that, Armbuster was quite likely thinking that there was only one way the Moccasins would be able to have a winning season—if every other team in the league contracted cholera. But he couldn't say that, and you ought to understand why. Instead, he mentioned Higgenbottom's health and talked about "improvement," which are perfectly safe because they are perfectly ambiguous.


## WRITING


At least two elements go high in the story, generally in the lead, and no later than the end of the second graf: (1) who won and by what score, and (2) the significance, if any, of the game. The order depends on the game itself and on the inclination of the writer:

> The New York Old Blues rugby team battered its way to an 11–8 victory over Princeton here yesterday, winning the Eastern Intercollegiate Rugby Championship.

or

> The New York Old Blues Rugby Club won the eastern championship here yesterday after battering its way to an 11–8 victory over Princeton.

Either way, or even reporting how the last goal was made, is acceptable. Notice the word "batter." It was not chosen randomly. Rugby, a body-contact sport of considerable violence, uses a

"scrum" in about the way football uses a line—basically to push
forward on the offense and hold back the other team on the defense.
The ball is moved toward the goal mainly with a powerful up-field
running attack during which the defense makes bone-jarring tackles.
"Batter," "pound," "smash," or "slam" are therefore all appropriate
for describing the action. There is no reason to tone down to the
point of making the story listless. But pick verbs carefully.

> The Pittsburgh Pirates clobbered the Los Angeles Dodgers
> 7–3 today, and in doing so, captured first place in their division.

Nobody got clobbered, trounced, drubbed, blasted, or wiped out
(except, maybe, the writer). The Dodgers were beaten. You get
clobbered in baseball when you lose 12–0, perhaps because your
outfielders spent the afternoon running into one another while the
pitcher was sending two hot dog vendors to the hospital with
concussions.

Records, depending on their importance, go high in the story or
at its very top. Common sense ought to tell you where. If you're
covering track, and the winner of the mile does it in record time,
that's your lead:

> Randy Gordon, an Ohio State sophomore, ran a record
> 3:56:25 mile in the fourth annual U.S. Collegiate Track and
> Field Championship here today.

You would then want to satisfy reader curiosity by putting in the
old record. You would not write that Gordon won the race. Since
he broke a record, his having won is self-evident, so it's the breaking
of the record that leads the story and sets its tone.

If, on the other hand, you're reporting a baseball game in which
so-and-so breaks the record for stealing bases under a threatening
sky, breaks his bat more times in the sixth inning than any other
player in history, or accomplishes any of the other statistical oddities
so loved by some baseball fans and those who write for them,
squeeze it in below the result of the game and its more important
highlights.

Give credit where it's due. Teams probably have five or six un-
sung heroes for every one who actually scores the points. They are

the interior linemen who open holes, practically unnoticed, so ball carriers can advance; rebounders who grab the basketball so the resident sharpshooter can pop it in from the outside; basemen who manage to keep runners from stealing while at the same time staying positioned to pick up any hit coming their way. The paradox inherent in good sports reporting is that you can miss the real story, or a good part of it, by keeping your eye on the ball.

# chapter twenty-one

# BUSINESS AND FINANCE

Stories having to do with numbers greater than 100, and particularly numbers in the company of decimal points, are dreaded by most reporters. Anything smacking of economics (money) is usually feared, loathed, and done badly. I once did business and financial reporting. In retrospect, I think I must have been in the vanguard of those who feared it, loathed it, and did it badly.

The reason most of us don't like consorting with numbers, I think, is that we consider ourselves to be artists of sorts, not accountants, and we therefore tend to think that coping with anything having to do with numbers that stand for money is beneath our dignity. "I can't even balance my checkbook, much less understand an annual report," we brag to friends and colleagues, perhaps in emulation of the way we want to think of Ernest Hemingway.

But Hemingway, a very sensible man in most regards, thought about money quite a bit, and for an excellent reason: He was fond of eating. Hemingway, Faulkner, Fitzgerald, and others of their artistic caliber knew that money is directly translatable to food, clothing, shelter, paper, typewriter ribbons or pencils, and other things necessary to sustain life and to make it more productive.

This is in no way meant to imply that money ought to be worshipped, but only that it ought to be understood for what it is, and for the ways in which it is used. You would not be experiencing what I'm sure is the boundless joy of reading these words had you, or someone else, not bought them. And I am sitting here, stringing them together, in full expectation that I will get paid for doing so. I believe in what I write, but that doesn't mean I have to be ashamed to earn part of my living from it, since writing and teaching are the products I sell in order to live the way I want to live.

Furthermore, the paper I used was made by a paper company, the typewriter by a typewriter company, and the finished book by a publishing company that processed it in several ways and then sent it to a printing company. While I wrote, I ate, and that brings us to the Glop Corporation (Glopco).

Glopco manufactures (makes) Catch-up, Uncle Barney's Bar-Bee-Cue Sauce, May-O-Naise, Sweet 'n Sour Hot Dawg Relish, Tangy-Tan French-style Mustard, 16 varieties of pickles, and several kinds of ice cream toppings and dips (including onion-cheddar). Its headquarters and main plant are in Milwaukee, and there are other plants in Atlanta, Dallas, and San Francisco. It employes 9,054 persons who do everything from sweep floors, to run mixing machines, to drive the red and white trucks that bring the products to stores in 31 states.

All this may not be very important to you, but it is most assuredly important to Glopco's president and board chairman, Merwin R. Grungus, to the board of directors and other company officers, to everyone who works for the company in any capacity, and to the millions of people who use Glopco's products—its "line." Whether they think about Glopco as part of their job, or only when they dip their spoons into its tangy lime ice cream topping, they can be said to believe in the "product" as much as I believe in mine. Those who work for Glopco want it to prosper, and to the extent that millions of customers enjoy what it sells them, they're kind of pulling for it, too. So are the thousands of others who have invested their money in Glopco, which is listed by the New York Stock Exchange (the "Big Board"), because those investors want the loans they have made to it to bring a profit.

What's really important here is that, irrespective of all the complicated numbers that are used to run Glopco, record its history, chart its progress, and plan its future, it's really only a vast collection of human beings, not digits, who are engaged in a common enterprise—the making, selling, and consumption of food. Glopco is actually a grown-up game, like monopoly-for-real. The numbers and code words are only used to keep track of the score. Current and fixed assets, accounts receivable, prepayments and deferred charges, accumulated depreciation, long-term liabilities, accumulated retained earnings, net earnings per share, and other code words are part of a specialized vocabulary used by the people who play the game in order to understand one another, exactly the same way that all nuclear physicists know what alpha-decay is, and all newspaper editors know what jumps, gutters, and flags are. Glopco, then, is in reality not numbers and code words, but people—just like you and me.

### The annual report.

As a general rule, large corporations must publish yearly reports on how they're doing, so anyone interested in finding out can do so. The annual report is to a company what the automobile brochure is to this year's model and its maker. Both are designed to attract "buyers" through the use of pretty pictures and clear and impressive verbiage. Both give figures for dimensions and performance. Both emphasize the positive and, as much as possible, ignore the negative.

Although they vary slightly in content, and widely in overall layout, most annual reports follow a standard format. Their heart—the numbers—are divided into three categories:

1. *The balance sheet,* which shows the company's financial situation as it stood on the last day of the year covered by the report (that's the last day of the *fiscal year,* which, as in many other games, is divided into four quarters). Two basic things to remember here: (1) not only are the latest year's numbers given, but also the numbers for the year before, so comparisons can easily be made, and (2) the balance sheet is divided into two columns—one for assets (+) and one for liabilities (−)—and their totals, at the bottom of the page, are in perfect balance. How they are made to balance can be very interesting, especially to the Internal Revenue Service.

2. *The income statement* is what it says it is: a statement, or table, showing how much the company made or lost during the year in question. Here, the amount of money taken in from sales is matched with the amount of money spent in order to operate the company. The result is a net profit, or a net loss, depending on which number is greater. As is the case with the balance sheet, and also with the accumulated retained earnings statement that follows, two consecutive years are also provided for comparative purposes.

3. *The accumulated retained earnings statement,* a formidable arrangement of words, is about *retained earnings.* To retain is to keep. So all this means is that the statement shows how much money the company has kept to invest or reinvest in itself. It shows, in other words, what kind of growth the company is planning with its available money. It could, for example, take money that might be used to pay higher dividends to stockholders and instead buy more equipment with which to expand. That might make short-term investors angry, but long-term investors who want the company to expand might very well prefer such a strategy to the more short-sighted one of making a few more cents in dividend payments.

Now, let's take a brief, but closer, look at some of the more important elements in these categories.

We said that the balance sheet is divided into two columns: Assets (how much Glopco has or expects to get), and Liabilities (how much it owes). The asset column, in turn, breaks down into these categories:

## CURRENT ASSETS

*Cash.* Money actually in the company's safe or on deposit in the bank.

*Marketable securities.* The amount of money Glopco has temporarily invested in such stable (and therefore predictable) areas as government securities. If there's an emergency, and the firm needs money fast, it sells its marketable securities.

*Accounts receivable.* The amount of money Glopco's customers owe it for merchandise they bought. They're usually given invoices that call for payment within 30, 60, or 90 days.

*Inventories.* The value of merchandise in the plants, generally divided into three categories: raw materials (like barrels of cucumbers), partly finished goods (like cucumbers soaking in brine), and finished products ready for shipment (jars of pickles packed in cartons).

*Total current assets.* The total value of all the above.

## FIXED ASSETS

Fixed assets are those which more or less stay put: land, factories, the office and its equipment, trucks, cars, manufacturing machinery, brooms, floor polishers, and whatnot. Their value, as listed in the statement, takes into account how much they have depreciated (lessened in value) through age and wear. The total of all this is listed as *Net Fixed Assets.* Then follow:

*Prepayments and deferred charges.* Glopco has a 10-year insurance policy covering fire, other kinds of damage, and accidents to employees. It prepaid that policy during the past year so the money it gave to the insurance company counts as an asset. It also leases some heavy machinery to other companies, which prepay for them. Deferred charges mean money that has been invested in such long-term areas as product development, research, or the introduction of a new product.

*Intangibles.* This includes the value of such things as patents and trademarks and, occasionally, an item called "goodwill," which is sure to bring snickers from accountants and tax lawyers. Goodwill represents the monetary value of, say, sponsoring Little League teams, or throwing a Halloween party at the local orphanage; things which intangibly enhance Glopco's good name. How do you fix a dollar value on that? It isn't easy, and that's why accountants and lawyers chuckle and wink when they see it. If Glopco's officers think that sponsoring Little League teams in each of the cities where it has plants is worth $1 million in goodwill, then its assets (and attractiveness to investors) goes up accordingly. . . .

*Total Assets.* That is usually the last number on the page and represents the total value of all of Glopco's assets (Current+Fixed).

Liabilities, listed opposite assets, show the negative side of

Glopco's worth, and are divided into two sections: Current and Long-Term. Both of these are followed by a category called something like Stockholders' Equity, meaning the amount of money that is invested in Glopco by stockholders.

## CURRENT LIABILITIES

*Accounts payable.* The amount of money Glopco owes to its creditors (for the nine new trucks and the Pound-Well Automatic Relish-Chopper, for example).

*Notes payable.* Money owed to the bank or some other lender.

*Accrued expenses payable.* Unpaid salaries, interest on borrowed money, pensions, legal and insurance fees or premiums, profit-sharing, and so on.

*Federal income tax payable.* What it says: the amount of money Glopco owes Washington in taxes.

*Total current liabilities.* The total of all of the above.

## LONG-TERM LIABILITIES

These are generally debts that are due more than one year from the date of the annual report, and can include things like bonds.

Consider, for example, the awesome-sounding 9 percent first mortgage bond with a 10-year maturity. It's almost enough to make your stomach knot, isn't it? Well, that piece of paper only says that the person who has it loaned Glopco, say, $10,000 at 9 percent interest payable twice a year for 10 years. That means that twice a year the mailman will deliver a check from Glopco for $450, which will total $900 every year, and $9,000 at the end of 10 years. Isn't that nice? The person will also be able to return that bond when it reaches maturity in 10 years and get the original $10,000 back, or sell it to someone else before then at whatever price it can bring in the bond market. It's called "first mortgage" because if Glopco is unable to make its 9 percent interest payments, and the company has to mortgage assets—sell things—in order to repay its debts, the holder of first mortgage bonds gets first crack at the proceeds.

Current liabilities plus long-term liabilities produce the line called (surprise): Total Liabilities.

## STOCKHOLDERS' EQUITY

This is the total amount of money—the percentage of the "action" —that stockholders have in Glopco. It breaks down into capital stock (preferred and common), capital surplus, and accumulated retained earnings. It's structured in the report like this:

### Preferred stock.

It's "preferred" because it has advantages over common stock, the nature of which depends on decisions by the board of directors. Generally, though, preferred stockholders get a fixed yearly dividend per share of, say, $2, are entitled to those dividends before common stockholders are paid dividends, and get an earlier "call" on the distribution of Glopco's assets if the company has to liquidate. Holders of preferred stock can also have more voting power in company affairs than do the other stockholders. Stock, preferred and common, is listed in the annual report according to its fixed dollar value.

### Common stock.

Its holders are not entitled to that fixed yearly dividend of $2 voted by the board of directors, nor are they the first to be paid dividends, nor do they have an early call, if any, on the proceeds of liquidation. Common stock dividends, on the other hand, bounce according to the fortunes of the company. Unlike preferred dividends, which are fixed and which therefore can't go higher than that amount, common dividends can either go unpaid or be more than that paid to holders of preferred stock. They are, then, more of a gamble.

### Capital surplus.

This is the total amount of money paid by stockholders to the company that exceeds the "par value" (the fixed, legal value) of each share. If Glopco's common stock has a par value of $1 a share, and it has one million shares to sell, all those shares are worth a total of $1 million. But if that stock is in such demand that it sells for $2 a share, the capital surplus is that additional $1 million.

### Accumulated retained earnings.

Most simply, they are what's left after the dividends paid to stockholders have been subtracted from net profits. If net profits for the year ended were $500,000, and dividends paid out came to $400,000, accumulated retained earnings amount to $100,000. That $100,000 gets plowed back into Glopco.

### Total liabilities and stockholders' equity.

It's the negative counterpart of *Total Assets* and is the same number, showing that the books balance (on paper, if not in reality . . .).

### The income statement.

The income statement, or earnings report, is what most investors and business reporters look at first when they want to see how a company is doing. While the balance sheet is supposed to show a company's soundness (or lack of it) on a given day—what it's worth—the income statement records operations for the year as a whole, compares the result with the previous year (and often with several years) and allows a little projection for the coming year.

In a nutshell, a company's income statement compares the amount of money it made from selling its product or service with the amount of money it spent in order to stay in business. If it made more than it spent, the income statement shows a net profit; if it spent more than it made, the statement shows a net loss. In essence, the company works exactly the way you do. If you make more than you spend, you're solvent; if you spend more than you make, you're in debt. If you were to set up your own income statement, it would be a rough miniature of Glopco's.

The standard income statement in an annual report lists *net sales* by their dollar value, and then subtracts from that the cost of sales and "operating expenses" (another ambiguous area), depreciation, and sales and other expenses, and arrives at a so-called *operating profit or loss*. It then adds *other income,* like the dividends and interest that are collected from investments Glopco has made, and arrives at a *total income* figure. Interest on bonds and federal taxes are subtracted from the total income, and what's left is the *net profit (or loss) for the year.*

The annual report will also list *net earnings per share.* You hear this expression quite a bit around stockbrokers and investors, who always seem to be talking about a company's common stock that "earned $1.25" or some other amount. *Earnings per share* show how much money one share of common stock made during the particular period. It is always given in annual and quarterly (see below) reports and is always compared with the previous applicable figure. It is calculated by dividing the number of common shares outstanding (the number people own) into the amount of earnings available (net profit minus preferred stock dividends). If Glopco has a net profit of $100,000, and is committed to pay $50,000 in dividends to preferred stockholders, that leaves another $50,000 to be divided among, say, the holders of its 40,000 common shares (notice, again, that preferred shareholders get paid first, while common shareholders split what's left). When you divide $50,000 by those 40,000 common shares, you get $1.25. That's how much your share of common stock earned in terms of the company's overall profit. If a common share earned $1.05 the previous year, and 76 cents the year before that, you know that things are improving for the common investor.

Finally (we're almost out of the financial report morass), reports are also listed after each quarter. These are called, appropriately enough, quarterly reports, and they're usually abbreviated to a few lines that give investors the bare bones of what they want to know. As was mentioned, companies divide their fiscal year into four three-month quarters: the first, second, third, and fourth. Here's a typical quarterly statement:

| | GLOPCO | |
|---|---|---|
| | 1977 | 1976 |
| Qtr. sales | $9,961,000 | $8,031,000 |
| Net income | 215,000 | 61,000 |
| Shr. earns | 25¢ | 7¢ |

If this were the second-quarter statement, it would not only contain the above information—about the second quarter—but also the overall picture at the end of the first half-year:

| | GLOPCO | |
|---|---|---|
| | 1977 | 1976 |
| Qtr. sales | $9,961,000 | $8,031,000 |
| Net income | 215,000 | 61,000 |
| Shr. earns | 25¢ | 7¢ |
| 6 mos. sales | 18,961,000 | 15,731,000 |
| Net income | 365,000 | 92,000 |
| Shr. earns | 43¢ | 11¢ |

The six-month figures combine the number from the first quarter (which were released three months ago), plus the numbers for the just-released second quarter. It is therefore what it says it is: a summary of sales, net income, and earnings per share for the first half of the year, compared to the same periods for the previous year. Merwin R. Grungus, his board of directors, and everyone else associated with Glopco ought to be congratulated—but not by us since, as business reporters, we view Glopco and its competitors with cool dispassion. And we report accordingly:

Glopco made a second-quarter profit of $215,000, up from $61,000 for the same period last year, the company announced yesterday.

First-half profits amounted to $365,000, up from $92,000 from the previous first half.

The Milwaukee-based condiment maker reported second-quarter sales of $9.96 million, up from $8.03 million last year, and a second-quarter earnings jump to 25 cents, up from 7 cents for the same period last year.

First-half sales were $18.9 million, up from $15.7 million last year, while earnings came to 43 cents, up from 11 cents.

Glopco's president, Merwin R. Grungus, said that increased sales and profits resulted from a five-year equipment modernization program in the firm's Dallas and San Francisco plants. The modernization was completed in August.

Notice that: (1) the latest figures are always given first, since they are the news; (2) the previous corresponding figures follow immediately in each case for comparative purposes; (3) profit (net income), which is taken to be the most important thing in a financial statement, leads the story; (4) figures in the millions are reduced to two decimal places in the story, since they are easier to read that way, and will appear in full in an accompanying box or list; (5) readers were told that Glopco is headquartered in Milwaukee and makes condiments; (6) Merwin Grungus was given the opportunity to explain his company's success, but he was not quoted directly, since what he said didn't warrant a direct quote.

### Footnotes.

Read them. Many annual reports contain this statement: "The accompanying footnotes are an integral part of the financial statements." They certainly are, and they can be explosive. They can, and often do, mention liabilities from claims or lawsuits, new contracts, pension and retirement plans, profit sharing, changes in the value of stock because of dividends or splits, changes in the way fixed assets are depreciated, and bankruptcy. Most seasoned business reporters routinely scan the footnotes right after the income statement. And you no longer need a magnifying glass to study them, either—they now have to be printed in type as large as the numbers in the financial statement.

Are earnings stories "interesting" to readers? The answer, obviously, is that, like every other kind of story, they are very interesting to those who care and uninteresting to those who don't. But many do care, including everyone who holds a responsible job with the company, everyone who is considering investing in the company or who has already done so, and those who compete with it. Since

Glopco is a publicly owned corporation (as opposed to one that is privately held, and which therefore doesn't offer stock to the public), the public has every right to know about its financial condition. This is particularly true in the case of such public service operations as utilities and transportation companies or those related to them. Checking oil companies' reports toward the end of the 1973–74 Arab oil embargo, during which petroleum was supposedly in very short supply, revealed that the major corporations were making handsome profits: in one case, about 400 percent. . . . That fact helped launch Senate hearings.

In the last analysis, though, meaningful investigative reporting of companies has to go well beyond formal company reports. Nowhere in a financial report will you find reference to product adulteration, false labeling, industrial espionage, tax fraud, bribery of officials, lobbying activities, specious bookkeeping, merger or acquisition plans that could violate antitrust laws, or any of the scores of other, often intricate, bits of maneuvering that unfairly empty some pockets to fill others. This is not to say that all businessmen are crooks. They are not. But the temptation to be crooked, or at least to push the law and accepted doctrines of fairness to their limits, is greatest in business because, again, businessmen play monopoly for real money.


### Sources.

There are four basic sources for corporate investigative work: dissident stockholders, unhappy employees or officials, consumer groups, and the government.

The annual meeting is the one time every year when Merwin R. Grungus has to answer stockholders' questions, face-to-face, in an auditorium. And the stockholders who bother to travel to Milwaukee or to some other city in order to attend the annual meeting are hardly bashful coupon-clippers. In most cases, those who show up for Glopco's annual meetings own a considerable amount of its stock, and they therefore follow the company's operations the way pony players follow the morning line. They will rise, annual report clutched beneath white knuckles, and try to make their annual question to Merwin Grungus a good one:

"How do you account for the fact that, in spite of marketing surveys showing that Slopco controls 94 percent of the Boston market, you want to open a plant there? And where, exactly, is the money for that white elephant supposed to come from?"

Talk to that stockholder after the meeting and, if what you hear makes sense, follow up.

Unhappy employees or officials know a great deal about what goes on inside Glopco for the very good reason that they work within its walls. As was said in the section on investigative reporting, your problem here is one of sorting pure spite from pure news, but if it is real news, you at least know that your source is highly knowledgeable.

Consumer groups frequently monitor entire industries, particularly for false advertising or labeling and inferior or dangerous merchandise. Not only are there private, nonprofit consumer groups for most industries, but many cities have their own departments or bureaus of consumer affairs. As a business reporter, you ought to keep in touch with these, letting them know that you're prepared to listen to bona fide complaints. I say "bona fide" because, in their exuberance, some of these groups occasionally shoot first and ask the key questions later. Double- and triple-check.

Everyone who manufactures anything in America has the law peering over his or her right shoulder, or so it seems. Glopco is answerable to the Securities and Exchange Commission (SEC) for the way in which it markets its stocks and bonds and generally handles its public financial affairs; the Internal Revenue Service (IRS) for the amount of taxes it does or does not pay; the National Labor Relations Board (NLRB) for relations with its employees; the Environmental Protection Agency (EPA) for smoke emissions or other kinds of pollution; the Federal Trade Commission (FTC) for the honesty, or lack of it, in product advertising and for false labeling, shoddy merchandise, or unfair business practices. Although you won't find it in the annual report, this, plus fierce competition from Slopco and Great Goo, is why Merwin Grungus puts away three highballs before dinner and has been told by his physician that his heart is beating with dangerous irregularity.

Financial reporting can go well beyond coverage of companies. It extends outward, like a series of ripples, to include entire industries, such specialized areas as labor and commodities, and to the national and international economies as a whole. These areas can be dry if they are perceived and reported that way, or they can be quite the opposite.

Take commodity futures, which generally draws the most yawns from the confidently ignorant. Corn, wheat, and soybean futures are set, for the most part, in the huge Chicago Board of Trade and the Chicago Mercantile Exchange. There, men in shirtsleeves who work in places called "pits" set the future prices of corn, wheat, and soybeans (among hundreds of other commodities) by bidding on them. Arms wave wildly, fingers appear and disappear into fists, and there is continuous shouting in three-quarter-time code. If you didn't know what they were doing, you might think that they were being attacked by bees. What they *are* doing, though, is establishing how much money farmers are going to be paid for what they grow, and how much consumers are going to have to pay for what they eat. If you've ever had to live on a tight budget, or have had to go without eating, you know that there's nothing boring about it.

Farmers in Kansas, Iowa, and elsewhere know this basic fact of economic life: when a commodity is in abundant supply, it is less valuable than when it is scarce, meaning that the less you produce, the more you get for it. That leaves the farmer in an interesting situation. If he underplants—works less—he can get more for what he *does* plant than he can if he kills himself to plant on every inch of land he owns. So, let us say, he plants less. Seeing that the corn crop is going to "short-fall"—not be abundant—the commodity traders are forced to bid up the price for whatever is available. That higher price is passed on to those who buy corn for canning, for sales in the vegetable store and supermarket, and for export overseas. The higher price *they* pay is, in turn, passed on to consumers who either eat less corn or divert more money from other items in order to buy the same amount they were eating three months ago. In any case, the higher price contributes to inflation, which diminishes the number of things that can be bought with a dollar, which prompts people to demand raises, which prompts employers to either say no or raise their own prices to offset the extra money they have to pay in salaries. If they say no, there could be a crippling strike. If they say yes, and their own merchandise is priced higher, the inflationary spiral moves still further upward. And among their customers are . . . the farmers, who now have to pay still more for what *they* buy, meaning that they need more money, meaning that they want to get more for their corn, meaning that. . . . You could report such a story in either of at least two ways:

Corn futures hit $6.70 a bushel in heavy trading yesterday, setting a four-year record.

The price, established while producers still hold perhaps 85 percent of the crop, is expected to rise another 25 cents or so before the end of the week.

Yesterday's bidding came 10 days after the Agriculture Department announced that it has estimated that this season's crop will come in at 3.1 billion bushels, a five-year low.

The price increase reflects . . . .

or

Max Williams, who owns 700 acres of choice farmland outside of Dubuque, Iowa, can grow corn whose quality rivals that of any in the world.

He can grow a lot of it on his land, but he has decided not to. It does not pay to grow all the corn you can these days.

Williams sat on his front porch one afternoon this week, looking at the half of his land that is bare, and at his new pickup truck. The truck cost him $220 more than it would have cost last year.

"There's no sense to it," said the lean farmer, sipping light coffee as he took in the emptiness. "It's getting to the point where working hard is unprofitable. The more you work, the less you have, so why bother?"

Williams was referring to the decision he made in March, along with thousands of other American corn farmers, to hold down this year's crop in an effort to push up its price.

It has worked, too. Corn futures went at $6.70 a bushel yesterday, setting a four-year record in very heavy trading. Unlike last year, then, Williams's crop is in great demand.

"When you figure that the land is being wasted, and that people in this world are hungry, it amounts to a kind of sin. But we have to eat, too, and we didn't eat very well last year and the year before."

The farmer went on to recall that last year's corn harvest, which came to a near-record 5.9 billion bushels, glutted storage facilities through the Midwest and drove prices down to "rock-bottom"—$2.73 a bushel.

"Hell, I've got three youngsters in college and two more about ready to go. After everything was said and done last year, I cleared less than $14,000. You can't do that for very long, even with all the free corn you can eat."

Clearly, the second version is about human beings, not merely numbers. It tries to translate the numbers into something more meaningful, and specifically, into a description of the farmer's plight. He, those he deals with, and their customers—the consumers—are really what the numbers are all about.

# chapter twenty-two

# RELIGION, EDUCATION, AND TRAVEL

## RELIGION

There was a time, not long ago, when religious news consisted of collecting assorted sermons on Sunday morning for Monday morning's edition. During the week, the "religion editor" reviewed books about motorcycle repair or how to grow geraniums in closets, or simply dozed off in the back of the newsroom somewhere. He was usually a good-natured fellow who wore Franklin glasses, said good morning to everyone, and was taken seriously by practically no one. He is gone.

He was retired by Pope John XXIII, who started the Catholic church's ecumenical movement, the Rev. Martin Luther King, Jr., who marched and died for racial equality in America, the Berrigan brothers and the Rev. William Sloane Coffin, who became activists against the war in Vietnam, American Jews who acted in support of emigration from the Soviet Union to Israel—and many others.

By the early 1970s, that kindly old religion editor was scratching his head in perplexed wonder because the Jesus People, Synanon, Arica, Scientology, Oriental "meditation" religions such as Zen, Sufi, and the Hare Krishna, "Moonies," and others were capturing the imaginations of the young, and even of the not-so-young. Acid-rock concerts were taking place in Unitarian churches; Roman Catholic liturgies were being given in English; Chicago Seven radical Rennie Davis had switched allegiance from the far left to the guru Maharaj Ji; Charles Colson, the Nixon aide who had bragged that he would run over his grandmother for his boss, turned into a "born-again Christian," and, it was revealed, so had then-presidential candidate Jimmy Carter. In Brazil, Ecuador, Argentina, and other Latin American countries, Catholic priests— *Catholic priests*—were becoming left-wing folk heroes and were being tortured or deported by their right-wing governments.

It began to dawn on American journalists by the mid-'70s that the unifying force of the Black Muslims, Billy Graham's influence in the White House, the role of Buddhists in toppling South Vietnam's Diem regime, the basis of U.S. support for Israel, the creation of Pakistan and Bangladesh, Soviet emigration laws and their relationship to East-West détente, the fighting in Northern Ireland and in Lebanon, the terrorist doctrine of Libya's Col. Muammar el-Qaddafi, and a great deal more, had to do with—religion. Not religion as a strictly spiritual phenomenon, but more as a social and political one.

When today's reporters talk about religion, then, they aren't really talking about yarmulkes, crucifixes, the Koran, Genesis, Easter, prayer beads, icons, Mecca, baptism, or contemplation. They're talking about a profound and continuing historical force, and one which has many facets.

It follows from this that whether or not you are "into" religion, you ought to understand that, to some degree, most people are. An estimated 2.6 billion inhabitants of this planet call themselves Roman Catholic, Eastern Orthodox, Protestant, Jew, Muslim, Zoroastrian, Shinto, Taoist, Confucian, Buddhist, or Hindu. Further, although all of them are engaged in the day-to-day business of supporting themselves and trying to stay alive, their religious convictions, however concealed, are matters of great emotion and sensitivity. As any number of "saints and sinners"—noble leaders and despots—have understood, you only have to probe long enough to get some kind of reaction. Tell an Irish Catholic who hasn't gone to church in 30 years that his religion is full of blindly obedient papists, or a Jew who hasn't attended synagogue in that long and who says he doesn't "practice," that Jews are cheapskates and a menace, and you will assuredly raise their hackles. It follows, in turn, that if you tell a Protestant in Northern Ireland that a Catholic is out to get him, or a Catholic that a Protestant means him harm, or do the same thing in India and Pakistan with a Muslim and a Hindu, you are raising the possibility of bloodshed. Religion can be highly volatile.

Religion can also be highly complicated. There are more than 250 traditional religious denominations (*not* sects) in the United States, ranging in size from the Roman Catholic Church's 48.5 million, to the American (Old) Catholic Church of New York's 200. There are more than 27 million Baptists divided into 21 denominations, more than 13 million Methodists in 12 denominations, more than six million Jews in three denominations, and more than four million members of the Eastern Orthodox Church who are divided into 21 denominations. There are also, of course, Lutherans, Latter-Day Saints (Mormons), Presbyterians, Spiritualists, Episcopalians, Mennonites, Adventists, Anglicans, Evangelists, Jehovah's Witnessess, Unitarians, Disciples of Christ, Friends, Independent Fundamentalists, and scores of others, including about 100,000 Buddhists and more than 350,000 members of the Salvation Army.

Almost all of them (Buddhists, Muslims, Black Muslims, and one or two others excepted) use either the Old Testament, the New Testament, or both as the basis of their theories. Interpretations, as you would expect, range from the very loose to line-by-line absolutist. Black Muslims follow the teachings of their prophet, Elijah Muhammad, and study the same Koran used by Muslims in the Arab world, the Far East, and elsewhere.

Religious leaders and those in their congregations don't like seeing names and titles misused. Since the collective group of Southern Baptist organizations calls itself the Southern Baptist Convention, for example, members don't like having their Convention called a church. Use "church" only on the local level. As another example, there are no clergymen or -women among Christian Scientists (members of the Church of Christ, Scientist): there are Practitioners, First and Second Readers, and Lecturers. Jews get understandably irked when their synagogues are called churches and rabbi is spelled rabi. Both the Associated Press and *The New York Times* style books cover the correct spellings of religious names and titles, plus their usages. If either or both of them don't have what you need, go right to the source—*ask*.

Religious ritual in houses of worship is rarely interesting to anyone except those in attendance and, of course, to their priests, pastors, preachers, rabbis, readers, elders, deacons, ministers, monks, and muftis. Good reporters are alert for stories that go well beyond the events that take place within the church or synagogue, itself—they see a bigger picture wherever they look.

A papal condemnation of birth control pills and devices may not make the most spectacular reading, for example, but the chain reactions it sets off down the line—including where you live—can be considerable. In their confrontation over birth control, both the Vatican and the ecologist are concerned with the same fundamental "sin"—the premature taking of human life. The only difference between the opposing sides has to do with the ages of the victims. The church insists that birth control and abortion amount to the willful taking of human life at its earliest stages. The ecologists are equally sure that not doing so, and therefore encouraging unsupportable population, brings the famines that kill those who have already been born. Another reaction has to do with how Roman Catholics themselves line up on the issue. Many have openly opposed the Church's position, others have quietly ignored it, and still others have followed it, well, religiously. Stories about the respective reasons for taking one stand or another could do much to shed light on the Church's authority in the midst of the modernization it is trying to make in the face of increasing secularism. To consider this a purely religious matter is to completely miss its significance.

## EDUCATION

Education is, and has always been, taken very seriously in the United States. But it's taken seriously for more than the usual reasons stemming from the Judeo-Christian and Greek philosophies about the inherent goodness of knowledge. There are at least three other reasons, all of them highly pragmatic:

1. Education in this country is, rightly or wrongly, equated with riches in terms of achievement and with aristocracy in terms of social status. Those who don't have generous gobs of money can at least fall back on their formidable array of degrees to prove their social worth. In a nonaristocratic society, a Ph.D. from Yale or Stanford is about as close as a poor boy or girl can get to being in the petty aristocracy (or so it was before the great post-war education explosion).

2. Education can be used as a social and political weapon, not only overtly (segregation, desegregation, and busing), but covertly by teachers and institutions wanting to get their ideologies across through the bending of "tender young minds." (That is precisely what *I'm* trying to do. I'm trying to convince you that what I believe is right, and that you ought to believe in it, too.)

Parents of college students are not terribly touchy about ideological messages because they like to think that their children are mentally robust enough to be able to separate sense from nonsense. The parents of grade school and high school students, however, worry about ideological infiltration and subversion quite a bit. And the local school, many parents feel, is where danger lurks—where the attack against their children's minds will be launched, perhaps turning them into irredeemable Communists, Fascists, miscegenators, hippies, dope addicts, or, at the very least, functional illiterates. This goes well beyond concern for the good old three R's; it is deadly serious political and social business. That's why there has been violence over desegregation and busing, why books have been taken off school shelves and burned, and why teachers have been investigated and fired.

3. A community's schools can be a source of prestige or embarrassment. Prestigious schools—those with regional reputations—boost community morale and enhance property value. This, in turn, attracts a better class of people, which brings in more tax money, which helps to improve the schools, which, as you might suppose, creates a spiral that moves upward, or just stays there,

rather pleasantly. Communities with poor or deteriorating schools face the opposite situation: neighborhoods don't attract better families, the morale of those already there tends to sag, and many residents leave, if they can, for something better. Property values fall.

Education in America, and especially on the primary and secondary levels, is therefore taken seriously to the point of occasionally being explosive. New York City's battle of a few years ago in which the central school board and neighborhoods fought bitterly over whether communities would, or would not, have more say in the running of schools was but one example. The dispute often involved angry demonstrations, sharp verbal attacks, a great deal of political manueuvering, sit-ins, vandalism, and even some fighting. The central board argued that central direction would maintain high and uniform standards. The neighborhoods, particularly those with ethnic minorities, countered that they understood their children's needs better than any central administration could. They eventually won but, ironically, budget cuts and other factors so weakened the system that by 1976 some blacks had started a private school.

As on other beats, the education reporter's first task is to understand the structure with which he or she is dealing.

At the top, in most communities, there is a school board whose members are either appointed or elected, and who serve without pay as a community service.

Next comes the school system's chief administrator (usually called the superintendent or chancellor), who is either hired directly by the board or is elected by the community as a whole. He and the board work closely together, at least in theory, on school policies, expenditures, major personnel movement (promotions, retirements, firings, hirings), and other technical matters. In theory (again), the board explains the boundaries within which the superintendent operates and allows him to do so unimpeded. He, on the other hand, does not try to change general policies or go over the heads of the board members.

So much for theory. In fact, most communities at one time or another have bitter disputes between the professional education administrator, who feels that Eternal High needs three more math teachers and new audiovisual equipment, and the board, which cannot, or doesn't want to, appropriate the necessary money. More often, the school board, whose members are usually among the staunchest, and therefore most conservative, members of the community, wants to fire a teacher for having done something "not in the best interests of ———." This can put the administrator in a serious quandary. If he sides with the board, many of the teachers in the system put him down as being an establishmentarian flunky who will not stick up for them. If he sides with the teachers, the board probably replaces him, or at least suggests doing so to the mayor or council.

On the next level are the district's principals, supervisors, directors, headmasters, and other middle-echelon persons. As a group, they are generally the worst prospects for information and quotes, and pursuing them is usually fruitless. That's because, like middle-level bureaucrats and middle-level everything else in the world, they have struggled up from the depths and don't think they've finished climbing. They have sacrificed a great deal, they feel, and have many rewards ahead if they can just manage to do their jobs decently and stay out of trouble. They see reporters as trouble—as pesky meddlers who will look under the rocks, emphasize their school's shortcomings while ignoring its virtues, twist the things they say and print only distortions, and otherwise commit havoc. Their response to reporters, then, is pretty much the same as it is in all federal offices and agencies and in the military: They tell reporters that they don't know anything and advise that the questions be asked of their superiors. Duck and cover, as we used to say.

Teachers are almost invariably the best professional sources because (1) they're "in the trenches" and therefore bear the brunt of the system's problems, and (2) the younger or the more spirited among them are altruistic enough to think that news stories about the problems can help clear them.

Students are tricky. The best of them are intellectually and emotionally as good or better than some of those under whom they're supposed to be learning. They are dependable observers, accurate quoters, and are generally mature enough so they can keep what happens around them in perspective. The worst of them—generally those with poor grades who get in various kinds of trouble—are often anxious to strike back at the system and will not hesitate to malign their teachers or the school in order to do so. Most, including the best and the worst, are prone to exaggeration. It is a quality that is easily forgiven in youth, but it is not so easily forgiven in reporters. When the youngster says that Eternal High's cafeteria serves the most vile rot on the face of the earth, he's probably comparing it to what his mother cooks and to what he gets at his favorite pizza place. No canned chicken in cream sauce, ladled over gummy rice, can stand up to that kind of competition. Be careful.

Education reporters in small towns or those who cover counties are generally responsible for the full gamut of institutionalized education, starting with the primary grades, and running through junior and senior colleges. Those who work in larger cities usually concentrate on primary and secondary education, public and private, and leave higher education stories to general assignment reporters who cover them on a spot basis (as particular stories develop).

There are basically two kinds of education stories: those which can be called cursory, and those which are investigative. The former include pieces on graduations, honors, enrollments, opening and closing dates for the school year, curricula changes, alumni affairs (including reunions), and building expansion. They are stories that ought to go on the record and that, because of the number of persons who either went to the particular school, have children in it, or pay taxes for it, are of some interest to the general readership. Investigative stories are what the name implies. In most cases, they take cursory stories a crucial step further, pinpointing specific instances of wrongdoing or exposing motives and attitudes not immediately apparent. A teacher's being fired is an obvious example. The first question occurring to a reporter who finds out that a teacher has been fired is—why? The superintendent or school board will doubtless have what seems to be an excellent reason, say, because of excessive absences or, as is more often the case, because of teaching that is "incompatible" with the standards of the school or district.

Incompatibility is usually a catchall that allows any organization to fire someone who somehow doesn't measure up, who has made enemies in high places, or who is simply doing something, however effectively, that goes against the grain of his or her superiors. It must be pursued.

You start by asking the superintendent, or whoever is qualified to talk about the matter, what "incompatibility" means in this case.

"Well," you might hear, "he's being paid to teach geometry, but he spends half of his class time taking students for nature walks. They all just walk through the woods, and we can't have that, because they already do such activities in biology. A mathematics teacher belongs at the blackboard, not in the woods." That would seem to make sense on the face of it. But having gotten such a reason, the next stop would be at the door of the fired teacher, and the first question would be:

"The superintendent says you were fired for spending half of your class time in the woods. Why does someone teaching geometry spend so much time in the woods?"

"Where else would I be able to find better examples than in nature?" he might answer. "What's more symmetrical than a leaf? Where is there a better example of a circle than in the cross-section of a tree? Where would you find a more dramatic example of angles than in a spider's web? Why should I copy all that stuff with chalk when they can see it in real life?"

Colleagues who teach mathematics and the fired teacher's students would be next. If, based on interviews with them, he appears to be an innovative thinker who captures his students' imaginations and teaches them well, you would have a serious digging job ahead, because either (1) the system in which he works does not respond to such innovations, or (2) there was another reason for his having been fired (he'd probably tell you if there was, anyway). On the other hand, the students would tell you pretty quickly if he didn't apply nature to geometry at all on the walks in the woods, but only wasted time. Your reportorial sense tells you whether to pursue the story or report it strictly as it appears after preliminary coverage only. If the latter is the case, then you at least have his side of the matter for inclusion in the story. In either case, you would not be content to lay the blame on "incompatibility" and let it go at that.

Hamilton McNamara, a geometry teacher at Eternal High School, has been fired for misuse of class time.

McNamara received a dismissal notice on Monday telling him that his contract will not be renewed for next year. The notice was signed by Superintendent of Schools Irving Bliss, who gave "incompatability" as the reason.

Bliss said yesterday that McNamara spends at least half of

his class time taking his students for "rather pointless" walks in the woods around the school. The superintendent added that McNamara had been warned on several occasions to end the excursions.

"Where else would I be able to find better examples than in nature?" the 41-year-old McNamara said yesterday. "Why should I copy all that stuff with chalk when they can see it in real life?" he asked, referring to circular cross-sections of trees, the symmetry of leaves, and the angles in spider webs.

Two of McNamara's colleagues, Janet Foorster and Malcolm Tribble, agree that applying geometry to nature is a good idea in theory. But several of McNamara's students, questioned yesterday, indicated that theory and practice do not come together in their teacher's class.

"We go on long walks and hardly ever talk about geometry," said Elsie Cavendish, a 15-year-old sophomore. Eight fellow students agreed.

"Every once in a while, he'll point out that a tree is a natural cylinder, but mostly, we just walk around without learning anything," added Jeffrey Greenberg, another sophomore. "I know from talking to friends in the other classes that we're pretty far behind."

Of the 27 students in McNamara's geometry class, none said they are satisfied with what they are learning. Nearly all said they like McNamara, but that he does not teach enough.

The deciding factor in this story is clearly the attitude of McNamara's students. It would be altogether different if they insisted that they were getting a great deal out of the course. In either case, however, checking county- or state-wide geometry test scores would probably settle the matter. You would compare the test scores of McNamara's students over, say, a five-year period with those of other students to see how they did on a comparative basis. Yes, it would be two or three days of very dull work, but that, again, is the true nature of investigative reporting. The stakes—whether perhaps 150 students a year were learning what they were supposed to be learning, and whether a person was being fired for doing something that ought to have brought commendation—would be anything but dull.

## TRAVEL

Travel writers are more prone to infectious adjectivitis than any other members of the craft. This is because they think (often correctly) that they are writing for an audience that associates faraway places with things exotic. Faraway places are rarely exotic, however, to the people living in them. Impervious to reality, and aware of the fact that if readers aren't whetted to travel they won't read travel stories, many travel writers "hype" their prose. They are hopelessly addicted to superlatives, metaphors, similes, and adjectives designed to tantalize readers and placate hotel and restaurant owners (many of whom, unfortunately, provide free lodging and meals for the service). There are travel writers who unashamedly skirt the globe living off those they write about and *for:* tourism offices, hotels, restaurants, airlines, nightclubs, inns, amusement parks, and others. They accept rooms, meals, travel expenses, and more in return for grinding out palpably patronizing nonsense.

The result is usually not only deeply dishonest, but enough to make intelligent and sensitive readers feel as though they are drowning in warm honey: The azure bay nestles within pine-covered mountains that look like giant green lobster claws from the monastery's sylvan setting . . . The Tuareg, mysterious and ethereal blue men of the Sahara, glide out of the mirages like frightening specters from another world. . . . The gaunt Gothic cathedral, rising from the forbidding woods along the Rhine, has many tales to tell the traveler who wanders by. . . . The tiny trattoria, wedged bashfully between the police station and an antique shop, boasts a veal scallopini tasting more like a cloud than terrestial fare. . . . The cheerful fishermen, their red and blue boats gliding across the mirrorlike harbor, are anxious to give their wives the night's catch for sale along the winding waterfront.

Well, the Tuareg aren't mysterious at all. They're nomadic herders whose family, clan, and tribal structures have been carefully studied and written about by any number of anthropologists (notably French), who have suffered profound social changes at the hands of Europeans, and who scrape to make ends meet by selling sheep and handicrafts to their neighbors and to tourists. And anyone who has ever ridden on a camel knows that it's anything but a glide. And of course those fishermen are anxious to sell their fish; it's their livelihood. But if they're really cheerful after spending 10 hours pulling haddock or herring out of the ocean and cleaning them, then they're more likely mad (which would be a pretty good story—a village full of crazy fishermen . . .).

The point, as was mentioned in the chapter on sports, is that you are dealing with people who are more like you and your readers than they are different. The travel writer's main job is to show readers what real life is like on other parts of the planet and to explain how the people who live there exist: what they're *really* like.

The essential philosophy, I think, ought to concentrate on bringing the peoples of the world closer together, rather than portraying them as jovial freaks, dancing around patches of edelweiss in secluded alpine pastures and living to eat cheese and make chocolate. Like athletes, the more intelligent and aware among them have little but scorn for the fools who couch them in exotic and mysterious metaphor, although they are perfectly willing to go along with the fiction so long as it brings in tourist money.

Here are a pair of core rules for travel writing: (1) report what happens or what you see, not what you think your subject or the folks back home want to read; (2) never accept favors in the way of meals, lodging, or transportation expenses from those you write about.


## Coverage

Almost all cities in the United States and in Europe, and very many elsewhere, have chambers of commerce or tourist offices where employees are paid to give away fact sheets, brochures, maps, and other material, and to answer questions. Here is your starting place. Go in, collect what you need, and study it. You will then have a fair idea of what those who run that city want you to know about its museums, transportation facilities, shopping, hotels, restaurants, discothèques, and history. The printed material will never say that you can get your brains bashed in by wandering through the Creeperbahn district, your pockets picked in such and such a medina, or your stomach pumped out after eating in any of the restaurants along the waterfront. It will never say that the Ritz Palace has maids with sticky fingers (even though, or perhaps because, it's rated as the best hotel in the city), or that the Lazy Daisy discothèque cuts its vodka with water. You can find out only by asking and sampling.

Tourist officials in Western Europe and the Middle East are a remarkably honest lot, I suppose because they know that it doesn't do their cities much good to have foreigners beaten up, robbed, cheated, or poisoned. Having gotten an idea of what's in the city, and having studied its general layout, ask a tourist official about the best the city has to offer and about the worst. Since most travel stories concern particular aspects of a place, rather than entire roundups, it's up to you to decide what you want to concentrate on. In Istanbul, for example, you might want to concentrate on the mosques, or on the Golden Horn, the outdoor restaurants lining the Bosphorus, the Topkapi museum, the Covered Bazaar, or food in general. All of those possibilities require comparison and homework, unless you're prepared to say that the minarets on the Blue Mosque are "pretty" and the yogurt at that little place off Taksim Square is "tasty." Research is just as important in travel stories as it is in any other kind of consumer work.

The best travel stories almost invariably have to do with people, not with hotels and restaurants, statues and boat excursions, scenic views and museums. Go out and meet people and find out what they do, how their families function, and how they're affected by the kinds of problems affecting your readers: politics, the economy, competition, the weather, sickness and medical care, and so on. Find out how young and old are treated within the family structure, how farming, or yogurt-making, or street cleaning compares to the way it's done back home, and how it could be improved. You will probably learn before too long that a beet farmer in Adapazari has more in common with a beet farmer in Louisiana than he does with any of his fellow citizens who live in Izmir, Ankara, Istanbul, or any of the cities in his country: Both worry about the weather, the low price they are going to get for their crops, the high prices they have to pay to feed and clothe their families, and the fact that both of their governments are always going to the dogs. Both are disdainful of life in the city, all politicians, international relations, and overindulgence in almost any form. Both are wary of what they read in the newspaper or hear on the radio. Neither really knows that the other is there. Good travel writing, as opposed to the gee-whiz, claptrap kind, can change that.

Judging the relative strengths and weaknesses of hotels, restaurants, nightclubs, and tourist attractions generally seems like great fun. But if you're prepared to print a story saying that a hotel is poor or a restaurant's food is bad, and bring to that any kind of conscience, you quickly realize that the responsibility involved takes away a great deal of the "fun." Consider the fact that it might take you six hours to research and write a story saying that the onion soup in such and such a restaurant ought to be registered as a poison. In doing that story, on the basis of having had the soup once, you may well be crippling or destroying a couple's life's work and only source of income. The story written and sent, you pack your suitcase and move on to Amiens, perhaps leaving a worthy little restaurant on the Left Bank unjustifiably mauled. What if the chef had an off-night, or there was an emergency in the kitchen, or you just didn't like their kind of onion soup? No matter; the deed is done.

You take enormous responsibility when you impose your taste on readers and your standards on chefs. Although there is a great deal of pure rubbish said and written in the world of gourmetdom by those who want to turn taste into science, it is nonetheless true that it is not work for the inexperienced. It is far more than a matter of knowing, in the pit of your stomach, "what's good." If you want to get into travel writing, or food criticism, there is a great deal of homework to do. Not only should you know when something tastes bad, or has been poorly prepared, but you ought to know why. If you presume to tell anyone that French cuisine is good or foul, you'd literally better be able to know which kind of sauce you're eating, how it was made, and what went wrong. If you're not prepared to say, you're not prepared to judge the chef who made it, anymore than he's prepared to criticize the structure and technique of your story. Read about it, think about it, and experience it again and again. It's very serious business.

The basic standard with which to judge any hotel, restaurant, or other tourist enterprise is this: does the customer get his money's worth? It's hardly surprising that the swank El Posho restaurant provides a better paella than the little café down the street. The real question, however, is whether the former's paella is worth perhaps 10 times more than the latter's. Hotels and restaurants ought to be judged according to what they say they have set out to do. If a restaurant has three-star pretensions (and prices its food accordingly), it should be judged by three-star standards. If the café has no such pretensions (and prices *its* food accordingly), it, too, ought to be judged in comparison with others in its class. Better an honest, unassuming hamburger, than an overpriced Beef Wellington.

Where restaurants are concerned, the quality of the dishes is usually inversely proportional to the view: the better the view, the worse the food. This is because the establishment is trading heavily on the fact that it is in a revolving tower above the city, or perched on a cliff over the ocean, and that its clientele comes as much or more for the view as for the cuisine. Having come to that conclusion, the management is tempted to skimp on the quality of what it buys in the market, and on the staff that prepares it. The basement bistro, on the other hand, has no view and will therefore survive or perish primarily on the strength of its menu.

When you have a question about a dish or a beverage, never be ashamed to ask. Coquilles Saint-Jacques and Salade Niçoise are pretty standard items on a French menu, and any decent cookbook should tell you what each is and how it's prepared. But when you walk into a restaurant and see "Crêpes Henri," which was invented by the proprietor, you can have no way of knowing that they are filled with Port du Salut cheese and a touch of fresh garlic. The waiter ought to be able to tell you. Similarly, few of us have the time or inclination to memorize every kind of wine (let alone vintage), so inquire. Oenology, like gastronomy, is pretty much a snob's game. This isn't to say that some wines aren't demonstrably better than others, but only that a great deal of nonsense gets passed along by "experts" who know less than they would have us believe. It is not only conceivable, but possible, that the house *ordinaire* is as good or better than the dusty vintage in the wine rack, and is therefore a far better buy.

Travel writing is consumer writing, and when you think about what travelers pay for transportation, accommodations, and food, you quickly realize that they are entitled to the best they can get in the way of help from those who scout for them.

# chapter twenty-three

# COURTS AND THE LAW

There is at least one good reason for lawyers to envy physicians, according to a lawyer friend of mine: the basic component of the physician's work—the human body—does not vary. Although methods of diagnosis and treatment are continuously improved, and physicians have to stay abreast of them, the human body remains essentially the same. The anterior longitudinal sulcus of a patient in Seattle is the same as the anterior longitudinal sulcus of a patient in Miami (assuming neither has heart trouble). A surgeon could therefore operate on either of them in exactly the same way knowing, as he would, that if you've seen one normal anterior longitudinal sulcus, you've seen them all.

Not so for the lawyer or the reporter covering the law. There are 50 states in this country, each claiming sovereignty, and each having its own set of laws. In addition, just about every municipality has its own legal statutes and, covering the whole confusing business, there is the pervasive mantle of federal laws enacted by Congress.

Not only are there enough laws on the books to fill a good-sized library, but many of them have proven to be in conflict with one

283

another, particularly where relations between the states and the federal government are concerned. That, in fact, was at the heart of the wrenching civil rights conflict of the 1950's—a battle of consitutions as interpreted by judges sitting in courts of law.

The court structure in the United States can be likened to a true pyramid. The Supreme Court of the United States, which sits in Washington, resolves appeals brought to it from the highest court in a particular state, generally called the appellate (appeals) or state supreme court.

Then comes the wide array of courts of first instance, or original jurisdiction, known as circuit, common pleas, or superior courts, which handle serious civil and criminal matters. In larger municipalities, or if the court load is heavy, other criminal courts with names like terminer, general sessions, oyer, or just county court are used. There can also be probate, or surrogate courts (which rule on wills), divorce courts, family courts, juvenile courts, and others. All courts of original jurisdiction are courts of record. Where the reporter is concerned, this means that what happens in them is privileged to be passed along to the public by the media unless the judge rules otherwise for a good and specific reason. If he or she *does* clamp a news embargo on a court proceeding, it is called a "gag" by the press.

At the base of the pyramid are the inferior courts of limited jurisdiction, sometimes known as magitrates' courts. Inferior courts in rural areas can be presided over by justices of the peace. Inferior courts, or people's courts as they are sometimes called, handle small claims, minor misdemeanors, traffic tickets, and the like.

The structure of the pyramid is such that, in theory, a case that is unresolved to the satisfaction of one party at the base can be carried ever upward from one court to the next until it lands in the U.S. Supreme Court for final adjudication (judgment). The Supreme Court, therefore, has the final word in any legal dispute involving a constitutional question—at least until the word, or decision, is overturned by a second Supreme Court ruling. That's why U.S. Supreme Court decisions are given so much play by the media —they are often of crucial importance, not just to the state or municipality, but to the entire nation.

There are two basic kinds of court proceedings: civil and criminal. Basically—and this pushes oversimplification to its limit—civil actions are almost always fought between two sides, neither of which is the state prosecuting for a violation of the law. I said "almost" because the federal government has lately begun using civil lawsuits to fight deceptive consumer practices. A divorce proceeding involving the end of a marriage is a good example of an ordinary civil suit. One or both of the persons in the action wants the divorce because they can't, or don't think they can, live together as man and wife. It's not because either of them is a criminal who has violated the law. The public prosecutor therefore has no grounds for prosecuting either or both of the parties, and stays out of the matter, since no law has been broken. Actions for damages or bankruptcy are civil matters and so, too, are battles for the control of companies, real estate, or money in which no crime has been committed.

Criminal cases obviously involve crimes. And where crimes have been committed (or *allegedly* committed), either an individual or, more usually, the state prosecutes. The public prosecutor—generally the district attorney for crimes against a municipality or county, the state's attorney for crimes against a state, or the United States Attorney for crimes against the federal government—tries to prove that so-and-so broke the law. Crimes of violence such as robbery, rape, and murder are obviously against the law. But so, too, are blackmail, bribery, intimidation, embezzlement, tax fraud, defacing property, violation of zoning ordinances, and a formidable list of other nonviolent offenses.

With all due respect to the intrepid Perry Mason, most court proceedings consist for the most part of constant tedium, dry language, and postponements. The army private's universal complaint applies to most court actions: Hurry up and wait. This is because the law is so important and complex that it has to be treated methodically and with painstaking precision. It is an offensive-defensive battle, often waged with great subtlety, with plenty of room for maneuvering and ingenuity. But, except in the most sensational cases—the Lindbergh murder trial and Patricia Hearst's robbery trial being but two—court actions generally don't produce very lively copy. There are things a reporter in court can do, though, to make his or her work easier and the stories resulting from it better.

## Train sources.

Judges and lawyers (both prosecution and defense) are political creatures. They are very ambitious and, as a profession, produce most of our politicians. If they don't learn the value of favorable publicity while campaigning for student office in college, they assuredly get the message by the time they leave law school. Not long after they start working in the courthouse and having lunch at the University Club, they begin bantering politics and getting into the swing of political life on some level. "Herb Miller is going to get the U.S. Attorney's job," one neophyte confides to another over crab salad, "and he's already positioning himself in the Democratic Club. Miller'll run for Congress in six years. You watch."

If that's true, then Herb Miller, public prosecutor, is acutely aware that (1) the more favorable exposure he gets in the press, the better, since this keeps his name in the public eye, in the party's eye, and in the eyes of the most important politicos in the city or state, and (2) those reporters who he favors with information will probably treat him better later on than those he ignores. For Miller, then, reporters are potential conduits for promotion, influence, and high office. Defense lawyers are equally ambitious, though more for building their practices (and bank accounts) than for political goals. Judges almost always want promotion to a higher court, and all the way to the U.S. Supreme Court, if possible, because of the increased prestige and salaries. Supreme Court judges, by the way, cannot be fired.

Therefore, let your best sources know that if they come to you first with accurate, clear, and undistorted information, they can expect to see their names in print if it is warranted. This does not mean a profile, an account of their "exploits," or any other form of pap, however brief. It means something like this:

> The government intends to prosecute Mario Macaroni, author of the best-selling *The Goddog,* on four counts of income tax evasion, according to the U.S. Attorney's office.
> The alleged nonpayment of federal income taxes, going back to 1976, involves an estimated $84,000 in book royalties and proceeds from the movie of the same name.
> "Artists sometimes have a tendency to think that their

creativity puts them above tax obligations," said Herbert Miller, Assistant U.S. Attorney. Miller is prosecuting the case.

"We see it differently, though. Anyone who accepts money for what he does is a businessman, and businessmen are supposed to pay taxes. So we're going to sue to recover the revenue," Miller said.

Macaroni is vacationing in Cannes, according to friends, and was not available for comment.

What occasionally happens, however, is that Miller calls, gives the information, and then tells the reporter to attribute it to . . . his boss, the U.S. Attorney. This doesn't happen because Herb Miller is as devoted to his chief as a cardinal is to the Pope. It's because one of the first memos Miller read after he took his job said that all press attribution goes to his boss, the U.S. Attorney, unless otherwise stipulated. Why? Because chances are that his boss also wants to run for something and is first in line. So you mention Miller's boss in the story. Miller's day will come.

Some of the most important court sources seem to have the lowliest, least glamorous jobs, but don't be fooled. Courts, again, run something like army regiments. The officers make the big decisions, but the sergeants keep everything moving. Depending on jurisdiction, the clerk sets the trial calendar with the judge, prepares the docket (a valuable abstract of cases), records motions, prepares judicial orders, and sells transcripts of the trial (which are mighty handy things to have, especially at deadline time). He or she is also responsible for seating the press. So be nice. The bailiff keeps order in the court. The stenographer makes a complete record of the proceedings. All three, if they are any good, know who's who and what's what.

## Break the code.

Legalese can be so complicated that even lawyers sometimes get confused by it. It has to be translated into standard English for the general audience, though. Most people don't know what a change of venue is, so the reporter has to tell them, even if doing so means using three times as many words. (It means changing the location of a trial, usually because any jury is likely to be prejudiced against the defendant.) Whether or not you cover courts regularly, you ought to have some rudimentary ability at reading legal documents and making sense out of them. This doesn't mean that you're expected to know what habeas corpus ad subjiciendum is. But words like plaintiff, subpoena, injunction, nolo contendere, mandamus, and deposition ought to be understood. (There's a list of them near the end of the chapter.) When you come across habeas corpus ad subjiciendum, grab one of the learned counsels, and ask for a definition.

"Oh," he or she will likely answer, "that's a writ challenging imprisonment. We don't think that Flagstone ought to be in jail." Good enough.

## Comment.

Try to get the accused's side of the story on the record or, if there is no accused, the positions of both parties to the dispute. You need as much for fairness. Comment, in this regard, goes beyond the plea ("guilty" or "not guilty") made at an arraignment or in court. It is a statement in as much detail as possible by the accused on how he or she feels about the situation. Once again: if that person doesn't want to say anything, write that he or she *declined to comment,* or *did not care to comment,* not refused to comment. If you can't get a comment on the day of the event, either because the accused is not available or because of time pressure, try for it the next day.

## Continuity.

Follow-ups are sadly lacking in almost all crime and court reporting. Most civil suits involving scandal, public officials, money, and the like, plus many criminal cases, involve so-called plea bargaining for a reduction of sentence. This means that an accused criminal will offer to plead guilty to a lesser crime in exchange for a lesser sentence (an obvious concession that he's guilty of something, anyway). Plea bargaining or a postponement of any kind can take years to reconcile. Too often, these matters are forgotten after the first flushes of an arrest or a court action, leaving the public (and the record) with a distorted picture of an event that is not concluded.

This frequently happens after arrests. Say a man is arrested downtown for drunken and disorderly conduct and the story makes the newspaper. Those in his community are going to read that he was arrested by the police and was charged. "Ah, ha!" neighbors and business associates will snicker, "Old Jim got smashed and was cutting up downtown, and the cops arrested him." Jim's wife and kids, parents and siblings, friends and partners, and, of course, Jim himself, will cringe with embarrassment. Jim's trial comes up three months later and he is . . . acquitted. It turns out that four drunks were carrying on as he passed by and that he was arrested and thrown in the paddy wagon with them. Where the law is concerned, Jim has been proven innocent of the charge in court. But if that court's verdict isn't put in the newspaper, the arrest story, standing alone, becomes the media's entire record of the event. That single story—". . . charged with being drunk and disorderly . . ."— may be committed to microfilm forever and certainly will be clipped and dropped into Jim's file in the newspaper's morgue. Worse, everyone in the community who does not know Jim personally will continue thinking that he was guilty (yes, if you're arrested for something, most people think you're guilty—why else would you have been arrested?) until the end of his days. That is manifestly unfair. You can avoid such a situation by keeping track of when postponements are due to come up on the court calendar, by noting when trials are supposed to take place, and by making certain that you learn their outcome.

You also ought to know that, sadly, even someone's official record doesn't always show the final disposition of his case. This is for the very simple reason that there are some policemen who can't bear the thought of having it recorded that someone they arrested was acquitted. It won't say that he was convicted if he wasn't, of course; it just won't show *any* disposition. You would therefore have to check court records.

### Indictments.

A grand jury is basically a screening device composed of 16 or more qualified citizens who decide whether the prosecution has a good enough case against someone so that it can go to trial. The composition of grand juries varies from state to state and federally, and so do the rules under which they work. In California, for example, there are 23 persons on a grand jury, at least 14 of whom must vote to indict in order for it to happen. In New York, the number varies between 16 and 23, at least 12 of whom are needed for an indictment. Defense evidence can be introduced to California grand juries; only prosecution evidence goes to New York grand juries.

Those who favor grand juries usually do so on the basis of their acting as checks against overzealous or vindictive prosecutors and because their secrecy means that suspects aren't exposed to unfavorable publicity. Those who don't like them argue that the selection of grand jurors can determine whether someone is prosecuted or not, that grand juries are little more than rubber stamps that almost always favor prosecutors, that they can therefore be used for harassment and violation of constitutional rights, and that they waste money because they duplicate other ways of accomplishing the same thing—preliminary judicial hearings and the filing of "information" by prosecutors.

According to general, but not uniform, custom, the prosecuting attorney presents evidence to the grand jury and acts as its legal adviser. The jury can order the prosecuting attorney to subpoena any witness it wants to question, and although that witness can consult a lawyer, he or she must testify before the jury without one. In most jurisdictions, witnesses are granted immunity from prosecution based on their testimony, unless they sign a waiver to the contrary. In some places, the prosecuting attorney is not required to inform suspects that they are under grand jury investigation, but if they learn that they are, they are entitled to appear on their own behalf. Finally, suspects are never granted immunity. If the grand jury thinks there is enough evidence against them to warrant a trial, it hands up (not down) an indictment.

It should be clear at this point that grand jury deliberations, which are always conducted in secret, are pretty one-sided affairs. They were designed that way. But it should also be clear that if the prosecuting attorney wanted to bring evidence to a grand jury purporting that you or I molest small animals, it wouldn't necessarily follow that (1) we are guilty, or (2) that the grand jury would decide that it had enough evidence against us to bring the case to a conviction in court. This being so, it is unfair to report, as some newspapers do, that a grand jury "is considering handing up an indictment against" so-and-so. A grand jury could in theory be considering handing up an indictment against the President of the United States for destruction of public property on his last campaign swing. This doesn't mean they *will* hand up anything. Such a story may seem sensational (it isn't until there's an indictment), but it assuredly isn't fair. Don't report grand jury deliberations (which are usually leaked by headline-hungry prosecutors who want to nail someone on page one) but only actual indictments. Then explain precisely what the indictment is for, what penalty a conviction would bring, some background to the case, a little about the accused, when the trial is scheduled to start, and how the accused feels about it all. It should be written clearly and pungently:

A Los Angeles County grand jury has handed up an indictment charging Bruno Troy, owner of North Hollywood's Step Inn restaurant, with the murder of his wife, Jill, last September.

Mrs. Troy was found shot to death in her car, which was parked on a deserted road near Malibu, shortly after 4 a.m. on Sept. 8. Police said at the time that robbery did not seem to be a motive.

If found guilty of first-degree murder, Troy could face life imprisonment. The trial is set to begin in Superior Court on Nov. 21.

"If I shot Jill, I'd be a zillionaire," Troy said after learning that he has been indicted. "I'd patent the gun because it would be able to shoot 3,000 miles. I was in New York when she was killed. I didn't do it."

## Trial procedure.

Bruno Troy's trial—a criminal, not a civil one—would begin with the selection of a regular jury. This is done very carefully because neither the prosecution nor the defense wants unfavorable jurors. The district attorney, for example, wouldn't dream of allowing 12 restaurant owners who didn't like their wives to sit in judgment of Bruno Troy. He and the defense counsel would screen prospective jurors in an effort to get as many as possible on the jury who might sympathize with their respective positions. It should be noted here that trial lawyers on either side hold most jurors in low esteem where intelligence and awareness are concerned. Every trial lawyer has jury "stories," the common denominator of them being that overestimating any juror's mentality is a serious mistake. (One recalls a juror who thought that rights are "waved" like a flag.) Anyway, when the jury has been agreed upon, all 12 members are sworn in.

The prosecutor makes the opening address. He or she explains the details of the crime and goes on to tell everyone how it will be proven that Bruno Troy murdered his wife, Jill, early on the morning of September 8th. The defense then either makes its own opening statement (explaining why Troy didn't kill his wife), or holds off making the statement until the prosecution has finished establishing its case.

Next come the witnesses for the prosecution: a police ballistics expert who tells the court that the .38-caliber bullet taken out of Mrs. Troy by the medical examiner came from a revolver owned by her husband; a barmaid from Santa Monica who is certain that she served the Troys drinks on the night of the murder and that they seemed to have been having a heated argument; an airline stewardess who swears that Troy was on her flight, which landed at Los Angeles International from New York just after midnight on the day of the murder; and others. The prosecutor questions the witnesses in such a way so as to make their testimony show that Troy is guilty. He *examines* them. The defense then *cross-examines* them, trying to find holes and inconsistencies in their testimony. If the scope of the cross-examination allows, the prosecutor can come back with more questions, and so can the defense after that.

Then it is the defense's turn to introduce witnesses. They are called to swear under oath that Bruno Troy loved Jill, had planned an expensive surprise birthday party that was to have taken place the week after she was killed, and, in fact, had been in New York on business the night she was murdered. Lying in court while under oath is called perjury and is a felony punishable by a prison term. All of the witnesses for the defense are then cross-examined in the same way as were the witnesses for the prosecution.

Both sides may now introduce rebuttal witnesses who can contradict or support what other witnesses testified.

Then comes the summation—the scene in the movies in which the lawyers try to convince the jury—with heartfelt rhetoric and as much drama as the judge can stomach—that Troy is obviously guilty and just as obviously innocent. The prosecution starts and is followed by the defense. In some places, the prosecution is also allowed to close the summation, leaving the defense in the middle. The prosecutor and the defense counsel then rest their cases and very likely both walk out of the courtroom and go to lunch together. Being on opposite sides of a court battle in no way means that they don't like each other.

The judge then charges the jury. He tells them, to make sure they understand what the law says in this case, what the possible verdicts are, and explains what each verdict means. He probably ends by reminding the jury that the state (the prosecution) must have been able to prove Troy's guilt beyond any reasonable doubt. If there is any reasonable doubt in their minds, he tells the jurors, they must find Troy not guilty.

The jury goes out. All 12 are escorted to a jury room and there they remain, alone, until they have reached a decision. All 12 must reach a verdict of guilty for a conviction. They must, in other words, be unanimous. If just one of them refuses to find Troy guilty as charged, the jury becomes "hung," and the trial has to take place all over again. If they find Troy guilty, they return to the court, and the jury foreman gives the verdict. If that verdict is guilty, the judge can either sentence Troy right there and then, or he can remand him (send him back to jail) until sentence is passed at a later date. (The judge would announce that date and the reporter would note it on his calendar.) This obviously wouldn't hold up the story, though, since the conviction itself is news.

> Bruno Troy, the owner of North Hollywood's Step Inn restaurant, was found guilty yesterday of murdering his wife, Jill, on Sept. 8.
>
> Superior Court Judge Harlowe Ballantine set Dec. 6 as the date of sentencing. Troy could get life imprisonment. His lawyer, Ruth Golden, said she plans an appeal.
>
> Mrs. Troy, a former model, was found shot to death in her car, which was parked on a deserted road near Malibu, shortly after 4 a.m. on Sept. 8.

Troy tried to establish his innocence during the six-day trial by proving that he was in New York at the time of his wife's murder.

Deputy District Attorney Carter Beanstock convinced the jury, however, that Troy flew back to Los Angeles hours before the murder and was with his wife shortly before she was killed. Troy's .38-caliber revolver was identified by police as the murder weapon.

Ms. Golden tried to show that an airline stewardess who identified Troy as having been on the plane was mistaken. The prosecution convinced the jury that Troy had returned to Los Angeles under an assumed name.

The jury, composed of four men and eight women, took a little more than two hours to bring in a verdict of first-degree, or premeditated, murder. The Troys had repeated arguments, according to friends, neighbors, and others who testified at the trial.

Notice that in both stories—the indictment and trial—background on the killing itself was provided for readers who might have missed the original crime story or whose memories needed freshening. In addition, Troy's main line of defense was put in, as was the composition of the jury, the time it took to bring in the verdict, and the fact that the Troys had had arguments. All this was done to give readers enough background so that the immediate news—that Troy was found guilty—made sense.

Major criminal trials are seldom as "clean" as this one. It is conceivable that there could have been one or more postponements, that the jury could have brought in a second-degree murder verdict, that there could have been a great deal of conflicting testimony, and more. It would all have to be explained clearly and concisely. This is one of the things that makes reporting on the courts difficult.

Here are some legal terms you ought to be familiar with when reporting court cases. It's important to remember, though, that as laws vary from one jurisdiction to another, so may the meaning of the terminology. Make sure you've broken whatever code is used before you write the story.

| Accessory | A person who assists another in committing a crime, either before the fact or after it. |

Someone who hides a fugitive is an accessory after the fact.

Adjournment

An allowance of more time to either the prosecution or the defense so it can find other witnesses or important evidence.

Administrator

Someone who is appointed by the court to oversee the estate of a person who has died without leaving a will (not a "last will and testament," which is corny).

Arraignment

The process in which a prisoner hears the charges against him and pleads to them (guilty or not guilty). Arraignments usually take place within 24 hours of the arrest.

Bail (or Bond)

Money, almost always supplied by a professional bondsman to the court, to help make sure the accused shows up for trial. The accused is released from jail only after the bail is posted. If he flees, he is said to have "jumped" bail, and the bail is forfeited. The amount of bail is set by a judge according to the seriousness of the crime and the likelihood that the accused will appear for trial. Bail can in some cases be set for as much as $4 million. In others, especially when the accused is known to be ferocious or is very likely to flee, he is held without bail (provided the jurisdiction allows the protection of society to be a consideration in the setting of bail).

Bench warrant

A court's authorizing an official to arrest someone and bring him to court.

Bill of particulars

A formal statement listing the details of an indictment, complaint, or information (the last, again, being an indictment, made directly by the prosecutor, not by a grand jury).

Change of venue

Changing the location of a trial because the defense counsel thinks that the accused will not be treated fairly by a jury. This is usually requested in towns after a particularly terrible crime—say, the murder of an entire family—when feelings throughout the community are running very high against anyone suspected of having been involved.

Commutation
A reduction of sentence, generally because of extenuating circumstances, such as the age of the defendant.

Concurrent sentence
A decision by the court that a convicted defendant serves only the longest of two or more terms set for him.

Consecutive sentence
Sentence in which the defendant serves the total of all the terms. For example, three years for robbery, plus two years for assault, equals five years in prison.

Contempt of court
Disruption of the court or any other offense against it by a witness, a lawyer or a defendant. It is punishable by a fine, imprisonment, or both. Improper examination or harassment of a witness by a lawyer after warnings from the judge can bring a contempt citation. So can unruliness by a defendant or a witness.

Corpus delicti
The element of the crime charged; its essence. Generally (and there are exceptions), there must be a body when someone is accused of murder. If there is no victim then, technically, there can be no murderer.

Deposition
Taking a statement under oath from a witness before a trial begins. Depositions are usually used in civil trials.

Directed verdict
The judge's telling a jury to bring in a particular verdict. But, you may ask, why bother having a jury if the judge is going to direct its verdict? Let's say Hank and Steve hate each other. Hank tells Steve that he's going to shoot him the next time he sees him. They meet on the street the next day, Hank reaches in his pocket, and Steve quickly

pulls out a pistol and kills him. It turns out that Hank was reaching for a tissue because his nose was running. But Steve is arrested and tried. Technically, Steve is guilty of second-degree murder, but because of the circumstances the judge could direct the jury to find him guilty of voluntary man-slaughter, which carries a lighter sentence.

**Double jeopardy**  Being tried twice for the same crime. It's unconstitutional.

**Extradition**  Returning a suspect from one jurisdiction to another so he can stand trial. Often, for example, suspects flee to other countries. An extradition treaty, if it exists, provides for that country's being able to return the suspect to the United States.

**Habeas corpus**  A writ calling for someone who is in custody as a crime suspect to be brought to court so that an inquiry can be made as to the legality of holding him.

**Injunction**  A court order requiring those named to stop doing whatever they're doing. Injunctions are probably most often filed to temporarily stop strikes and business activities until the court has time to hear the case and make a ruling. An injunction was used against *The New York Times* in 1971 to prevent publication of the Pentagon Papers (see Gag orders, below).

**Mandamus**  A court's ordering someone, even another judge, to do something. If a trial court erroneously rules that a confession is inadmissable, for example, the district attorney might appeal the decision to a higher court. If the appellate court agrees with the D.A., it could issue a writ of mandamus ordering the trial court to admit the confession as evidence.

**Mistrial**  The premature ending of a trial because of

some irregularity. This is generally asked for by the defense when evidence is improperly submitted or it is found that one or more members of the jury have been exposed to unfavorable publicity about the defendant during the trial.

Motion to dismiss    A motion made by the defense to end an action because there is insufficient basis for it.

Nolle prosequi    Literally, not to prosecute. Therefore, a decision not to continue the case.

Nolo contendere    This means that the defendant does not want to contest the charges against him.

Pardon    The ending of a prison sentence before it is completed as set by the court, either for good behavior, or because new evidence has been found in support of the person in prison.

Parole    The release of a prisoner on condition that he reports to a parole officer or board at regular intervals. Failure to do so could get him put back in jail.

Plaintiff    The person or group that starts the court action. It is therefore the *opposite* of defendant.

Plea bargaining    It's called "copping a plea," in street talk. This means that the accused agrees before trial to admit to a lesser crime with the understanding that he will get a lesser sentence. The case therefore doesn't go to trial, which saves the prosecutor's and the court's time, while getting the accused off relatively lightly.

Presentment    A grand jury indictment made on its own initiative or after allegations have been brought to it by private citizens.

Quash    A motion made by the defense saying that an indictment or any judicial order should be nullified.

Replevin    A writ ordering that property be returned.

| | |
|---|---|
| Reprieve | A delay in the start of a prison sentence. |
| Sealed verdict | A jury verdict written and sealed while the judge is absent. He opens it when he returns. |
| Subpoena | An order by the court directing someone to appear and testify (with documentary evidence, if appropriate). This has nothing to do with the guilt or innocence of the person who gets it and should not be confused with a summons. |
| Summons | An action order by the court against someone who has allegedly committed a crime or who is being brought to court as a party to some kind of litigation. Summonses are "served" in person by a representative of the court—a policeman, sheriff, or anyone else. |
| Writ of certiorari | An order from a higher court to a lower one directing the records of a proceeding be sent for examination and review. |

These terms and their definitions are for your information and don't necessarily belong in news stories. Since many readers wouldn't necessarily understand what a change of venue means, for example, it would have to be explained in standard English: "Leghorn asked that the trial be moved to River City because he does not think that his client can get an unbiased jury in Boylston."

### "Gag" orders.

"Gags" are usually imposed by judges to prevent the press from reporting what happens at a trial, the events concerning the case, or from talking to lawyers and other participants outside the courtroom. The reason for this, judges issuing gags say, is that publicity can affect the outcome of a trial and therefore interferes with the whole concept of impartiality—with the Sixth Amendment's guarantee of a fair trial.

The press, on the other hand, has argued that gag orders violate its freedom to report the news as guaranteed by the First Amendment. If the events at or about trials can't be reported, the journalists insist, then the public is denied knowledge of them. Furthermore, the argument goes, gags can be (and often are) slapped on legislative committee meetings and other political gatherings that directly affect the public, and on anything (such as the Pentagon Papers) that is summarily classified as being secret. Technically, this is called "prior restraint," but the word "gag" gives a good indication of the contempt with which journalists view such orders. They have therefore battled gags for decades.

On June 30, 1976, the United States Supreme Court issued an historic decision, and one which warmed the hearts of reporters and editors throughout the country. By a vote of 9–0, the Justices ruled that judges generally may not forbid the publication of information about criminal cases even when they think that doing so will help assure a fair trial. This does not mean that those involved in a trial are guaranteed the right to talk to reporters about cases. They can still be prevented from doing so. It does mean, though, that once a reporter *has* the information, he or she cannot be prevented from using it except in truly unique circumstances.

By coincidence, the decision came five years to the day after the Supreme Court handed down a 6–3 ruling in favor of allowing *The New York Times* to publish the Pentagon Papers. *The Times* began publishing the Vietnam war documents in installments, starting on June 13, 1971, but was forced to stop after the Justice Department almost immediately got an injunction against continued publication. When the Court made its ruling against prior restraint by the government, the series began running again, and was eventually published in book form.

In the 1976 decision, which was brought to the Supreme Court by Nebraska journalists who had been gagged while trying to cover a mass murder trial in their state, the Court said that gag orders almost always violate the First Amendment. Three of the Justices wrote opinions saying that gags are always unconstitutional. The others, while also condemning gags, left open the possibility of using them only in the most exceptional cases. The net effect, though, was to practically kill the possibility of a news organization's not being able to run stories about criminal cases. It amounted to a virtual ban on prior restraint.

The opinion of Justice William J. Brennan Jr., a First

Amendment absolutist, is worth quoting in part here. There probably isn't a journalist in the country who could have put it better
than he did:

> Secrecy of judicial action can only breed ignorance and dis-
> trust of courts and suspicion concerning the competence and
> impartiality of judges; free and robust reporting, criticism, and
> debate can contribute to public understanding of the rule of law
> and to comprehension of the functioning of the entire criminal
> justice system, as well as improve the quality of that system by
> subjecting it to the cleansing effects of exposure and public
> accountability.

# chapter twenty-four

# POLITICS AND GOVERNMENT

Politics as practiced in America can be a sordid, devious, and aggrandizing game more often than most of us care to think about. Weak and corrupt politicians at times seem to be everywhere. Instances of governmental waste and incompetence amount to folklore. In spite of it all, however, there is one factor that is so redeeming that it more than tips the balance: Politics *is* practiced in America.

The United States is the most socially responsive nation in history. It is also one of the relatively few remaining nations that is still politically responsive to the wishes of its citizenry. Today—now—it comes closer to epitomizing Aristotle's dream of a democratic state than did his own Athens. And the wonder of American democracy is a resilience that has allowed it to survive a series of jarring blows that would have shattered less sturdy systems like so much crystal.

The freedoms in America, relative to most of the rest of the world, are formidable. Take, for example, the gags we were discussing at the end of the last chapter. In most nations, gags are not a matter of court conflict. Since in many countries there is no freedom of the press, it doesn't occur to anyone to make much of an issue out of permanent gagging, or censorship. If an editor or a reporter doesn't like the system, he or she is simply "replaced." Period. Here, squabbles over gags turn into honest-to-goodness court battles, and go all the way to the highest court in the land. And, astoundingly, the Supreme Court—one of the three pillars of the federal government—rules in favor of the press and against other courts!

Good reporters are mindful of the imperfections of the body politic in which they live and work. They are skeptical about politicians and bureaucrats, and rightly so, since it is their job to act as the watchdogs of the political system. You can hear them snickering in every campaign, at every primary, at every convention, and on every election day. But ask any of them whether he or she would rather work someplace else—say in Eastern Europe, Communist China, Korea, the Soviet Union, or anywhere in Africa or Latin America—and you will probably be looked at as though you're slightly mad. American journalists basically work within the system and for its improvement, not to undermine and destroy it.

The system rests on local politics. Before a reporter is allowed to cover politics, he or she has enough experience—has been around long enough—so that the basics of local politics and government are pretty well digested. I therefore wouldn't try to turn this chapter into a mini-civics lesson, even if I could, since this book deals with beginning reporting. Yet a few words about local politics are in order. Then we'll touch on a few things reporters ought to know about politicians, but which aren't in the civics books.

There are two established political parties in this country, both of which have offshoots, and neither of which is as cohesive as it once was. Both are in a constant state of realignment and both have large splinter groups. If you asked a voter as late as 1960 how he was going to vote, the chances are he would answer: Republican or Democratic. Now, the traditionally conservative Republicans have a liberal "wing," and the traditionally liberal Democrats have an outspoken conservative "wing." In a loose sort of way, it's similar to the proliferation of Protestant denominations. Members of an existing church don't feel completely comfortable with all of its tenets, so they break off and start their own denomination, though still calling themselves Protestants. To make matters even more complicated, a liberal Republican from Texas is not necessarily in harmony with a liberal Republican from Rhode Island. Finally, there are those who vote ultraconservative, liberal, socialist, and, increasingly, a very large group calling itself "independent," which is unified only to the extent that its members don't follow any party line, but "swing" back and forth according to the candidates they believe in. Political alignments, voter moods, and issues vary considerably from one county to the next, let alone from state to state, and it is the political reporter's job to sort out the situation in his or her area and make sense out of it. That can be done only by close study—by reading the clips, going over voting records, attending speeches and rallies, and questioning the candidates and their representatives very closely.

You should be able to see by this point why political coverage goes to the most experienced reporters in a news organization. As opposed to, say, routine police stories, politics is complicated and potentially very serious in the long-run. On the one hand, politicians become justifiably angry when they are misrepresented in print or on the air. But on the other hand, they are often the most expedient of creatures and therefore need to be covered with generous doses of healthy skepticism. This is not work for "cubs."

The basic, and most important, political subdivision in a city is the precinct. In rural areas, it is usually the county as a whole. Each of the two major parties has precinct or county organizations throughout the country, and it is in them that the legion of loyalists does all the dreary things that carry elections: ringing doorbells, using loudspeakers in cars downtown or at the shopping mall, slapping up posters, handing out buttons, circulating petitions, stuffing envelopes, phoning voters, and the rest. These are the most wonderful people in the campaign (and always the least reported) because most of them work out of pure ideological conviction, rather than because they will get some office if their candidate wins.

Several precincts are generally grouped into a ward, run by a "boss," or "captain," who wields considerable power. It is on the ward level, in fact, that the power game begins in earnest. The ward boss sends money to precincts so bills can be paid, dispenses favors to the most loyal around him, maintains communication with anyone in his area who can contribute to the party, and occasionally intercedes for anyone in the party machine who gets into trouble with the law. Wards, in turn, report to the city or county committee, also run by a boss who does about what the ward boss does, but on a bigger scale. The most interesting aspect of the relationship between candidates and bosses, at least from a reporting standpoint, is that while the former constantly seek publicity, the latter almost always shun it—and with very good reason. The nature of the boss' wheeling and dealing behind the scenes is such that publicity would hurt, not help, him. It is usually from his office that city jobs are handed out to the most dedicated of the party loyalists or to members of their families—jobs starting on the level of bookkeeper in the sanitation department or secretary in a city hospital, to elevator inspector or welfare claims supervisor, to the head of an entire department or agency. It is in his office, too, that the big money behind campaigns is collected and dispensed, high-ranking police officers are "taken care of" in embarrassing emergencies, balky union leaders are made to see the wisdom of not ordering strikes before elections, and a good deal more. Those are not things that can be accomplished in the presence of reporters. So while the candidate is talking himself hoarse on some street corner or, having been elected, is handling the visible affairs of the city or county, the well-greased machine on which he rides moves silently, but relentlessly on.

It follows from this that everyone who is elected to office owes favors—*everyone*, from a city councilman, to the mayor, to the governor, to a senator, to the President of the United States. They owe favors to those who support them—farmers, union members, industrial leaders, bankers, other politicians, or to any other group or individual that lends support. There is nothing sinister about this, at least theoretically, in a democratic system. Those who support a candidate have a right to expect something in return. It becomes sinister, however, when the public is needlessly subjected to hardship or expense through the repayment of such favors. The creation of unnecessary government jobs is a case in point, and so is a tax structure that benefits the supporters of the winner, while penalizing those of the loser. The awarding of contracts, a common element in the political reward system, should make the point.

Say that a new sewer is involved. There are two ways in which taxpayers can get hurt because of the repayment of a favor here. First, they can be charged for a sewer that is not needed. Second, they can pay more for that sewer than they should. A municipal decision to install a new sewer system can be made, even though the existing system is functioning quite nicely, because a large construction company bankrolled part of the mayor's, and several of the city councilmen's campaigns. Then, that same company unfairly wins the bidding that ordinarily goes with such municipal projects. Here, the ordinary voter loses. If, however, a new sewer system really is needed, and two bids come to about the same amount, it is not unreasonable to expect that the firm that supported the administration should win the contract. The catch, of course, is that all things ought to be equal in such a circumstance. But they never are, and that's why the spoils system has always been one of the investigative reporter's most fruitful working areas.

The political reporter working on a campaign is always caught in a morass of charges and countercharges, feints and lunges, brilliant rhetoric and abysmal droning, statesmanship and the worst sort of vindictiveness, recriminations, half-truths, and outright lies. Polls are either deliberately fashioned to show that the electorate wants Blowharde, or they are systematically interpreted to his advantage. And the "advantage" doesn't always mean showing that a majority wants Blowharde. Naturally, he is delighted if the polls shows that he has 68 percent of the vote, because it means (we are told) that the electorate understands and appreciates what he has done. A poll showing that he has only 39 percent of the vote, though, makes Blowharde an "underdog" fighting a hard, "uphill" battle, a beleaguered knight with a vision, pushing resolutely on, despite heavy odds. Americans, after all, are supposed to sympathize with underdogs.

In the middle of all this, along with the reporters, are members of the campaign staff, and notably the public relations, advertising, and polling specialists whose job it is to package poor old Blowharde until he looks like something under a Christmas tree. They form a small army that reconnoiters the electorate and the opposition and then provides the candidate with whatever weapons he needs to wage a particular battle. They slap a yarmulke on his head in a synagogue and tell him to say that "Israel must survive." An hour later, they hand him a plate of manicotti in an Italian neighborhood, and he announces that his maternal grandfather came from Milan. (The audience probably stirs at this because it comes from Naples and Palermo, where the Milanese are not liked.) That afternoon, the public relations specialists have told Blowharde, he will tell a group of bankers that the area needs tax incentives in order to bring in more industry. Later, after a shower, a second shave, and a third change of clothes (this time a slightly rumpled suit and scuffed shoes) he will explain to the transport workers' union that if the city were to stop wasting money on highway and road construction, they'd be making as much money as the police and firemen. Wherever he and Mrs. Blowharde are led, they smile, wave, pose for pictures, sign autographs, and shake so many hands that they have nightmares about it. And so it goes, day after grueling day, as the campaign progresses.

Reporters rarely have trouble with candidates in major campaigns—in no small part because they find it increasingly difficult to get near them. The campaign team handles and arranges everything. Its members write Blowharde's speeches, compose handouts for the press, conduct polls, mastermind the approach he takes on specific issues, occasionally tell him how to dress for specific occasions, give him lessons on how to speak, instruct him on his opponent's weak points and fashion ways in which he can exploit them, and school him on how to look and behave on television (if, indeed, they decide that it is to his advantage to appear on television). With increasing regularity, the packaged politician is sent to "media events," or happenings that have little or no news value, but that are staged in order to get maximum publicity, particularly on television. When a politician announces his candidacy four times, the first is news—the next three are media events. So are taking lessons on the use of chopsticks in a Chinese restaurant, kissing Cherry Bomb at the premiere of *The Goddog,* or singing "P-L-A-Y, Possum" at his college's alumni dinner, all in front of the cameras.

Who, then, *is* S. Erasmus Blowharde? As it turns out, it's becoming increasingly hard to tell, perhaps even for Blowharde himself. This is obviously a serious problem for the voters, who are more and more casting their ballots for looks, charm, and the neatly turned phrase. But it is also a problem for the political reporter, who has to make sense out of what he or she sees and hears, particularly in interpretive stories were explanations are necessary. The reporter, however, has two valuable tools with which to do this: a cool and dispassionate approach, and the record.

During Richard M. Nixon's 1968 presidential campaign, and

during the years of his first term, Spiro Agnew delivered a series of speeches and issued a string of remarks that left most of the press and many of the Eastern "establishment" shaking their heads in disbelief. He sailed through the now-famous effete snob and negative nabob litany, picking up fire from outraged editorial writers as he went, and otherwise drawing great attention to himself. Agnew, first as a candidate and then as the Vice-President, became an irresistible target for radicals, liberals, and Democrats of almost every stripe. Wristwatches with his picture on them were sold in department stores and, it was snickered on campuses and at cocktail parties from coast to coast, "Mickey Mouse wears a Spiro Agnew watch." Opponents of the Nixon administration had a field day punching back as hard or harder than they were punched. That, however, was precisely the Nixon team's plan. Like a mechanical fox, Spiro Agnew led the hounds away from the real fox by so goading and tantalizing them that they abandoned their primary quarry in favor of chasing a less important one. To a lesser degree, and in varying ways, this happens in many campaigns and during virtually every term of office.

Experienced political reporters are not easily drawn off the scent —drawn away from the issues. They know, for example, that charges and countercharges tend to get nastier as a campaign winds down, dirty tricks increase, more wild accusations are made, and an element of deliberate distortion creeps into the battle. Politicians, like most of us, tend to be "immediate," which is to say, as expedient as the moment requires. Unlike most of us, though, they are out to govern or, in fact, do govern. They are out to wield power. The price we ask in return for that power is accountability, which, in turn, rests on fundamental honesty.

Beware of wild charges and the raising of false issues. It is the responsibility of the political reporter, not only to substantiate charges made by anyone running for, or already in, public office, but to keep the most outlandish and vicious of those charges in careful perspective. Even if they are manifest lies, printing them invariably wins support from some voters and puts the accused candidate on the defensive, since he or she has to deny them (which keeps the malicious accusation alive):

## FERGUSON DENIES HIS WIFE IS ALCOHOLIC

Well, he can deny it all he wants, but a good deal of damage will have been done. The average reader, seeing such a story, carries in the back of his mind the nagging notion that it wouldn't have been in the newspaper unless there was "some truth to it." He will go to the polls with that thought.

A politician who styles himself as a "friend" of labor, college students, the middle class, ghetto dwellers, blacks, businessmen, or any other group is accountable for such statements. And, as you should know by now, the best way to check out what he says is to go to the leaders of such groups and ask them—*for the record*.

> Sen. S. Erasmus Blowharde said last night that, if elected to a third term, he will push hard for low- and middle-class housing projects in Grove City's East End.
>
> Speaking at a press conference at the Hotel Dorset, the Democrat said that it is time for the residents of Grove City's ghetto to be able to "live like human beings, not like animals."
>
> He accused his opponent, Harold Ferguson, of indifference to those in the East End, as well as to the poor elsewhere in the city and state. Ferguson is a liberal Republican.
>
> "My opponent's record speaks more eloquently about where his sympathies lie than I am capable of," the Senator said. "He's a liberal in name only."
>
> Mildred Garner, president of the East End Citizen's Association, is not optimistic about Blowharde's promise.
>
> "It sounds wonderful," Mrs. Garner said after hearing the speech, "but we've got two problems with it.
>
> "First, if the Senator's announced plan comes true, we'll still be penned up in the East End. Second, he's been in the Senate for 12 years and the ghetto is still there. What's taken him so long?"

Which brings us to the political reporter's second tool: the record. Everyone in public office takes stands on issues. Mayors are ultimately responsible for the overall running of their cities. To a greater or lesser degree, they get involved in union negotiations, tax structures, fiscal allocations, social services, transportation, housing, medical facilities, school affairs, public utility services, and just about everything else affecting a city. Their public (as opposed to private) stand on such matters is a matter of record. And that record ought to be checked for accountability, particularly at election time, or when controversy is in the air. The same applies to comptrollers, housing administrators, district attorneys, and everyone else in authority who belongs to a city's or state's executive branch.

Legislators—city councilmen, assemblymen, representatives, senators, or whatever—are even easier to check because they vote on specific issues (Yes, No, or Abstain)—and those votes are printed in the official record of the proceedings, year after year. It's only a matter of pulling the appropriate book off the shelf to find out that Blowharde abstained the last time the East End redevelopment bill came up for a vote. You would want to know *why* he did that. A transcript of anything he had said on the floor of the Senate before the vote might provide the answer and that, too, is on record. At the very least, you would want to raise the question at an appropriate time during the campaign.

Politics is what you do to get elected, some reporters like to say, and government is what you do after you're elected. This, of course, is oversimplified. Both politics and government are conducted simultaneously all the time by everyone in elective office. "They're always running," according to the saying. Yet the definition sets the basis for the essential difference: politics concerns the acquisition and maintenance of power, while government exercises that power.

Government, whether in a township or on the federal level, is a balancing act between groups having specific responsibilities. The "groups," be they called city council, Department of Defense, mayor's office, United States Senate, circuit court, or whatever, are always designed to check and balance one another and to carry out specific services on behalf of the citizenry. They are there to serve you and me; to preserve and, if possible, improve our existence.

Government on all levels has grown with the nation; some say too much, others, not enough. Most cities of any size today are not only loaded with agencies and offices designed to minister to the needs of their inhabitants, but have elaborate channels of communication with their state and federal counterparts. Laid out, nationwide, on a chart (the mere thought of which is horrifying), the entire structure would look like Buckminster Fuller's ultimate geodesic dome—an almost incomprehensible array of angular sections held together by thousands upon thousands of interlocking lines.

City governments are usually patterned on the federal, or constitutional model. That is, they have three branches: executive, legislative, and judicial. The mayor and the various departments or agencies that report to him form the executive branch. The city council, or board of aldermen, constitute the legislative branch. They enact laws, usually pass on the budget, and watch the executive branch as closely as possible. Councilmen and aldermen are elected from the various precincts of the city, and unlike the mayor, who represents everyone, a big part of their job is to make sure that no one gives their particular districts short shift when improvements are made or money is handed out. The judicial branch—the courts —does what courts generally do. It is supposed to act independently of the other two branches, but since so many judges are political appointees, this is rarely the case. If judges are appointed, they owe their jobs to the politician who appoints them. If they are elected (which means they run on a ticket) they owe what they have to the party machine under whose banner they won.

Because the various branches, and occasionally agencies or departments within branches, are designed to balance one another, they are in a more or less constant conflict situation. This is not bad, but good, because that's the way the checking and balancing works. The nature of the human quest for power being what it is, people are tempted to invest themselves with emperorlike authority unless there's someone around who has been empowered to say, "You can't do that." The political reporter—on all levels of government—stands in the midst of the conflict situation and observes what is happening around him or her.

What's happening, let's say, is that the municipal transportation department has completed a study that shows conclusively that a subway would unsnarl traffic in the downtown area, greatly ease pollution, rejuvenate the shopping district, and draw much of the middle and upper classes back into the heart of the city making it, a Public Affairs Department handout explains, a "vibrant and energetic lodestone for the entire area." (Public Affairs Department handouts always say things like that about proposed bridges, subways, airports, outdoor markets, and shopping malls.) Working in conjunction with the department of finance or the comptroller's office, which is also in the executive branch, a cost estimate has been reached. The mayor says that he's in favor of the project and, along with the comptroller and city engineers (carrying an easel and assorted maps), he appears before the City Council because he has to get its approval.

Up goes the easel and out come the maps. There's even a chart, done in pretty shades of red and blue, showing the projected amount of money that will come into the city after the subway is completed. The subway system map, however, shows not only what parts of the downtown area it will serve, but also where it will go along the fringes of the city—this, after all, is its purpose—to bring people in so they can work and shop.

Councilman Gerald L. Flinte, who represents the impoverished East End, now notices something interesting. The proposed system has two spurs. One of them ends at the far north end of Grove City, almost at the high, ivy-covered gates of the posh Knollwood Country Club. The other extends to the southwest, right along a series of upper-middle-class neighborhoods full of apartment houses. Councilman Flinte asks the mayor why there is no spur to the East End.

"Because," the mayor answers, "those are the neighborhoods with the dollars we want and the cars we don't want. A line running to the East End is under active consideration, Jerry."

"Am I to understand that the poorest people in this city are going to be denied the cheapest and fastest way to work? Do I understand correctly that you are going to use their tax money to finance a rapid transit system to the gates of the Knollwood Country Club and to Cherrydale Village?"

The conflict situation in its fullest, finest flower.

There is no way to appreciate, much less report, a city's ongoing conflict situation—its "politics"—unless you grasp the nature and motivations, the responsibilities and loyalties, the functions and ideologies, of all of the participants. You ought to start with a city organization chart and the clips, and then make the rounds, department by department, talking with the most important persons on your beat. And, as is the case with police and the courts, the most important persons from your standpoint aren't necessarily those with the most important titles. Key clerks in every municipal department are usually gold mines of information. And by all means go to as many meetings as possible. City council meetings, particularly in

proviso, but they are not necessarily separate laws, and they vary enormously in quality.

New York State's Freedom of Information Law, which went into effect in September 1974, pertains to records in all state and local government agencies, boards, committees, and legislatures. Groups that don't perform governmental functions—political parties, for example—don't come under freedom of information provisions. Information that any other law makes confidential is not open to the public, and neither is information that was given to any agency in confidence and contains trade secrets or other business details that, if made public, could unfairly harm a private individual or group. Here, though, are areas available to the public: opinions and orders in cases; statements of policy and interpretation, plus any documents or tables which led to the statements; minutes of meetings and public hearings; audits and tabulations made by or for the agency, board, committee, or department; instructions to staff (including manuals) if they affect the public; police booking records; records of names, titles, and salaries of employees (law enforcement agency records are available only to the press); final determinations of the members of governing bodies and the records of the final votes; any other records that any other laws make open.

Every New York State governmental agency is required under the provisions of the Freedom of Information Law to tell the public exactly where its records are available for reading or copying. It must also have a Records Access Officer in charge of helping people to get what they want. Finally, the agency has five working days in which to say whether or not it intends to make the records available. A refusal can be appealed to someone else in the agency. A second denial could result in a review by the state supreme court.

Sunshine and freedom of information laws are designed to give the public greater access to governmental matters that affect it, however indirectly. These are fine, as far as they go, and can be of considerable help to newspersons. But it is important to remember that they supplement other kinds of news gathering; they don't replace them. All of the information coming out of a committee hearing, whether made available orally through "sunshine," or in writing through freedom of information statute, leads to live sources who have to be questioned. There is no shortcut.

The political or governmental affairs reporter works among those who either want, or have sheer power, some of it obvious, some carefully hidden. If he is really good at his work, he does a great deal more than report and write about what happens on his beat. He also spends a great deal of time contemplating power—where it comes from, what it is, why some are hopelessly addicted to it, and how it is used or misused. He comes to understand that political power, on any level, can bring out the best or the worst in those who wield it. He also knows from close observation that political power, an amorphous, untouchable thing, can bring pleasure or misery to those for whom, or against whom, it is used. To many professional journalists, these qualities make "the power game," and everything that goes with it, the most fascinating and challenging of the reporting specialties.

part four

SURVIVAL

# chapter twenty-five

# THROUGH THE FIRST WINTER

There are only two kinds of absolute dictators left in the world, a colleague of mine once said in despair—ship captains and newspaper editors.

He knew that there were others, of course, but the remark reflected the frustration we first-year news clerks felt after our initial encounters with unyielding editors. We used to say that such and such an editor had the ABCs down cold—he was Arbitrary, Blind, and Capricious.

Twelve years, four jobs, eight beats, and more than 1,000 stories later, I began teaching basic news reporting in college. And in every class I have had, there have been students who have looked at the assignments I graded and then told me, in effect, that I am Arbitrary, Blind, and Capricious. It makes me smile.

The paradox of the American news organization is that it wages a constant battle for democracy while at the same time being one of the most undemocratic institutions ever hatched in a free society. It must be so. If every reporter picked the story he or she wanted to do, and had it run exactly as written, their combined product

319

would be almost unimaginable. There might be six stories about the same baseball game, 17 movie reviews (nine of them about the same movie), 14 news analyses (each 4,000 words long), and a staggering number of pieces about gourmet cooking, French restaurants, and television programs. Crime and the courts, science and education, religion and transportation, business and labor, would go practically unattended. The Paris bureau, with five times the staff of the home office, would send in a daily barrage of stories about bistros, wine, and the Grand Prix. Given the fact that there was a news hole of, say, 40 columns, reporters would get into shouting matches over whose story took precedence. It would be Pandemonium.

Editors have two basic functions. They are supposed to assure the integrity (balance, fairness, and correct length) of news stories, and do the same with the product as a whole, whether it be a newspaper or a news show. The managing editor of a newspaper, or the news director of a radio or television station, is like an orchestra leader. He has to keep perhaps 100 or more "musicians," most of whom think of themselves as virtuosos, playing in harmony. Like an orchestra leader, the editor tries to do the best he can with the "talent" he has. He dreams about what he could do with a reporting staff built around a dozen or more aggressive, obedient, and thoroughly knowledgeable Pulitzer Prize winners who are versed in everything from Aabenraa to Zygote and who can write Hemingway-quality stories in something under an hour. That kind of reporting staff will never exist, though, and neither will the ominiscient editor. Editors, too, make their share of mistakes. The difference between a good editor and a bad one is that the former understands this. While maintaining the authority he needs in order to get the job done, and never hesitating to make even the most unpopular decisions, he nonetheless keeps himself sufficiently flexible and imaginative so that good stuff from anyone—beginners included—is encouraged and rewarded. The unfailing mark of a good editor, like any other good administrator, is that of being able to get the best out of those who work for him.

From the beginning reporter's point of view, the first year or so is a tremendously difficult one, with a formidable number of things to learn. Arguing with editors is almost always counterproductive for two reasons, one professional and one emotional. Professionally, you've got to figure that he knows a lot more than you do, not only about reporting, but about things peculiar to the newspaper and its place in the community. By virtue of the fact that he is an editor— even a relatively poor one—he has a wider view of the news operation than any of his beginning reporters and most of his experienced ones. He sits in the eye of the news flow every day, considering your work and those of your colleagues, and comparing them.

The emotional reason, so far as I am concerned, amounts to a law: early impressions are infinitely more important than later impressions. It is a rather sad commentary on human relations, but I think a true one, that first impressions usually *do* stick. (Sensing this, many students go out of their way to "psych out" their teachers during the first days of class.) When a reporter who has done his first dozen or so stories in excellent fashion produces a bummer, the editor assumes that he has had a bad day. When a reporter whose first dozen or so stories were bummers produces one that is excellent, the editor may put it down to luck. Similarly, when a beginner does good work uncomplainingly and gains the respect of his editor during the initial period, he is taken seriously later when something happens that is really worth arguing about. The reporter who starts arguing with his editor from day one, on the other hand, is quickly put down as being something of a disciplinary problem and is listened to with a lot less than full attention ever after. During that first year, then, make your counterpoints politely, but firmly, and back off when you run into serious resistance. Don't snarl and complain about it to your fellow reporters. Be mature enough to understand that you just might be wrong and, further, that you aren't the only musician in the orchestra. Your day will come when they hand you the first violin (or the baton).

Here are other hints for survival, some minor, some pretty important:

1. Never whistle or sing in a newsroom. Your little ditty is guaranteed to leave someone else's concentration in shambles, and that's far from appreciated.

2. Don't bother any of your colleagues who are working. Writing —putting words on paper out of thin air so they make sense—requires a great deal of serious thought. If a colleague is doing that,

don't lope over to read him or her your lead, tell an anecdote, or crab about an assignment. And, particularly, never ask anyone how to spell a word. What goes through your victim's head is something like, "Why don't you look it up, yourself, you lazy twit?" If you're too lazy to use a dictionary, your reporting ability has to be questioned.

3. Never pirate a colleague's story or idea for a story, even if it's mentioned in the most casual way. It is morally wrong to steal anything, including ideas. More pragmatically, you will lay the basis for an office feud whose bitterness will erode the organization's overall effort and haunt you until the day you leave.

4. Be alert for stories that others can handle better than you can. You will from time to time trip over good stories that you either don't have time to cover, or which are better suited to the reporter on that particular beat. Tell him or her about it or write a detailed memo to the editor. Conversely, don't bombard beat reporters or editors with good-looking, but actually shallow, story ideas in order to promote yourself. Doing that will earn you the reputation of being either a politico or a dope.

5. Adhere to deadlines. Editors know that stories seldom develop to suit the clocks on the walls in front of them. They therefore also know that from time to time you will be late getting stories in. Don't abuse it. The rule is to get finished as quickly as possible. Turning in a story two hours early eases the copy editing jam-up later and is therefore deeply appreciated by everyone down the line, editors, copy editors, those on layout, and the souls on the picture desk who have to select photographs to go with your story and write captions for them.

6. Write what you've told them you're going to write. Learning a couple of minutes before deadline that all eight of the victims of the hotel fire turned out to be parakeets is the kind of thing that sends editors to their Gelusil bottles. If a story changes, keep your editor advised, since he's planning to play it according to what he thinks its value is. Editors have orderly, methodical minds. They positively despise last-minute surprises.

7. Don't get "lost." On the theory that they don't get poor assignments if they're not around, some reporters spend three times as long as they need to on stories, just so they can stay out of the office. What they don't know, or perhaps choose to ignore, is that their time is usually carefully accounted for by someone on the desk. Eventually, they are called to task for hardly ever being around when they're needed, and they suffer the consequences. Be stingy with your organization's time, first, because you're not paid to waste it, and second, because efficiency is noted. When on short assignments, and especially those that require movement (police or major accident stories, for example), keep the desk advised where you are. There is always a possibility that other, more pressing news, will require your being diverted.

8. Your progress is under constant evaluation, and one of the ways in which they judge you, is by the number of page-one stories you get. Page-one stories are obviously the day's most important (or so the editors think), and they are therefore noted by any number of persons in the organization. Without turning into a "bonus player," a "grandstander," or a "hot dog," to use sports terms, bear in mind that the more page-one stories you get, the better. That in no way means you ought to let less important news slip away, but only that you should be especially alert to any with page-one potential.

9. Keep a neat scrapbook filled with every bylined story you do. Not only is it a handy reference for any story you want to refer to later, but it is the portable record of your accomplishments (and potential), and it will therefore be important should you want to change jobs. Keep it at home. The rule for scrapbook preparation is this: lay it out in such a way so that it reflects the pride you have in your work. Hard-covered 11½ x 14 ring binders with plastic-covered black pages are probably best. The black pages set off the stories to best advantage, while the clear plastic oversheet protects them and reduces yellowing. Use a single-edge razor and a ruler, not scissors, to do the cutting. Glue the neatly cut clip on the page with rubber cement and make note of the date on which the story appeared on or beside it. Get as many clips as possible on each page, rather than trying to spread them out, since pages are

expensive. Some journalists spray each completed page with artist's fixative to further reduce yellowing. Unless you've got a statewide, or national reputation, you will sooner or later need a scrapbook for job hunting. If you drop a bunch of yellowed clips on an editor's desk, or hand him a sloppy scrapbook held together by a shoelace, you will not be making the best possible impression.

10. Avoid the "Cult of Personality." Newsmen and -women are in business to dispense the news, not make it. Television news, which has a heavy entertainment component, is increasingly putting its own reporters on camera as participants in events. This is done in an apparent effort to promote them as personalities—as being just as "human" as those in their audience—and therefore increase their followings (and ratings). We therefore see Greg Squarejaw not only reporting a pie-eating contest, but sitting there and eating one, while grinning contentedly at the camera. There should be no place for that kind of thing on television because it takes time away from legitimate news. This is a far less serious problem in the print media, but it still happens, particularly in the area of self-promotion outside the office. There is nothing wrong with accepting invitations to appear at forums or conferences, or to make speeches to civic and school groups. But beware of self-inflation within the community— of turning into a "star." The more blatantly visible you become, the more those who are suspicious of the news media will have grounds to challenge your impartiality. Unlike the movies, the news media arouse passions which often run very deep, especially where politics is concerned. Since a sizable segment of the community probably won't like what your organization stands for in the first place, and indeed will be looking for any chance to snipe at it, don't help by taunting it with your "celebrity status."

## BEHIND THE "SHIELD"

Unlike James Bond's legendary 007 number, a press card is not a "license to kill." Reporters function on a day-to-day basis under the same local, state, and federal laws as do other citizens. Stealing information, for example, can get you the same jail sentence on conviction that it will get the guy down the street, and so will harboring a fugitive or being an accomplice to a crime. These are rarely problems, though.

Aside from libel and gags, the legal area in which news organizations are most sensitive is the one having to do with the confidentiality of sources.

Say you're working on a story about the use of drugs on a college campus. In order to get as much hard information as possible, you interview several students who not only take drugs, but sell them. You get their names and they give you plenty of solid information, but only after you have promised them confidentiality—that you won't name them in the story or tell anyone outside your organization who they are. A week after the story appears, you get a grand jury subpoena calling on you to divulge everything you know about those who talked to you. How can drug operations on the campus be smashed, the district attorney asks, if someone other than one of the criminals has information about it, but won't divulge it? How can I turn over for prosecution those who gave me confidential information with the understanding that I would protect them from exposure? the reporter wants to know. It's a conflict of ethics—are a reporter's sources "privileged," or do the interests of the state come first?

Privilege is a fairly common rule in many professional relationships, including doctors and their patients, lawyers and their clients, priests and the parishioners, and husbands and their wives. It is not common, however, between reporters and their sources. Only about a third of the states in the union have so-called "shield laws" which allow reporters to respect the confidentiality of those who give them information on the understanding that it will not be attributed. The others, and the federal government, have no such laws. A newsman or -woman who refuses to disclose sources in those jurisdictions can be slapped with a contempt-of-court citation and jailed. It has frequently happened, too.

News organizations, the American Civil Liberties Union, the Reporter's Committee on Freedom of the Press, and other groups have argued that forced disclosure not only severely cripples news-gathering capability, but violates First Amendment rights. It is preposterous to think of getting serious information about drug use on a campus, the press would contend in our example, if no one but the law enforcement and school authorities, plus a scattering of none-users, talked about the situation.

The debate between those who insist on full disclosure of sources and those who are equally insistent that it prevents healthy journalism will go on for some time. Meanwhile, you ought to familiarize yourself with the status of source confidentiality in your own state. If there is a shield law, it has provisions about which you ought to be aware, since there is no such thing as blanket protection in all circumstances. If there is no shield law, you can be treated like any other citizen who willfully withholds criminal information from the authorities.

## TRUE COMPETITION

The spirit of competition runs through virtually every page in this book—competition in getting information from those who have it, competition with other news organizations, competition with outsiders who don't want you to gather unfavorable material, and competition with others within your own organization. News reporting, then, is by definition a highly competitive undertaking. But the fiercest—I will say the worst—competition is waged inside yourself.

The most fundamental way in which a professional reporter measures his or her real worth is by the outcome of the clash of competing instincts.

There is, after a while, an instinct that tells you that a feature that took the better part of a week to write doesn't quite work. It's not that it's wrong. You know in the solitude of your mind that the newspaper would run it as written, possibly even after complimenting you on it, and that no one would be able to challenge you on its contents. Yet your instinct tells you that you haven't gotten the most out of the material—that it can be better. You will then do one of two things. You will either convince yourself that another try isn't worth the effort, or you will make that effort knowing that there is a good possibility that you will lose again—that it still won't be right. The important thing to remember in such circumstances, though, is this: the story may not improve, but you will. You will end the next version of that story as a minutely better writer than you were when you started it, if only by virtue of the fact that new problems appeared of which you were unaware. But the whole business is between you and yourself. It's strictly a matter of how far you want to go, of how hard you want to push yourself in order to realize the limits of your potential.

This kind of inner competition is by all odds the loneliest, and often, the most frustrating. But that is precisely what makes winning so sweet.

# COPY EDITING
# SYMBOLS

| | | | |
|---|---|---|---|
| ⊙ | Period. | *stet* | Let Stand (for use when something has been inadvertently crossed out). |
| ⋀ | Comma. | ~~God~~ | Delete. |
| = | Hyphen. | ⌐God | Graf. |
| : | Colon. | god | Capitalize. |
| ; | Semicolon. | GØ∅ | Lower case. |
| ⩛ | Apostrophe. | God | Italics. |
| 'y ⋁" | Quotations. | ( ) | Parentheses. |
| ⊥⁄ₘ | One em dash. | (Neb.) | Spell out. |
| ◡ | Close up. | (God our) | Transpose letters, words, or sentences. |
| # | Insert space. | | |

Copy editing marks and symbols were designed to be as clear and specific as possible. When you make pencil changes on your copy, remember that they are instructions to someone else who should not have to guess about what you've done. Although it is often impossible to be completely neat when editing copy, and particularly on deadline, every effort should be made to help those who will have

to further work on your copy.  You therefore ought to press on
your pencil, print neatly, and put letters in their correct case (upper
or lower) :

The bandits escaped in a/station wagon, according to

police.


Use an arrow to take out unwanted words and to join the remaining parts of the sentence.

The bandits escaped ~~in a station wagon~~, according to

police.


A continuous line, from the last letter to the first, runs one sentence into another or joins two grafs.

She has the highest grades in her class ~~and always eats~~

~~a good breakfast.~~ Next year, she says, she will be able to

take a job after school.


Block out, "X," and flag a graf you want killed.

~~The bandits escaped in a station wagon, according to~~
~~police.  They sped east on Middlebury Boulevard and were~~
~~out of town within 10 minutes of the robbery.~~

# GLOSSARY

| | |
|---|---|
| Add | Additions of any kind to a news story. |
| Advance | A story based on an event that has not yet happened, such as an upcoming speech whose text has been provided, or one describing a new line of automobiles. |
| Angle | The approach to a story or a part of it. A story full of interviews with the survivors of a fire, for example, approaches the event from the "human interest" angle. |
| Art | Any illustration—photograph, drawing, chart, map, or graph—that goes in a newspaper. |
| Bank | The part of a headline (head) that follows the top line or lines set in the boldest type. This is also known as a deck. |
| Banner | A head going at least halfway, and often all the way, across the front page. |
| B Matter | Advance material, written ahead of time, and then "topped" with the actual news. Biographical material about a politician expected to announce as a candidate would be B matter, and would be added to the story saying that he plans to run for office. |

| | |
|---|---|
| Beat | A reporter's regular area of responsibility. Also, the professional word for what laymen call a "scoop." |
| Body | The part of a story following the lead. |
| Book | From two to ten attached sheets of copy paper on which stories are written. These make automatic carbon copies for distribution around the newsroom. |
| Box | A short story, usually enclosed by a border on all sides, but occasionally only by lines at the top and bottom. |
| Bulldog | An early (generally the first) edition. |
| Bulletin | A brief story, usually of no more than 50 words, about a major breaking news development. |
| Byline | The name of the reporter or reporters who cover a story. It is placed between the head and the first graf only on instruction from the editor. |
| Caps | Capital letters. |
| Caption | The words that describe and support any kind of illustration. A picture caption under a picture describes what the picture shows. |
| Center spread | Both pages in the center fold of a newspaper. It's also called a "double truck." |
| Clip | A newspaper clipping. |
| Copy | What is written by a journalist. It is written on *copy paper*, picked up by a *copy boy* or *girl*, and read by a *copy editor*. |
| Copy boy or girl | Junior members of a news organization who are responsible for picking up reporters' copy and bringing it to the copy desk for editing, as well as doing other unskilled chores. |
| Copy desk | Where copy editors prepare stories for print and give them heads. |
| Correspondent | What some reporters call themselves when they leave town. . . . Increasingly, and in an effort to break the "trench coat image," |

they are calling themselves reporters, no matter where they go.

| | |
|---|---|
| Coverage | Getting the news. |
| Credit line | Attributing the source of a photograph or other illustration. It usually goes beneath the picture. |
| Crop | To reduce the size of a photograph so as to eliminate what is less important before it is printed in the newspaper. |
| Cut | Any engraving of a newspaper illustration. |
| Cutline | The part of the caption, usually set in bold-face type, that directly describes an illustration. |
| Dateline | The location and date on which a story is sent. Datelines are never used on local stories written for local consumption. |
| Deskman or -woman | A copy editor on the copy desk. |
| Dummy | A drawing made on vertically ruled, otherwise blank paper, to show positions of stories and illustrations. They are blocked out in the appropriate column or columns and identified by slug and type of head. |
| Dupe | The carbon copy of a take. Also called a "black." |
| Ears | The small boxes on either side of the newspaper's name that appear at the top of the front page. Ears usually contain a brief summary and prediction of the weather, notice of an important story inside the newspaper, or the credo or motto of the news organization. |
| Edition | The particular version of one day's newspaper. The first edition is sometimes *remade* as often as three times, meaning that there are four editions before it is "put to bed." |
| Editor | Editors are those who generally work only in the office to process what reporters turn in or perform administrative functions. The managing editor, at the top, is responsible for the |

overall news operation. Desk editors are in charge of the various news divisions (city, state, suburban, national, foreign, sports, culture, and financial, for example). Copy editors do the actual editing of stories for publication and write headlines for them. In addition, there is usually an editor in charge of the editorial page and another who is responsible for the Sunday section.

File    To send in a story.

Filler    Relatively unimportant, or expendable news, used to fill columns. Filler material is usually short. An important story that goes only four-fifths of the way down a page, for example, will often be followed by a filler.

Flag    The name of the newspaper as it appears at the top of page one. This is often confused with "masthead" (see below).

Flash    A few words that describe a very important news event, such as a crash or an assassination. It is often used for the results of sports events.

Folio    The name of the paper and the page number as they appear in small print at the top or bottom of the page.

Folo    The abbreviated form of follow-up, meaning the events that follow the initial news.

Fudge    To avoid reference to factual material because it is not in hand. In an election story for which the final vote is not yet available, for example, the reporter might simply write that so-and-so won by a wide margin, and get the numbers in later. Fudging is also an editing and printing technique for getting very late and important news onto page one without stopping the main presses.

Futures    Upcoming stories that are noted in a "future book" by date.

| | |
|---|---|
| Handout | The widely accepted slang term for publicity release. |
| Head | All headlines, large and small. HTK means "Head to Kum" in printer's jargon. It is written on top of the story sent to the printer when the head is to be written later. |
| Hellbox | Where printers drop type that is not to be used. |
| Hold for release | An order that news is not to be released until a certain date or time, or until permission is given. |
| Insert | An addition to a story, generally no more than one or two grafs, that is written so that it can be smoothly placed between two existing grafs. |
| Italics | Type that is slanted slightly to the right, generally used for *emphasis*. |
| Jump | The continuation of a story (usually from page one) onto an inside page. |
| Jump line | The line telling the reader what page to turn to for the jump. On the jump, it is used to tell the reader where the story started ("continued from page C1"). |
| Kill | The word used to knock out a story, a part of one, a head, or an illustration from the news columns at any stage of their preparation or printing. Because the word is so dramatic, and potentially confusing, it should never be used as a slug. |
| Layout | The arrangement of any kind of type or illustration or a combination of them. |
| Lead | Sometimes called "lede" to differentiate it from the metal used to make type. It is the beginning of a story and, depending on complications, can be anywhere from a word to two or more grafs long. |
| Legman or -woman | A reporter who gathers news but who doesn't do the writing. |
| Lobster | The very late shift on a newspaper or wire |

|  | service, generally from midnight to about 10 A.M. |
|---|---|
| Lockup | The composing room deadline for getting all pages set and to the stereotype department in preparation for printing. |
| Makeup | Putting the various parts of pages together in the composing room; fitting stories, illustrations, and advertisements onto individual pages. Doing this so they are interesting and attractive amounts to a minor art form where newsmen and newswomen are concerned. |
| Markup | A galley proof or clipping of a story that is pasted on paper and marked by a copy editor to show where changes should be made. |
| Masthead | It lists the newspaper's ownership, top editors and other officers, place of publication, and bureaus, if any, and usually appears on the editorial page. |
| Morgue | The library where clip files are stored. |
| Must | It means that a story must be used. It can be written on top of a story only by an editor authorized to do so. Because of possible confusion, it is another word that ought never to be used as a slug. |
| New lead | A new beginning for an existing story, written so that it can smoothly pick up the existing story at some point. New Leads (or Nuleads or New tops) can be as short as a graf or as long as several takes. |
| Overnight | A story written earlier for use in an afternoon newspaper's first edition. Morning newspapers use the term to refer to an assignment to be covered the following day. |
| Overset | Type—usually filler material or the bottoms of more important stories—that is left over and eventually discarded. |
| Pica | Twelve-point typewriter type |

|                 |                                                                                                                                                                                 |
| --------------- | ------------------------------------------------------------------------------------------------------------------------------------------------------------------------------- |
|                 | (like this); or a linear unit of measurement of 12 points. One inch of space is the equivalent of 6 picas.                                                                        |
| Pick up         | The part of a story that comes after an addition, such as a new lead or an insert.                                                                                               |
| Pix             | Slang for pictures.                                                                                                                                                              |
| Play            | The way a story is positioned or displayed. It gets more "play" on page one than it would inside, for example, or when it is used in full, rather than being cropped or cut.      |
| Pool            | The selection of one reporter or a few of them, generally by broad agreement, to cover an event and share what they get with everyone else.                                      |
| Pox             | Slang for police.                                                                                                                                                               |
| Proof           | Galleys of stories that are in type, but that have not yet been published. The story is on long strips of paper so that corrections can be easily written in.                    |
| Replate         | Redoing the contents of one or more pages between editions. This is also called a "makeover."                                                                                   |
| Rewrite person  | A writer who redoes the stories of others, or who takes reporters' notes by phone or wire and turns them into complete stories ready for publication.                            |
| Ride            | Allowing an important story to be as long as the reporter thinks it should be, or at least, quite long. An editor then tells all concerned to "Give it a ride."                  |
| Rim             | The outer edge of a copy desk, which is almost always shaped as a half-circle.                                                                                                   |
| Rocket          | A very important message or, more usually, a question, sent by an editor to a reporter.                                                                                          |
| Runover         | The same as jump.                                                                                                                                                                |
| Shirttail       | Additional news, related to a story but not necessarily a part of it, that gets tacked onto the bottom and is separated from it by a dash. If the story is about the Secretary of |

|  | State visiting another country, for example, a shirttail might be a short story about a Senator's reaction to the trip. |
| Short | A brief story. |
| Sidebar | A story related to a main story, but concentrating only on one element of it, and usually one that is not covered in the main story. |
| Slot | Where the chief of the copy desk, called a slot man or woman, sits. He or she hands out stories to be edited and makes certain they are properly edited before they are forwarded for publication. |
| Slug | The name or title of the story (generally one word) that is written at the top of every consecutively numbered take. |
| Split page | The first page of the second section of a two-section newspaper. It is also called the "second front." |
| Spread | A longer story, usually one that can go at the top of an inside page. |
| Stereotype | The curved plate cast from the mold of a page set in type. It is locked on the press and, going round and round, prints the page on the paper passing under it. |
| Stet | The term used by editors and reporters meaning to restore something that was changed or killed. |
| Stringer | Someone who reports on a part-time basis and is paid either by the story or with a low, but regular, wage. |
| Take | One page containing as little as a line of copy. "Short takes" are used on or very near deadline and often contain a single graf. |
| Tight | Indicating that space is at a premium in the newspaper as a whole, or that a writer should keep his or her story as short as possible. |
| Trim | To cut a story, generally with some delicacy. |

Turn rule

An order to a printer to look for changes that are coming. Generally abbreviated on copy as "T.R."

Wrapup

A summary of events relating in a general way to a news situation. Also called a "roundup."

# FURTHER READING

The books below are among my favorites. Some are devoted strictly to technique and to the fashioning of prose. Others provide a good "feel" for journalism, for reporting, and for what reporters really do.

Berger, Meyer. *The Story of The New York Times.* New York: Simon and Schuster, 1951. (An adulatory, but fact-filled, history of that newspaper's first 100 years.)

Babb, Laura Longley (ed.). *Writing in Style.* Boston: Houghton Mifflin, 1975. (A selection of the best features from *The Washington Post's* Style section.)

Bernstein, Carl, and Bob Woodward. *All The President's Men.* New York: Simon and Schuster, 1974. (An account of the Watergate story by the two reporters who broke it.)

Crouse, Timothy. *The Boys on the Bus.* New York: Random House, 1972. (A wittily written minor classic about those who covered President Nixon's 1972 campaign.)

Gora, Joel M. *The Rights of Reporters.* New York: Discus, 1974. (An American Civil Liberties Union-sponsored handbook on First Amendment principles, protection of sources, libel, and other legal areas.)

Kendrick, Alexander. *Prime Time.* Boston: Little, Brown and

Company, 1969. (The life and some of the best reporting of CBS's Edward R. Murrow.)

Knightley, Phillip. *The First Casualty.* New York: Harcourt Brace Jovanovich, 1975. (A highly critical appraisal of war reporting from the Crimea to Vietnam.)

Liebling, A. J. *The Press.* New York: Ballantine, 1961. (An acerbic classic on the state of the press from the pages of *The New Yorker.*)

Lipsyte, Robert. *SportsWorld.* New York: Quadrangle, 1975. (A sobering view of American sports and those who cover them by a former reporter-columnist of *The New York Times.*)

Newman, Edwin. *Strictly Speaking.* Indianapolis: Bobbs-Merrill, 1974. (A clever and highly readable defense of good English by one of NBC's most respected newsmen.)

Reston, James. *The Artillery of the Press.* New York: Harper & Row, 1966. (A plea for more responsible reporting of foreign affairs by one of journalism's senior statesmen.)

Rivers, William L. *Finding Facts.* Englewood Cliffs, N.J.: Prentice-Hall, 1975. (A tightly written handbook on reportorial observation, interviewing, and source material.)

Sandman, Peter M., David M. Rubin, and David B. Sachsman. *Media.* Englewood Cliffs, N.J.: Prentice-Hall, 1976. (A widely used, first-rate overview of the American media).

Snyder, Louis L., and Richard B. Morris (ed.), *A Treasury of Great Reporting.* New York: Simon and Schuster, 1962. (A compilation of some of the best reporting—"Literature Under Pressure"—from the 16th Century to the mid-20th.)

Stone, I. F. *In a Time of Torment.* New York: Random House, 1967. (A collection of many of the most incisive pieces from the now defunct *I. F. Stone's Weekly.*)

Swanberg, W. A. *Citizen Hearst.* New York: Scribner's, 1961. (An astoundingly good biography of the founder of the news dynasty.)

Talese, Gay. *The Kingdom and the Power.* New York: World, 1969. (An engrossing classic about *The New York Times* and those who run it.)

Zinsser, William. *On Writing Well.* New York: Harper & Row, 1976. (A delightful treatise on the art of writing good nonfiction by a newsman-turned-Yale professor.)

# INDEX

Major topics are indicated by heavy type.

341